D1602867

Gallica

Volume 6

THE MEDIEVAL WARRIOR ARISTOCRACY
GIFTS, VIOLENCE, PERFORMANCE, AND THE SACRED

The process of identity formation during the central Middle Ages (10th–12th centuries) among the warrior aristocracy was fundamentally centered on the paired practices of gift giving and violent taking, inextricably linked elements of the same basic symbolic economy. These performative practices cannot be understood without reference to a concept of the sacred, which anchored and governed the performances, providing the goal and rationale of social and military action.

After focussing on anthropological theory, social history, and chronicles, the author turns to the "literary" persona of the hero as seen in the epic. He argues that the hero was specifically a narrative touchstone used for reflection on the nature and limits of aggressive identity formation among the medieval warrior elite; the hero can be seen, from a theoretical perspective, as a "supplement" to his own society, who both perfectly incarnated its values but also, in attaining full integrity, short-circuited the very mechanisms of identity formation and reciprocity which undergirded the society.

The book shows that the relationship between warriors, heroes, and their opponents (especially Saracens) must be understood as a complex, tri-partite structure – not a simple binary opposition – in which the identity of each constituent depends on the other two.

ANDREW COWELL is Associate Professor of the Department of French and Italian, and the Department of Linguistics, at the University of Colorado.

Gallica

ISSN 1749–091X

General Editor: Sarah Kay

Gallica aims to provide a forum for the best current work in medieval French studies. Literary studies are particularly welcome and preference is given to works written in English, although publication in French is not excluded.

Proposals or queries should be sent in the first instance to the editor, or to the publisher, at the addresses given below; all submissions receive prompt and informed consideration.

Professor Sarah Kay, Department of French and Italian, Princeton University, 303 East Pyne, Princeton, NJ 08544, USA
The Managing Editor, Gallica, Boydell & Brewer Ltd., PO Box 9, Woodbridge, Suffolk IP12 3DF, UK

Already Published

THE MEDIEVAL WARRIOR ARISTOCRACY

GIFTS, VIOLENCE, PERFORMANCE, AND THE SACRED

Andrew Cowell

D. S. BREWER

First published 2007
D. S. Brewer, Cambridge

ISBN 978–1–84384–123–4

D. S. Brewer is an imprint of Boydell & Brewer Ltd
PO Box 9, Woodbridge, Suffolk IP12 3DF, UK
and of Boydell & Brewer Inc.
668 Mt Hope Avenue, Rochester, NY 14620, USA
website: www.boydellandbrewer.com

A catalogue record for this title is available
from the British Library

This publication is printed on acid-free paper

Printed in Great Britain by
Biddles Ltd, King's Lynn, Norfolk

CONTENTS

ACKNOWLEDGEMENTS

I would first like to thank various colleagues who read parts of this book in draft form: Vincent Barletta, Steven Epstein, Bruce Holsinger, Peggy McCracken, and Michelle Warren. Their comments were extremely valuable, and of course any remaining errors are entirely my own. I would also like to thank the extremely thoughtful and meticulous anonymous reader of the manuscript, as well as the very efficient staff at Boydell and Brewer.

Parts of Chapters 4, 5, and 9 were presented at various MLA conferences, and I would like to thank the organizers and participants for the opportunity to receive valuable feedback at those sessions. None of the book has been previously published.

I would also like to thank my graduate advisors at UC-Berkeley, R. Howard Bloch and Joseph Duggan, whose continuing influence can be seen in this book, both in the anthropological orientation and in the focus on epic, on performance, and on socio-historical context.

Finally, thanks to my wife, whose undergraduate and graduate work in Pacific anthropology resulted in all kinds of interesting books lying around the house which turned out to be crucial to this project; and thanks to the Arapaho people for their willingness to support my field work with them on linguistics, anthropology and ethnopoetics. The perspective provided by those years of research, while not directly a part of this book, has provided valuable insight at many points.

Introduction

Individuality and Identity in the Middle Ages

Within the field of medieval studies, a number of interrelated terms and concepts centered around the idea of the individual and individual identity have drawn a great deal of critical attention over the years. If we begin by citing Louis Dumont's definition of such an individual from his *Essays on Individualism* – "the independent, autonomous, and thus essentially nonsocial moral being" (Dumont 1986:25) – then broadly speaking, we can say that during much of the history of medieval studies, scholars largely rejected the possibility of such individuals in the Middle Ages. But in the 1960s and 1970s, a number of scholars began to point to at least the avatars of modern individualism in the Middle Ages. Among the most prominent examples which one could cite are Marie-Dominique Chénu's *L'Eveil de la conscience dans la civilisation médiévale* (1969) and Colin Morris's *The Discovery of the Individual 1050–1200* (1972). This trend produced a contrary response, epitomized in its early form by Evelyn Vitz's argument that medieval individual identity was always a matter of merely quantitative difference (being more beautiful, more heroic, etc.) and never a question of qualitative distinctions which we might call (from a modern perspective) "individualistic" (Vitz 1975).

While the two sides of the argument have continued to grow in richness and complexity over the ensuing decades, the recent trend has been to focus more on the social limits and constraints on individualism in the Middle Ages – especially the period prior to 1200 – while at the same time recognizing the existence of forms of individual autonomy which were expressed in culturally specific ways which may not match – and even less lead to – classic modern forms of the autonomous individual. Peter Haidu argues in a recent book, for example, that the independent individual was in fact the antagonist of the Church (2004:10), and suggests that the Peace of God movement was in large part designed to rein in excessively individualistic feudal lords not only militarily and politically, but psychologically as well, through an ideology of individual submissiveness (2004:9–38). In a recent edited volume entitled *L'Individu au Moyen Age* (Bedos-Rezak and Iogna-Prat, 2005) Brigitte-Miriam Bedos-Rezak argues that true individualization was seen as a mark of alterity (2005:43–57), and Dominique Demartini shows how extreme realizations of individuality were linked to "la folie" (2005:145–65, esp. 147). More generally, the editors argue in the

Introduction that the focus in medieval studies of individualism needs to be on models, as opposed to selves (2005:25).

This is a very important point, because it suggests the need to look at the question of identity and identity formation rather than the question of the individual per se. In all cultures, every individual has one or more identities, defined in relation to culturally-established categories and models. In the case of many (some would argue all) potential identities, the individual's actions, behaviors and "performance" work to establish, maintain, and alter the individual's specific identitie(s). And in every culture, the available identities are largely constrained by culture-specific models, which it is crucial to understand.[1] Moreover, the category of the individual becomes a reality only within the framework of culture-specific models of identity which allow enough variety and fluidity within a given identity category, as well as enough creative combining of multiple categories, to allow full-fledged individuals with unique identities to emerge. The scholars mentioned above, along with several others, have recognized the culture-specific valences of medieval identity and (more-or-less attenuated) medieval individualism: the importance of what Michel Zink has called "literary subjectivity" (Zink 1985; Haidu 2004); renewed focus on the theological bases of individualism (Dumont 1986:23–59; Den Bok 2005); and focus on the pagan and Germanic heritage and its contribution to the idea of the individual (Gurevich 1995:19–88).

Gurevich's work stands out for its anthropological approach, as well as its focus on identity formation outside the realm of Christian religious models. This type of approach has been the least used by medievalists studying the individual and identity formation. Likewise, non-Christian models of identity formation have received comparatively less attention than others, especially for the earlier Middle Ages, when relatively little documentation is available other than from Church sources. Yet as Sarah Kay's provocative, anthropologically-inspired study of epic and romance has shown (1995), there is great potential in this area for further studies. This book is inspired by the idea that a better understanding of the anthropology of the real-life warrior aristocrat, as seen in medieval chronicles, as well as of the speculative persona of the hero, as seen in medieval epics, has much to offer for an improved knowledge of the forms and limits of individuality and identity formation in the early Middle Ages. In focusing on texts and events primarily from the eleventh and twelfth centuries, this project offers a prehistory of sorts to the more well-known models of the individual and individual identity seen in the ideology of Chivalry, with its close ties to the religious concepts of introspection, faith, and submission. A cultural model of identity did exist outside religious circles, which made available the concept of full-fledged individuality for at least one group. That group was the "warrior aristocracy"

---

[1]   I recognize that individuals' collective performance alters the form of culturally-available identities over time and creates new ones as well; and also that individuals can play with, challenge, and even escape such culturally-formed identities, but that will not be the focus of this book, except tangentially in Chapters 8 and 9.

of the tenth through twelfth centuries in western Europe, including England, France, Spain, Germany and southern Italy. This group should be understood to include all warriors who were also (roughly speaking) independent leaders or lords, or who aspired to be so, whether technically noble or not.[2]

The three fundamental claims of the book are: first, that the social practices of gift-giving and violent taking were fundamentally congruent and mutually reinforcing symbolic activities, which were absolutely central to the formation of individual identity and the creation and maintenance of social authority among the warrior aristocracy; second, that the rationale behind these performative practices cannot be understood without reference to a socially-consecrated notion of a sacred, essential "keeping," which functioned as the governing anchor of performance; and third, that ambitious warrior aristocrats made use of this social model of giving, taking and keeping – incarnated especially in the persona of the medieval hero – to conceive of themselves as full-fledged individuals capable of acting and existing apart from the networks of reciprocity which bound together medieval aristocratic society. In other words, again using Dumont's definition of the individual as an "independent, autonomous, and thus essentially nonsocial moral being" (Dumont 1986:25), we will see that medieval warrior aristocrats possessed a model which allowed them to conceptualize and imagine such a form of individualism, and potentially to pursue it. But such pursuit carried extremely high risks not only for the individual, but for his society. As a consequence, the society of the warrior aristocracy developed social mechanisms to restrain and inhibit it, and thus to restrain and inhibit the development of full-fledged individuality on the part of its members, largely through entrapping them in networks of reciprocity which inhibited the pursuit of the sacred "kept." This study will thus offer a way of bridging the divide – at least in the case of the warrior aristocracy – between scholars who have argued for the existence of specifically medieval models of full-fledged individuality and identity, and those who have focused on the limits and constraints to such individuality in that era.

The Middle Ages, Anthropology, and the Problem of Modernity

Symbolic exchange systems involving ritual giving and violent taking were clearly central to questions of power, authority, identity-formation, and alterity in the earlier Middle Ages. There has been a major revolution in the understanding of such symbolic exchange systems within the field of anthropology in the last twenty to twenty-five years. This revolution has been driven to a significant extent by more general theoretical work on the notion of "performance" as elaborated by Victor Turner, Clifford Geertz, Pierre Bourdieu, and others. The recent work

---

[2]   The question of legal nobility in this period is complex, but my broader term is designed to include all who might be called "lords," as well as those mounted warriors supported by the lords or linked to them in relationships of a fundamentally military nature.

in anthropology has significantly modified and sometimes even overturned ideas on symbolic exchange and reciprocity put forward by earlier functionalist and structuralist anthropologists such as Marcel Mauss and Claude Lévi-Strauss, as well as economic anthropologists such as Marshall Sahlins and Christopher Gregory. Yet the full implications of this revolution have not yet been fully integrated into medieval studies of the warrior aristocracy.

The need to take fuller account of the recent anthropological studies of symbolic exchange, identity formation, and power relationships is all the more important due to the exciting work being done to integrate post-colonial studies into medieval studies, both as a tool for better understanding medieval culture, and as a means of critiquing medieval studies and medievalism itself.[3] This work has brought interesting new perspectives to the understanding of social and individual aggression and power, the dynamics of alterity, and the ways in which identity formation occurs within such contexts. But as interesting as this work is, it relies on theoretical approaches closely tied to the context of modern colonialism and decolonization, within the larger framework of modern bureaucratic states, literacy and electronic media, global capitalism, and vast differentials of power and access to technology between colonizer and colonized. The era of the epic may have been, as Robert Bartlett has argued in *The Making of Europe*, central to the origin of the colonizing impulse. Yet this was also an era in which bureaucratic states, literacy, capitalist markets and large-scale power differentials were often marginal at best to social organization. Anthropological studies of public oral performance traditions and gift cultures in the context of small-scale structures of authority based heavily on individual, "heroic" identity and military power obviously would complement post-colonial theories nicely.

Yet we must also recognize that recent anthropological studies of the above phenomena also occur in a colonial or post-colonial world wherein the particular phenomena in question are themselves marginal to the larger forces of global capitalism, literacy, and the like, and not central to overall social organization as they were in the earlier Middle Ages. Thus the era of the medieval warrior aristocracy resists the easy, straightforward application of contemporary anthropology, as it does post-colonial studies. The question of our own alterity to the Middle Ages must be confronted. The notion of the "gift" is a key theme which this book uses to confront that issue, as well as to explore the world of the warrior aristocracy. An important argument of this study is that the notion of the gift must be redefined for the medieval context, and resituated in relation to the issues of violence, performance and the sacred. Once this is done, we can see the epic, gift-giving, and the trope of the epic hero/giver as social tools for managing the problems of individual identity formation and power relations among the warrior aristocracy. We will also see that mechanisms of individual identity formation are replicated on the level of group identity, which will significantly compli-

---

[3]   See Fradenburg 1997:219; Dagenais and Greer 2000; Cohen 2000; Holsinger 2002; Ingham and Warren 2003.

cate the role of the gift among the warrior aristocracy. Moreover, we will see that these same tools were absolutely central to development of and reflection on indigenous theories of identity, difference, and the relationship of power and performance to the sacred. The remainder of this Introduction begins the process of redefining and resituating the gift.

Anthropological Renewal: Beyond Gift and Commodity

It is virtually a truism of anthropology that the gift stands in opposition to the commodity. Indeed, since many theorists have argued that gift economies are actually systems of "total prestation" (Mauss 1967:3) in which the "economy" is "embedded" (Polanyi 1977:Ch. 4) in a more fundamental social, moral, and political system, it could be argued that the gift stands in opposition to the notion of an "economy" itself, and in particular to the Western capitalist economy. Marcel Mauss's founding 1925 essay on the topic, *The Gift*, opposes the practice of the gift to both communism and capitalism (Mauss 1967:Ch. 4). Claude Lévi-Strauss sees gift-giving and generalized reciprocity as a feature most evident in non-market economies (1969:459ff). More narrowly, Marshall Sahlins' most extensive writing on the gift occurs in a 1972 book entitled *Stone Age Economics* which stands in many ways as a critique of capitalist models of affluence. Christopher Gregory's influential 1982 book *Gifts and Commodities* explicitly establishes the opposition of gift and commodity as fundamental. Marilyn Strathern's provocative study of *The Gender of the Gift* also takes this opposition as given.

Not only do all of these anthropologists establish a broad distinction between gift and market, or gift and capitalism, but they use their descriptions of gift cultures to critique a number of the assumptions of western capitalism. In the more recent instances, such critiques are of a primarily methodological nature, arguing for the inapplicability of key capitalist concepts of economic analysis to the understanding of gift cultures.[4] But especially in the earlier works, the capitalist or more generally market-based economy itself is the target of critique. This is perhaps the central point of Mauss's essay and Lévi-Strauss's project.[5]

The importance of the gift as an external viewpoint from which to critique the economics of the West is even more apparent in the work of the various literary and cultural theorists who have picked up on the work of Mauss and Lévi-Strauss. Georges Bataille presents the gift as a form of resistance to capitalist expenditure (Bataille 1985:116–29). Jean Baudrillard argues that capitalism is in fact a perverted version of the symbolic economy of the gift (1972:7–58), then goes on to critique both Marxism and capitalism for their obfuscating "economisation" of the true spirit of the gift (1973). Hélène Cixous uses the gift as a trope not only of anticapitalist, but also of antipatriarchal tendencies in feminist writing (1981,

---

[4] See especially Strathern 1988 and Callari 2002.
[5] See in particular *Tristes Tropiques*, especially Chs. 6 and 38.

1989). Lewis Hyde speaks of the "erotic life of property" that inheres in the gift, as opposed to the lack and emptiness found in the commodity (1983). Jacques Derrida, most recently, has deconstructed this broad opposition between gift and economy, but that deconstruction nevertheless accepts the terms of the opposition as its focal point, and ultimately re-institutes them in a post-structuralist version, with the gift acting as the "supplement" to the "economy" of circulation and exchange (1992).[6]

Scholars of the Middle Ages have largely adopted the same perspectives in their use of sociological and anthropological sources to understand the medieval past, seeing the gift as both opposed to the commodity and clearly non-modern. While medieval studies long resisted such sources,[7] an anthropological turn began in medieval studies just prior to World War II and intensified afterwards, with the rise of the "Annales" school of historians and oral-formulaic approaches to epic. Scholars of the Middle Ages have adopted the standard modernist anthropological perspective on the gift, often speaking of the opposition of gift and sale in historical studies, or gift and commodity as they appear in literary texts.[8] This is not to say that such studies simplistically accept such an opposition in a straightforward way – indeed, they almost all examine the ways in which it is inadequate and even impossible to maintain from a methodological standpoint – a point also made by recent anthropological analyses of exchange systems more generally.[9] Nevertheless, it is this particular dichotomy which is the focus of interest, and the majority of the studies operate from the assumption that even if we can see the inadequacies of the two terms in retrospect, that they were socially operational categories. Perhaps the best recent book on medieval epic, Sarah Kay's work of 1995, argues for a poetics of the gift and the commodity, the former characterizing the epic, and the latter the romance. She argues that the two poetics represented two opposing rhetorics for confronting the issues of social order and individual relations.

It would be quite audacious to argue that such a vast theoretical apparatus and accompanying set of interpretive results is wrong, and I do not intend to do so. However, I do intend to argue that it is fundamentally incomplete, and that its theoretical incompleteness is especially critical when we attempt to look to the past using the perspective of anthropology generally, and notions of gifts and

---

[6] Boon 1999:211ff offers an interesting critique of Derrida's "economism," which he suggests is due to a lack of sensitivity to anthropological evidence.

[7] See Bloch and Nichols 1996:26ff on the way in which medieval studies explicitly resisted the impulses of modernism, and posed philology as its own, alternative, "anthropology" of language (1996:29). See also Patterson 1987 for a more extended analysis of similar tendencies in the study of Chaucer and medieval English literature.

[8] See Kellogg 1989, Shell 1978 and 1982, and Vance 1986 on the transition from gift to commodity in medieval literature. See Little 1978 for a representative study of the transformation within medieval society. Specific recent discussions of the gift versus sale issue can be found in Bouchard 1987 and 1991 and White 1988.

[9] See especially Appadurai 1986b, Thomas 1991, Humphrey and Hugh-Jones 1992, and Parry and Bloch 1989.

exchange more specifically. The incompleteness, moreover, is not so much theoretical as ideological: key components of the practice of the gift have been not so much unseen as downplayed or ignored in both modern theory and in literary-historical analyses due to the particular historical conditions (spreading global capitalism) and ideological intentions (a critique of the universal, economistic claims of that capitalism) under which gift theory has evolved. It is important to recognize that the modern practice of the gift is often a form of sociopolitical opposition to the sale, wherein both terms are articulated and theoretically elaborated as much by the subjects of study as by the anthropologists themselves. As Lévi-Strauss observes (anticipating recent questions on who the real authors of ethnographic monographs are), one could "see the indigenous Melanesians themselves as the real authors of the modern theory of reciprocity" (1987:37–8).

If one returns to the anthropological literature, a second opposition becomes apparent: that between the gift and violence. This opposition appears in several forms: in both Mauss and Lévi-Strauss, there is a recognition that confrontation between two groups ultimately offers the choice of either gift-giving, friendship, and solidarity, or confrontation, violence and warfare.[10] The gift is essentially a classificatory mechanism, which establishes and maintains bonds between various allies, and delineates the enemy as the one to whom one does not give.

One can also find another connection between the gift and violence in a different context. In the work of recent scholars of the Pacific region in particular, there is a greater or lesser focus on the way that the gift fosters competition and tension *within* a group, as individuals compete to gain status and prestige through maximum giving. Mauss did in fact recognize this phenomenon, being much influenced by descriptions of the potlatches practised on the northwest coast of North America (1967:31–7), and he spoke specifically of "obligations" to give, receive, and return the gift (1967:37ff).[11] It is only in the most recent work of anthropologists such as Marilyn Strathern, Annette Weiner, Maurice Godelier, and Jacques Godbout that this aspect of gift-giving has begun to receive special attention, however.[12] Interestingly, competitive gift-giving can be seen in this body of work as itself a form of sublimated violence.

Despite this recognition of violence as both the opposite of the gift, and also as potentially a component of the gift, the more fundamental opposition of gift and commodity continues to dominate critical theory, literary studies, and anthropology. Yet if one turns to medieval documents of gift ceremonies,

---

[10] For Lévi-Strauss, see 1969:59–67; 482–3; for Mauss, see 1967:11.

[11] Lévi-Strauss likewise recognized the competitive side of the gift quite clearly: he talks of its use to "surpass a rival" and even to "crush him" (1969:53). But he focuses on marriage, which he does not see as an overtly competitive form of exchange for the most part (but see his discussion of hypergamy in 1969, ch. 4) in that the dowry gift is a positive instrument for the accomplishment of the marriage. Thus competitive giving receives far less attention in his work, though of course marriages themselves are highly competitive.

[12] See especially Godelier and Strathern 1991, Godelier 1999, Weiner 1992, Strathern 1988, Godbout 1998, and Komter 1996a.

one is struck far less by issues of gift/commodity opposition than by the tension and immanent violence surrounding the practice. Indeed, the violence was often more than immanent: in one case, Roger of Montgomery was donating a marsh to a monastery. After inspecting the property, he suddenly "threw his son, Robert of Bellême, dressed in a miniver cloak, into the water, in witness and memory that the domain of the abbot and monks extended up to there" (Tabuteau 1988:151). The reason for this memorable and unexpected event was of course to make the gift ceremony, and the land boundaries in question, all the more memorable to the son. Gift-giving was a serious matter, and not to be entrusted merely to Latin charters, but to the minds and words of the living.

There are many other medieval examples of the beating of witnesses at dona- tion ceremonies for the same reasons – to make sure that the exact details of the gifts were remembered by those giving, receiving and participating.[13] On one occasion, after a gift, "they there whipped many little boys and [then] refreshed [them] well in the record and memory of this deed" (Tabuteau 1988:149). An account of a Norman gift ceremony involving Humphrey of Vieilles reports that at one point during the ceremony, Humphrey struck his son "for the sake of memory." He then had an apparently unwilling assistant struck with another blow, as well as the assistant's son. The unfortunate assistant is recorded as asking (no doubt indignantly) why he had been struck, to which Humphrey replied that it was so "you will live a long time and you will be a witness of this business when there is need." That said, Humphrey turned and struck yet another bystander.[14]

These acts of violence practised on the bodies of the witnesses to the gift bear witness to the orality of medieval culture, and to the fact that without such witnesses and their memories, there was really no gift at all. The gift was less an act of exchange between two individuals than a public ceremony intended to secure public order through the establishment of the controlling existence of these witnesses, whose existence guaranteed the sanctity of the bonds established between giver and receiver, and also helped insure the obedience of both parties to these bonds. (Indeed, in the Middle Ages, the parties often waited until the king should happen to be present before transacting especially important gifts.) In many charters, the description of the actual transfer of property occupied far less room than the many clauses of assurance that were designed to assure the permanence of the gift. In effect, the ceremony was inscribed into a series of constraints and social pressures to ensure continued respect for what had taken place. At the same time, the giver and receiver, to the extent that they also liter- ally enacted, in bodily gesture and language, the process of the gift ceremony, also enacted a series of rituals (often quite similar to the rituals of homage and investiture familiar to feudalism) that formed the basis of peaceful coexistence

---

[13] The practice was probably endemic to gift and oral culture. See James 1988:210 for an example from the Frankish kingdom and Homans 1974:368 on English villagers of the twelfth century.
[14] The charter is cited in Tabuteau 1988:148–51.

and social order. Thus the gift ceremony promised the avoidance of the implicit alternative of violence and social disruption. In fact, many assurance clauses make this alternative quite explicit.[15]

In another aspect of the ceremonies, various symbolic objects were often physically attached to the medieval manuscripts that recorded donations, serving through their presence to authenticate and reanimate the ceremony that the manuscripts recorded. Interestingly, the most common such object was a knife (see Clanchy 1993:36–41). The knife, whatever its multiple meanings may have been in the individual cases of exchange, suggests the extent to which the gift ceremony represented not just the preferred alternative to socially destructive violence, but was itself the sublimated version of the repressive violence necessary for social control.[16] Indeed, as we have just seen, the violence was not at all sublimated in some cases. Upon reading the descriptions of the experiences of the witnesses, one thinks of Foucault's analysis in the first part of *Discipline and Punish* of how, in the early modern era, state authority was inscribed onto the subject in the form of the tortures and executions. Marshall Sahlins has noted that the gift effectively replaces the state in many contexts (1972:171), and one could see in these sometimes physically violent gift ceremonies and in their sublimated symbolic objects a force of social authority that would indeed eventually be replaced by the often violent authority of the state itself in the later Middle Ages and Renaissance. The medieval gift ceremony thus offers implicit images of two kinds of violence: a socially disordering and destructive variety, and a socially ordering and constructive type. The gift ceremony stands in opposition to the first, and as the ritual enactment of the second. A key point of the analysis in this book will be to separate the two types.

Yet behind these two forms of violence lies a third: the fierce competition between individuals in medieval society to establish social prestige and power through giving. As Bourdieu (1977; 1966) has argued, there is always a third party to an exchange – the larger public. In this case, he means not simply the witnesses to the ceremony, but the more general public which those witnesses incarnate, and which always sat as judge to the larger contextual implications of the gift. As much as a noble donor to a monastery may have been establishing bonds of solidarity with the monastery, he was also implicitly establishing priority in relation to other rival nobles, by giving when they were not, or by giving more than they had given. It has been widely recognized that medieval nobles competed fiercely in gift-giving in order to attract and retain the military followers necessary to protect and expand their domains and their power (Bartlett 1993). In other words, gift-giving could be as much about establishing a name

---

[15] See Tabuteau 1988, Chs. 6–10 for a very detailed study of clauses of assurance of various types. See also Bouchard 1987 Ch. 1, and 1991, Chs. 1, 2 and 4 on the various parts of gift charters and their relationship to potential problems which arise with the exchange.

[16] There were also cases of cutting off the hair of the giver. (See Clanchy 1993:38.) Thus the knife and the inscription onto/by means of the body itself were combined in a single gesture.

and an identity – as an individual – as about establishing connections with other groups. It could differentiate between people as well as draw them together in solidarity.

Reconsidering the Medieval Gift

It will be the contention of this book that in examining the medieval past, we must shift our focus from the opposition of gift and commodity to that of gift and violence. This is not to say that the former opposition did not exist: it is clear that markets existed essentially throughout the Middle Ages, and one axis of the gift's function was always in relation to the commodity (though we will also need to rethink exactly what a "commodity" was in the early Middle Ages). Yet the other axis – of gift and socially destructive violence – was actually far more crucial for the warrior aristocracy of the late tenth through twelfth centuries. For this group, it is the contention here that the strict gift/violence opposition seen by Mauss and Lévi-Strauss must be rejected, and that the gift itself must be examined much more closely as a form of aggression and even violence which served as much or more for differentiation and identity formation as for establishing bonds of solidarity – both outside and inside social groups. We will need to rethink the definition of the terms "gift," "violence," and "commodity" in a medieval context, seeking to disentangle historical commonalities from socio-cultural particularities.

Critiques of the gift/commodity opposition have grown increasingly forceful among recent anthropologists, certainly. The gift has been drawn closer and closer into the economic circle, or else had its theoretical utility questioned altogether. In *The Social Life of Things*, Arjun Appadurai argues that the process of exchange is less important than the objects exchanged, and Nicholas Thomas, in *Entangled Objects*, also argues for a move away from questions of process to considerations of specific product. In *Money and the Morality of Exchange*, Jonathan Parry and Maurice Bloch write that rather than any "unbridgeable chasm between gift and commodity exchange," the studies in the book stress that "one may evolve rather easily into the other." They note that "the radical opposition which so many anthropologists have discovered between the principles on which gift and commodity exchange are founded derives in part, we believe, from the fact that our ideology of the gift has been constructed in antithesis to market exchange." They continue, "We cannot therefore expect ideologies of non-market societies to reproduce this kind of opposition" (1989:8).[17]

But while they downplay the overemphasized axis of gift/commodity opposition, such critiques do little to highlight the alternative axis of gift and violence.

---

[17] It is perhaps not an accident that Mauss's essay on the gift (1925) dates from just a few years after the widespread general use of the term "capitalism" itself. See Holton 1985:12 on the origins of this term.

In fact, by bringing the gift into the (capitalist) economy of the post-Enlightenment era, they elide the larger social, moral and psychological roles of the gift, and more generally make alterity a purely cultural phenomenon, as opposed to one of social organization.[18] This book argues for the need to recognize the societal alterity of the medieval warrior aristocracy more cogently, and suggests that the status of violence – especially the violence of giving – is key to this recognition. The false alterity of commodity ("us") versus gift (the medieval "other"), which is primarily a product of our own present, must be replaced by a deeper alterity centered on the status of violence as enacted in the gift. This makes the Middle Ages look less like a mirror image of the contemporary Others of the Euro-American, capitalist world of the twentieth century, and more like a very different Other which challenges some of our most fundamental categories of sociological, economic and anthropological analysis.

Of course, once we begin questioning the validity of modern categories for the study of the Middle Ages, we might be tempted to go all the way in this endeavor and throw out the category of the gift itself. Kathleen Biddick has argued recently that virtually all our cherished analytical categories are inadequate to the Middle Ages, although she sees the offending categories as more the product of the nineteenth century than the twentieth (1998:16; 58). But it seems hard to know where to start without approaching the past with some category. The idea that we could find a true set of purely medieval categories of analysis and understanding is not something that Biddick is willing to accept either. But it seems equally fruitless to reject the concept of categorization, and with it the historically constituted categories which include "the gift." Instead, it will be more useful to continue to adjust and critique the "same old terms." As Bruce Holsinger has recently pointed out, the very theoretical notions which we might seek to use to critique the discipline of medieval studies are themselves in part a product of that discipline, so that we are always caught in a feedback loop in which old categories infuse the new; we can never really escape the old terms (Holsinger 2002). It can in fact be argued that the modern notion of the gift actually began with the medieval courtly romance, which produced an implicit theory of the gift in opposition to that seen in the epic. We – as moderns and as theorists – are all ultimately still captives of the romance eroticization of the gift, as seen in such prototypical examples as Marie de France's lai *Lanval* of the twelfth century. Whereas Holsinger focuses on medieval studies as the source of many critical theoretical notions, one could equally well extend the analysis backwards and show how medieval studies was itself the product of the social practices and theories of the eighteenth and early nineteenth centuries: medieval studies found in the Middle Ages that which its own contemporary social and political ideologies needed it to find – Montesquieu's feudalism and so forth. The scholarly discourse of medievalism was as much a product of the political

---

[18] For more on the issues of society and culture in the alterity debate and the stakes involved within anthropology, see Adams 1998:297ff.

struggle between absolute monarchy, the state, and individual liberty during the Enlightenment and Romanticism as it was a product of the study of medieval documents and monuments.

One could pursue this tangled encounter regressively all the way back to the warrior aristocracy. Such an investigation is beyond the scope of this book, however. It aims to focus on the tenth, and especially the eleventh and twelfth centuries, when a vernacular discourse of the gift becomes fully accessible to us in the epic literature of the time, complemented by a great increase in the wealth of Latin sources. That discourse, it will be argued, is largely a product of the decline of centralized authority which occurred during and after the late Carolingian period, and it continues to reflect notions of that period well into the twelfth century, until the issue of commodification replaces that of social strife and violence as the central focus of the gift.

Medieval Conceptions of Identity and Difference in Performance

Once this new awareness of the gift is available, it opens the way to see the fuller subtlety of the discourse of the gift in medieval culture. In particular, once we begin to look not just at the gift in opposition to violence, but at the gift *as* a form of violence, then the strict oppositions of gift/identity and violence/alterity suggested by Mauss and Lévi-Strauss begin to collapse. This key finding about the gift and violence then leads back to the other central topic of the book: an examination of the conceptions of the individual, the individual's social group(s), and the Other among the warrior aristocracy. The gift, as both a social practice and a literary and ritual trope, is fundamental for understanding the ways in which identity formation for both aristocratic individuals and aristocratic groups was fundamentally entangled, as well as for understanding the ways in which both of these were entangled with notions of alterity.

John Miles Foley has argued that advances in the understanding of the medieval epic are at a standstill due to inadequate theories of verbal performance (1991:5–6). The early epics have often been taken as surprisingly realistic artifacts, which supposedly allow us to see medieval culture naively portrayed, or at least to listen in on straightforward medieval debates about cultural organization.[19] While almost no one doubts that romances were self-aware, rhetorical works, the epic often remains a genre of lyric "intensity" peopled with heroes who populate a "transparent" world (Boutet 1999:250–51). Epics are said to reflect worlds of – or beliefs in the possibility of – homosocial solidarity, or to represent the breakdown of such modes due to the incapacity of the warrior aristocracy and its particular social discourses to adequately confront social and

---

[19] See Sarah Kay's contention that the epic has been removed from the category of literature, and moved into that of "history" (1995:10).

linguistic complexity.[20] But recent ethnopoetic studies of epic performance reveal the ways in which this genre is in fact highly reflexive and self-aware, though in ways that do not correspond to typical literate indices of these qualities.[21] Such contributions will allow us to see the medieval warrior aristocracy not just as users of gifts and reciprocity as means of negotiating issues of identity, social order, violence, and alterity, but as active theorizers – in the epic – of these issues and of the limits and weaknesses of their own cultural models and ideals. Louise Fradenburg has noted how the Middle Ages has often been used as a "marker of fantasy and excess," and more specifically how the "hypereconomy" of the gift has been a key component of this marking function, since the gift is seen as that which "exceeds calculation and rationality" (Fradenburg 1997:210). In this Batallian perspective, exceeding rationality and calculation is often insepa-rable from lacking or abandoning them. In contrast, we must restore the rational, calculating component of the gift, as a form of social and poetic practice which is a theorization of excess rather than an engagement in it.

In summary, this book examines the way in which the gift and performance were necessarily connected as means by which the medieval warrior aristocracy examined and negotiated identity and alterity. But it also serves to focus atten-tion on the particular modalities of our own alterity to the Middle Ages.

Organization

The first two chapters define gift-giving, and then examine the violent, aggres-sive gift in both anthropological theory and medieval practice, with a case study of William the Conqueror and the Normans more generally. These chapters argue for the importance of the symbolic economy of the gift. Chapters 3 and 4 then look at the opposite side of giving – taking – and argue that the same symbolic economy operates in both domains, with the gift and violence seen as equivalent forms of reciprocity. Chapter 4 offers a case study of symbolic identity formation in *The Poem of the Cid*. Chapter 5 then addresses the tension between performa-tive models of culture such as those enacted in giving and taking, and alternative medieval visions of essential or transcendental identity and authority, embodied in sacred kingship, blood nobility, or legalistic definitions of social standing and class. It turns to anthropological studies of the sacred kept – as the anchor of systems of giving and taking – to examine the way this tension is resolved.

Chapters 6 and 7 broaden the focus from the in-group identity issues which occupy the first five chapters. They look specifically at the persona of the epic hero and examine how he can become simultaneously the perfect exemplar of

---

[20] See Kay 1995:1–30 for a very perceptive study of the tendency to read the epic in such terms – especially, she argues, when the critics are themselves male.

[21] More extensive discussion and references will be provided in the following chapter, but I will mention here specifically the work of Richard Bauman and Victor Turner.

his own culture taken to its limit, but also Other to it. These chapters argue that the hero was a specifically ritual/literary personage, used as a touchstone for examining the complex boundaries and interconnections between the self and the group, the performative and the sacred, and the group and the Other.

Chapter 8 pursues a reading of *The Nibelungenlied*, examining the ways in which this text seeks to suppress many of the inherent conflicts and weaknesses of the performative, giving-and-taking culture of the warrior aristocracy. The final chapter examines the ways in which the categories of the gift and the sacred were fundamentally re-imagined in the Old French *Coronation of Louis*, postulating the ideological construct of Chivalry as an alternative mode for establishing both individual and group identity.

1

The Power of Giving

In the medieval French epic *Girart de Vienne,* the attested version of which has been dated to around 1180, a poor knight named Renier arrives at Charlemagne's court, and offers to serve the king so that he and his brother may win "honor and reward" (l. 681). Charlemagne is not willing to take the young men into his household, but does offer them a nice sum of money, lodging, and new suits of clothing – fine gifts indeed for poorly dressed, unknown strangers. By the rules of classical gift theory, the strangers should be required to accept such gifts, and to reciprocate at a later time. Additionally, bonds of solidarity should be established between the parties, thanks to Charlemagne's generous offer. But instead, Renier reacts angrily, stating that "n'ai song d'avoir, ne sui pas marcheant" ("I need no money, I am no merchant born") (l. 695) and continues "einz mes lingnage n'ala avoir querant" ("None of my line have longed for wealth before") (l. 701). He says that if he owned the whole palace, he would simply give it away (ll. 697–9).[1] The exchange is the first encounter in a relationship which, though temporarily patched up, will ultimately turn into catastrophic rebellion.

Why does Renier unequivocally reject the gift, especially in such angry words, and why does he feel that it is an insult, as Charlemagne apparently indeed intended? This scene seems to correspond to nothing in Marcel Mauss's famous depiction of gift-giving which forms the basis of classical theory. A clue is the mode of Renier's arrival: after being turned away by courtly retainers, he has kicked down Charlemagne's door in order to gain entrance, and now makes an offer – a "gift" – of service which he clearly expects will not and cannot be refused, due to his own self-image as a great (though impoverished) warrior of a high noble family. His gift of service is as aggressive as his mode of entry, and Charlemagne replies by both refusing the offered gift, and then giving an aggressive counter-gift of his own in return, which the impoverished knight has no hope of reciprocating, thus shaming him. The gift – especially in the form of money – emphasizes Renier's dependent and powerless position in relation to Charlemagne. In refusing Renier's offer of service and instead giving him material goods, Charlemagne challenges Renier's self-image as a warrior capable of winning honor and rewards on his own. The gifts represent not symbolic rewards for brave and loyal military service, but rather a form of alms to the poor, for someone implicitly unable to earn his rewards. This gratuitous gesture on the

---

[1]   This and many other such examples are discussed in fuller detail in Noble 1986.

part of Charlemagne further reinforces his superiority to his adversary, since it reveals that he is so wealthy he can give away cash to complete strangers, for no reason, and out of no self-interested motivation. Renier wants to win honor, but Charlemagne merely gives him the things which should really be secondary, symbolic rewards of honor. It is a crushing insult, disguised as a magnanimous gift, in response to the equally aggressive initial gift offered by Renier.

The scene is really about the confrontation of two aggressive and proud individuals, who have very high self-images, and regard themselves as fully self-sufficient in terms of their ability to perform militarily and socially. The confrontation is played out in a series of aggressive gifts which seek to force the receiver to share the giver's own self-image, thus imposing the giver's personal identity onto the recipient. Each of the aggressive gifts is rejected, as a prelude to the conflicts which will dominate this epic of revolt. But most importantly, this scene further underlines the violence and aggression of medieval gifts which we already encountered in the introduction; their highly symbolic character; and the importance of social image, self-image, and what will be called here the "integrity" of the heroic individual. These will be the subjects of this chapter.

Classic Gift Theory

Gift theory was first given coherent form by Marcel Mauss in his essay on *The Gift* (1925), a text itself crucially influenced by Malinowski's reports of the Kula Ring in Melanesia (1922). The theory acquired greater resonance with Lévi-Strauss's work on generalized reciprocity (1969). This section will provide a critical outline of the classic theory, since it has been highly influential in medieval studies.[2]

Mauss was concerned with societies where gift-giving is constitutive of the social order. It is a social process wherein economics, morality, and political relationships are embedded in the act of gift-giving (Polanyi 1977:48). Gifts include not just material items, but services, hospitality, and other intangibles. The act of giving is understood as being fundamentally symbolic, in that the objects given are less important than the act itself. This act serves to create ritual bonds between donor and recipient, and the objects given symbolize those bonds. Such bonds often include a hierarchical component, so that the recipient feels an obligation or debt towards the donor.

The objects given also symbolize the social status of the donor: gifts are considered to be "inalienable," not in the sense that they cannot leave their owner, but in the sense that the imprint of the original owner remains with the gift. In gift cultures, relationships are between people, mediated by things, whereas in a contrasting commodity culture, relationships are between things (commodities), mediated by people (as workers – see esp. Gregory 1982:16, 41). Dense networks

---

2   Key texts are Mauss 1967, Levi-Strauss 1969, Sahlins 1972, and Gregory 1982.

of exchanges and the resulting bonds ultimately constitute the social order. Such forms of social order are crucially dependent on the three imperatives of gift cultures: to give, to receive, and to give in return. All members of a gift culture live under these imperatives, so gifts in general are seen less as voluntary acts than as part of the obligation involved in being part of the culture.

Everyone in a gift culture does not necessarily give and receive equally, however. The goal of the ambitious individual in such a culture is to give the most, rather than to accumulate the most, since true wealth consists in the social connections and the high status that derive from giving. This is not to say that objects are not important: certain objects are sometimes specifically designated as "gift objects," and their only utility is in this context. (The most famous are the kula shells of Melanesia.) These objects are often ranked in value, and ambitious individuals seek to possess and give objects of the highest rank. Mauss recognized the existence of competitive forms of gift-giving, most famously the potlatch.

Lévi-Strauss (1969) suggests that the gift is the basic act of social identity in gift cultures. Such societies offer two choices in an encounter – giving and social solidarity, or violence. Even more fundamentally, the gift is one form of a deeper process of general reciprocity, upon which all human societies are organized. The most fundamental gift is the exchange of women by men in marriage. Thus he explicitly links the process of gift-giving with social reproduction. In this context, the incest taboo becomes the essential form of a more general social rule: to exchange is good and necessary, to keep is bad and socially destructive.

A fundamental tension runs through classic gift theory: it stresses how gift-giving creates social solidarity, yet it recognizes that gift-giving in specific instances can be competitive or even antagonistic. This second aspect of the theory has received far less attention than the first, however. Mauss recognized the existence of antagonistic gift-giving, but focused far more on "solidarity." Lévi-Strauss essentially elides the question of antagonistic giving, in that individual competitive drives all are subsumed into a more general system of social solidarity and reproduction (not unlike capitalist theories of individual competition). Other influential students of the gift from the 1970s (Marshall Sahlins) and 1980s (Christopher Gregory) share in this same tendency.

Indeed, Mauss, Levi-Strauss, Sahlins and Gregory all share a fundamental orientation in their approach to the gift, despite quite different theoretical backgrounds. They are all interested in the way that gift-giving works functionally in whole societies, to organize and reproduce the society. This interest is most explicit in Levi-Strauss, but Mauss – a key figure in the rise of functionalism in anthropology – shares this interest. Sahlins's work is related to the evolutionary functionalist perspective which dominated American anthropology in the 1960s and 1970s (Julian Steward, Marvin Harris, Leslie White etc.). Gregory writes from a neo-Marxist perspective, which again focuses on social reproduction. As a result of this functionalist perspective, all the theories tend to share a general perspective on human subjects which diminishes their agency and sees them as

strongly produced by their physical and cultural environment.[3] Thus the individual and the individual act of exchange receive far less attention than the group
within which the strongly-bound individual acts. Individuals and individual acts
are only particular instances of the social.

But beyond these theoretical issues are ideological ones. The four theorists
share a general desire to critique Euro-American modes of socioeconomic organization, particularly in the way they produce social anomie. Mauss devotes an
entire chapter of his essay to this goal; Lévi-Strauss discusses his critical-outsider
perspective in detail in *Tristes Tropiques*; Sahlins wrote *Stone Age Economics*
as a critique of Western stereotypes of "primitive" societies, and more particularly as an attempt to examine alternative, even superior models of "affluence";
and Gregory seeks to better understand the ways in which non-Western societies can successfully resist the homogenizing, capitalist socioeconomic forces
of colonialism and globalization. It is thus not surprising that the role of the
gift in creating social solidarity should receive far more attention than its role
in fostering individual competition and social tension. The gift is a theoretical
vehicle for thinking critically about the Euro-American West.[4] Gift-giving as a
forum for competitive identity formation through antagonistic giving – potlatch-
style – looks a little too much like contemporary western society to be very
appealing for close attention. The excessive socialization of individuals and acts
in gift cultures turns out to be not just a secondary product of certain types of
theoretical orientations, but a primary necessity if the cultures are to serve their
functions as perspectival positions from which to engage in Western debates on
politics, economics, and ideology.

Medievalists have long focused on the solidarity of gift-giving. A paradig-
matic example is Erich Kohler's *Ideal und Wirklichkeit in der höfischen Epic*
(1970), which argues that medieval courtly literature served to elaborate a social
model which would allow for the continuing solidarity of the aristocracy through
the process of gift transfer from upper to lower ranks.[5] This is simply a more
focused version of the general conception of the fief and feudalism which reigned
supreme in medieval studies until recently: the vision of a world where gifts
were exchanged and bonds were formed,[6] and where such peaceful exchanges
responded to and resisted external forms of violence. The medieval epic in

---

[3]   Boon 1982:Chp. 3 offers a very thorough evaluation of the forms of solidarity in anthropological theory and their relationship to what I will call the "colonization" of the Other through
non-agency. Rhoda Halperin offers an interesting critique of classical economic anthropology
on the grounds that it consistently constructs economies for other cultures (1994:1), and that
such structures inevitably dominate the agency of individuals (1994:15).

[4]   Richman 1990 analyzes the special strength of this phenomenon in France. On the same
subject, see Clifford 1988:117ff and Adams 1998:361ff.

[5]   See Bouchard 1987, 1991 and Tabuteau 1988 for excellent recent studies of this aspect
of medieval gift-giving – in particular, in relation to the Church.

[6]   There have been many recent critiques of the concepts of fiefs, vassals, and feudalism.
For one detailed historical study, see Reynolds 1994. For a general survey of the scholarly
trends, see Bouchard 1998.

particular has been treated in a very (functionalist) anthropological fashion, and the role of gifts has received considerable attention, while the courtly romance is often interpreted as being a genre of markets, commodities, and of the disruption of the economic and social solidarity of the epic world of the gift.[7] But we need to think instead about how this supposed solidarity might be disrupted from within, rather than from without, just as it is in *Girart de Vienne,* where gifts and revolt are intimately connected. And we need to think more about the importance of gifts for individuals, rather than communities.

The Antagonistic Gift and the Self

The competitive, antagonistic side of the gift – internal to a given group – has drawn increasing attention among recent (post-1980) anthropologists and social theorists, who have noted the tension between issues of group identity/solidarity and individual identity within gift cultures.[8] Gift-giving can be seen on a continuum, from non-antagonistic giving which works towards group solidarity to antagonistic giving which works towards the social elevation and differentiation of the individual.[9] As Annette Weiner notes, gift-giving is often about creating heterogeneity, not homogeneity (1992:10). This and the following sections will first present a general overview of anthropological theories and studies of the antagonistic gift, and then offer a case study of William the Conqueror's use of such gift-giving strategies.

Receipt of a gift is usually understood as a putting into debt of the recipient by the donor.[10] In antagonistic contexts, such gifts can often be understood as truly aggressive acts, which lead not just to moral debt and obligation, but to actual shame and loss of social status (see Bourdieu 1977:13 on the example of Kabyle society). William Miller's analyses of gift-giving in the Icelandic sagas emphasize that the repayment of the gift was as imperative as the repayment of an insult or an assault, and failure to repay meant being excluded from the world of honor (1993:16). More generally, he points out that the "idiom of gifts" was equally the "idiom of honor and feud" (1993:16). The giver acts aggressively not only towards the recipient, however, but also indirectly towards other potential givers in the society, who have not given to the recipient.[11] The donor unequivo-

---

[7]   See Kellogg 1989, Duggan 1989, Bloch 1983, Kay 1995, Vance 1986, Shell 1978, 1982.

[8]   See especially Godbout 1998:112 on the calculation and self-interest involved in the gift, and Miller 1993 on the connections between giving and individual honor and status.

[9]   Bourdieu notes that gifts can create either solidarity or enforced dependency (1977:192), but he does not focus on issues of hetero-generation.

[10]   Gregory 1982:19; See Mauss, p. 63 "charity wounds him who receives." William Miller likewise notes the "obliging force" of gifts (1993:5) and the "continuing tyranny of the norm of reciprocity" (1993:5).

[11]   These two aspects of the gift could be considered tactical (direct) and strategic (indirect) aggression, to use Guy Halsall's terms. See Halsall 1998:17–18. See also Godelier 1999:42 on

cally gains in honor and prestige, and the goal in such settings is always to be a donor.[12] Thus in a competitive gift culture, the ambitious individual might seek ideally to always give and never to receive.[13] Yet things are never quite so simple. A key corollary of the above general rule is that one should seek to give first.[14] The eventual counter-gift is not seen in the same way as the first gift, since it is an owed return. When the counter-gift is more highly valued or ranked than the initial gift however, it shifts the honor of giving to the second donor, and converts an occasion of debt repayment into an opportunity for aggressive riposte (Gregory 1982:53–4). In addition, one can seek to give more, or to give better things. In certain cultures which seek balanced reciprocity, to give more than can possibly be returned is a grave error which threatens to disrupt social equilibrium (Bourdieu 1966:198, 204). But in other cultures, one may seek to crush rivals with extreme examples of giving, so that social equilibrium is replaced – at least temporarily – by the establishment of rank hierarchies such as in "potlatch" and "big men" societies.

The idea of giving more or giving items of higher value would seem to contradict the standard assumption that it is the act of giving, rather than the thing given, which is predominant in a gift exchange, or the idea that counting and measuring are antithetical to a gift culture (Little 1978:4–5). But if objects given in a gift culture do not have a value like a commodity does, they nevertheless have a rank.[15] Kula shells, for example, are intricately ranked, as were the "coppers" used in potlatches. Indeed, there are even different spheres of exchange, which are incommensurable; no number of low-rank shells can compensate for a high-rank shell (Gregory 1982:49–50). Thus an additional goal would be to give gifts of the highest rank (Gregory 1982:52).

In aggressive situations, one not only tries to avoid receiving, or to reciprocate overwhelmingly; one may go so far as to reject gifts, as a way of "affirming the selfhood whose status an acceptance would threaten" in the words of social psychologist Barry Schwarz (1996:71).[16] He suggests that gifts, in their personalized nature, function to impose the identity of the giver onto the receiver (1996:69; see also Komter 1996b:119 and Weiner 1992:64). In sum, one should seek to: give, give first, give the most, give the best, avoid receiving, and if things are received, to reciprocate aggressively and even overwhelmingly. Writing about antagonistic Middle Eastern gift-giving, Paul Dresch notes that "the gift

the implicit third party always present to the gift, as well as Miller 1993:55–9 on the crucial role of the observers in arbitrating the full meaning of the gift.

[12]   Godbout 1998:112; Gregory 1982:51, 55

[13]   See Schwarz 1996:72 on the necessity for the leader never to be in debt to the follower. Schwarz also cites Georg Simmel on this same idea (1996:77).

[14]   See Gregory 1982:48 on the idea that gifts have an "ordinal relationship," and also Simmel 1950:392 on the notion of the first gift as the only truly free one.

[15]   Gregory 1982:49–50. See also Nicholas Thomas 1991, with his general call to pay more attention to what is given rather than to how it is given (esp. the Introduction).

[16]   See Godbout 1998:127 on Freudian and Girardian perspectives on this same idea.

is about compulsion" (1998:116). In saga Iceland, gifts could "importune ... annoy" (Miller 1993:6), "challenge" (Miller 1993:17), "insult ... [and] injure" (Miller 1993:16). Thus people "maintain ascendancy by regulating the indebtedness of others to them" (Schwarz 1996:72), and sometimes even create *de jure* relationships of dependence (Testart 1993:107–8; Gregory 1982:55).[17]

These ideas on gift-giving can be integrated into even broader theories of consumption, of which gift-giving is one example. Mary Douglas and Baron Isherwood have discussed the ways in which "goods ... are needed for making visible and stable the categories of culture" (1979:59). Much like gifts, the broader category of goods "also make and maintain social relationships" (60) and "are good for thinking" (62); they serve as "a nonverbal medium for the human creative faculty" (62). Consumption, like gift-giving, "uses goods to make firm and visible a particular set of judgements in the fluid processes of classifying persons" (67). They argue that societies are organized around access to "information" (79), and that access to this information (conveyed through goods [gifts] and consumption [gift-giving]) determines social status and the ability to maintain that status. They suggest that those who have access to this information will seek monopoly control over it, by erecting barriers to others' entry into the system of information, by consolidating their own access, and by techniques of exclusion (89). A person can ultimately even seek to "take charge of the information himself" (79). In such settings, "refusal to transact" (140) can become a characteristic behavior as well on the part of those who already control information and power.

The ultimate conclusion of this process of heterogeneration is potentially the attainment of individual integrity and – ironically – an escape from the processes of reciprocity and exchange which supposedly hold the group together, and which were used in pursuit of the goal of integrity in the first place.[18] As the concept of integrity will be central to this book, and is not a well-defined theoretical term, let us briefly discuss it in greater depth. Integrity[19] has elements in common with "honor" as understood in anthropology and Mediterranean area studies,[20] but as used here, it represents something more idealized and more extreme than honor – specifically, a state of freedom from social bonds and obligations, such that

---

[17] A recent explication of the full ramifications involved in the distinction between aggressive and antagonistic (or "agonistic") gift-giving and the opposite ("non-agonistic gifts") can be found in Godelier 1999:42–84. I will note here in passing that aristocratic gifts to churches and monasteries would be classed as broadly non-agonistic under Godelier's schema, though we will have occasion to question this distinction later.

[18] "Exchange" is the transfer of one service or material item "against" another. "Reciprocity" is a more general term referring to relationships in which transfers of lands, goods or services either regularly occur or are expected to do so, but where a given transfer is not seen necessarily as an exchange.

[19] The term is used by anthropologists Campbell (1966:144) and Marcus (1987:52).

[20] Key studies of Mediterranean honor societies are Peristiany 1966, Peristiany and Pitt-Rivers 1992 and Gilmore 1987a (which offers a series of critical perspectives on the field).

the individual is "whole" (Latin *integer*) and completely self-dependent.[21] This is a potential, but never fully realized state. Integrity will have two interrelated components – socioeconomic, and also a psychological one – but for the moment we will focus on the first, and return to the second in Chapter 2.

The modern analytic term "honor" was originally theorized primarily within the context of Mediterranean area studies (Peristiany 1966; Gilmore 1987a). There, it is typically linked to the sexual chastity of women and the social prestige of the men who maintain the chastity of women in their own families while also projecting a strongly sexualized aggressiveness. Such studies tend to focus on small communities, peripheral to modern states and bureaucracies, with relatively little range of distinction in rank among the members of the community, and with few true class distinctions. Typically, there is limited movement up and down on the scale of social rank (expressed as more or less honor), and all individuals strive to maintain a rough equality of honor. Honor also includes a goal of general non-dependent status within the community – a quality shared by most or all heads of households. It can be understood as maintaining a "full social personality" (Peristiany 1966:11), both in one's own eyes and in the general consensus of one's honorable peers. And finally, codes of honor are seen as involving strong in-group/out-group distinctions.[22]

The preceding context is too specific to apply to the medieval warrior aristocracy; that society was much more stratified and larger-scale than those described. The more general use of "honor," which is applicable here, rests on the fact that in certain communities one's "social personality" (Peristiany 1966:11) as judged by the mutual consensus of the other members of the community is as important as – or more important than – one's formal title, juridical rank, or economic wealth in enabling one to act successfully in the community. The ability to "act successfully in the community" is expressed as "power." A medieval warrior aristocrat possessing a great deal of honor thus also had a great deal of power – the effective correlate of honor. Such a person could attract adherents, command their obedience, and use them to accomplish goals. Honor is thus the measure of a generalized, consensus social judgement attached to an individual, and power represents the physical and material assistance which members of the community are willing to give to that individual, based on the social judgement. From this perspective, honor accruing to an individual expresses underlying socioeconomic power, which is banked in the form of honor. The honor is convertible to goods and services which are the means of exercising power.

This explanation of honor and power makes power highly personal in nature, vested as much or more in individuals – and the adherence of members of the

---

[21] See Miller 1993:111 on the connection between honor and "autonomy of self."

[22] Peristiany 1966:9–18 and Gilmore 1987b:1–17 are good introductions to honor and Mediterranian studies; Gilmore provides a survey of debates within the discipline. Key questions are the relative importance of sexual elements, and the unity of the concept of "honor" itself, with an important distinction proposed by Julian Pitt-Rivers between "honor = precedence" and "honor = virtue" (discussed in Gilmore 1987b:90).

community to those individuals – as in institutions (see Bourdieu 1977:125, 130). But members of a community do not simply adhere to individuals: rather, they adhere to that particular individual's general social identity: while honor is a general currency or evaluative measure of social standing, each individual in a society where power is highly personal has a specific identity. As we have seen, honor associated with gift-giving is highly contextualized, and high-status gifts are closely associated with specific individuals.

To summarize, ambitious medieval warrior aristocrats constructed a social identity through acts of giving, with the identity being the general sum of such acts. Each individual's identity was unique, and was established in relation to the various other individuals with whom he exchanged or refused to exchange. For the average person, multiple exchanges with multiple people, some involving relations of superiority and others involving relationships of inferiority, would lead to a plural set of identities. One's social identity in a given social context was the product of a social consensus among those making up the context in question, and it was this identity which correlated with power; this identity determined to what extent one could attract adherents, command obedience, and achieve social goals. But although every individual act of exchange and every individual identity might be unique, these acts and identities could still be judged relative to each other, as having more or less value, since members of the society shared a general set of criteria for an idealized individual and idealized actions. In this framework, honor was the abstract measure of the value of an action, and more generally, of the value of one's identity.

Studies of honor have used the notion of a "social personality" much like we are using here the term "social identity," although they have tended to see this personality as single, rather than potentially multiple. The social personality is defined in relation to an idealized social persona (Peristiany 1966:9–10), and can be analyzed as the primary form of socialization and integration to the group. The persona includes a range of more specific behavioral values which vary depending on the community. In some communities, the idealized social persona can be considered bounded, and excessive pursuit of certain values is seen as negative, as too individualistic (Peristiany 1966:16; Bourdieu 1966:197–8), while in others (including the warrior aristocracy), honor is relatively unbounded, and by giving more and more, one can accrue more and more honor, without thereby being seen as violating the social persona.

The society of the medieval warrior aristocracy constitutes a challenge to many modern analytical uses of the term "honor." Modern honor societies are often seen as fundamentally oriented toward group solidarity, with a strong "us versus them" ethos in relation to outsiders, and as possessing a strong cultural consensus among their members that inhibits excessive individualism (Gilmore 1987b:3, Pitt-Rivers 1966:35) – much like the way that many gift-based cultures have been viewed. In contrast, medieval warrior-aristocrat society allowed for a much wider range of individual distinction from one's peers, and the strict us/them divide was likewise much less clear-cut. Indeed, the idealized social identity for the medieval warrior aristocracy was integrity, not solidarity.

Note however that attaining this ideal would ironically mean an escape from the need for concerns about social evaluations of one's honor, as one crossed into a realm of self-sufficiency and autonomy. While honor was an element of the system of reciprocity, integrity transcended both honor and reciprocity. Moreover, if one could attain a status of integrity in all contexts, relative to all other individuals, then one could escape plural identity and constitute a single, "whole" identity for oneself, which would allow a complete escape from the social constraints of reciprocity and the social judgements associated with each act of reciprocity.

"Integrity" does not have a standard medieval lexical correlate, though notions of desire and will (Latin "voluntas" and derivatives, Middle High German "über-muot") play a key role.[23] The closest literary correlate I have found is the term "singularity" as used by Sarah Kay in her reading of *Girart of Roussillon* (Kay 1998–2003). That term describes the desire "to possess an irreducible unique-ness" (1998–2003:12). More generally, as we will see, integrity is extremely closely linked to the concept of the hero.

The desire for integrity is a widespread phenomenon. Anthropologist Paul Dresch has studied the wariness towards trade among certain Middle Eastern cultures. There, any form of trade becomes a potential source of dishonor; while peasants might go to markets, feudal lords would not (1998:126). The indig-enous vocabulary for such goals centers on the concept of "honour" (127), a word which refers to an "ideal autonomy" (127). Such peoples are examples, for Dresch, of the "heroic style" (127).[24]

In a European context, Frankish aristocrats pursued a strategy of scattered land holdings in order to maximize the variety of their internal production and avoid recourse to merchants (James 1988:215, 219). Georges Duby has studied the occurrence of the ideal among medieval Carolingian lords (1968:44; 1973:68, 125), for whom exchange was a process which should occur only within the confines of their own demesne. Charlemagne's capitulary "De villis," on the running of his manors, clearly illustrates the drive towards self-sufficiency on the feudal manor: its exhaustive listing of plants for the garden is exemplary of this goal.[25]

A desire for integrity seems at first paradoxical given the functioning of the medieval rural economy. A lord received vast amounts of goods and services – and money as well – from serfs and peasants, and also from vassals. But these

[23] The best lexical study of the honor ethos in Old French is Jones 1963. For German, see Müller 1998:237–42.

[24] Parry 1989 in Parry and Bloch 1989:82–5 offers a more general analysis of the notion of autarky in both classical and medieval Europe, with many references. Polanyi 1968 contains extensive analysis of the idea in Aristotle.

[25] "De villis" is in *Monumenta Germaniae Historia*, Legum, Sectio II, Capitularia regum francorum, vol. 1 (Alfred Boretius, ed. Hannover, 1883).

transfers derived from juridically inferior individuals who were dependent on the lord.[26] They would thus not be considered threats to his integrity or self-sufficiency. It was exchanges with equals or superiors which were to be avoided. Thus in medieval Iceland, newly arriving settlers often refused gifts of land, preferring to take it through duels or outright violence. William Miller notes that on an island, land was a type of gift difficult to reciprocate, leaving the recipient in potentially permanent debt.[27] For the medieval manor, recourse to trade and commerce for items otherwise produceable on their own lands could become a form of dishonor (LeGoff 1988:211).[28] Of course it is not being argued here that such desires could ever be fully realized – only that they were a powerful ideological model. The aggressive gift, the overwhelming and unreciprocable gift, and the refusal to receive from outside the circle of one's clearly recognized dependents must all be understood in terms of a competitive drive for absolute individual heterogeneity and integrity.

William I as Giver and Conqueror

The *Gesta Guillelmi* is an account of the life of William the Conqueror. It is by William of Poitiers (himself a knight), and will serve well to illustrate the above points. Although the text has been disparaged as more propaganda than history, that is of less importance here than two facts: first, it was written by an ex-knight turned cleric; and secondly, due no doubt largely to its author's background, it offers a relatively direct view of the political discourse of gift-giving, identity construction, and integrity – a view which is largely submerged in other, more monastically-inspired accounts of William's life.[29] What we are investigating

---

[26] I use the term "juridical" here to indicate either strictly legal or more customary distinctions which explicitly recognized relationships of dependence and superiority. See Flori 1986 on the juridical basis of nobility in this era, but also Barbero 1991 on the important de facto distinctions which existed. See also Evergates 1995.

[27] Miller 1986:49–50. See also Gurevich 1968:130.

[28] The Benedictine Rule foresaw the same goals of independence for monasteries (LeGoff 1988:211; see also Duby 1988b:122).

[29] The relative importance of the vocabulary and economy of the gift in William of Poitiers's chronicle stands out in comparison to others. In William of Jumièges's *Gesta Ducum Normannorum*, this vocabulary is largely replaced by a more abstract, moral vocabulary which contrasts William's religious faith and rationality on the one hand with his enemies' "madness" (93) "arrogance" (103), "treacherous zeal" (103), "insane" provocations (107) and "pride and arrogance" (121) on the other. William, like most medieval clerics, thus substitutes a transcendental religious discourse for a more secular, performative one. On the historical reception of William of Poiters's chronicle, see Alba 2001:82–3. See Alba 2001:49ff on William of Jumièges's version of the events. Golding 2001:1–9 provides a general overview of all the sources on William. Orderic Vitalis likewise often fails to appreciate the mutual logics of giving and taking as part of a symbolic economy of aggression. See the *Historia Aecclesiastica* (ed. Chibnall) III:64–7 (on Robert of Grandmesnil); III:154–5 ("he was always ready to seize the property of others and dissipate his own in order to win a worthless reputation for

here is not just the social practice of the gift, but also the gift as a social trope – a carefully and elaborately constituted, idealized social model of both the practice and meaning of the gift, which guided thought and behavior in relation to social interaction and individual identity. We are less interested in whether the things William of Poitiers describes happened just as he says they did than in the assumption that his choices of how to describe (or invent) things reflect typical choices and strategies used by the warrior aristocracy. A key point of this book is that the gift was – in both social imagination and social practice – a locus of both reflection on and enactment of social and individual constitution. The gift was not simply a hegemonic or ideological force which created and maintained order. Rather, as a social trope, it provided a series of manipulable symbolic tools for "doing things" and "thinking about things." What is often lacking in monastically-inspired chronicles is attention to and understanding of these symbolic tools: they are replaced by other tropes of the gift drawn from a monastic or clerical tradition.

The narrative recounts William's birth and the circumstances around it that led some to question his noble standing. It then narrates how he gradually consolidated his power within Normandy through military means. He then turned his attention to England, and used a visit by the English nobleman Harold to Normandy as a way of establishing his claim to that throne. When Harold later saw events otherwise, William invaded, and defeated him at Hastings in 1066.

A crucial moment in William's narrative occurs when Harold comes to visit Normandy from England, to take an oath of obedience to William (thus forming the basis of William's claim to the throne). In the narrative, this oath is intimately linked to the great number of gifts and services which William provides. William first had to obtain Harold's release from captivity: he had fallen into the hands of a Norman lord upon landing. Afterwards, he lavished both lands and money on him. William thus essentially paid the ransom that Harold would otherwise have had to pay, as the text makes clear (69), and places him in a relationship of debt. He then provided Harold "every kind of hospitality" (71) – with all the attendant obligations for the guest. After receiving Harold's oath of fealty, he then "provided him and the men who had accompanied him with knightly arms and the finest horses" (71) and "treated his guest and envoy as his companion in arms so as to make him by that honour more faithful and beholden to him" (71–3). Knightly arms and horses are the kind of thing that a lord would typically give to his military dependents, and that seems to be part of their symbolic function here. This suspicion is increased by the phrase "make him ... beholden," which needs to be understood in the strongest sense: on several occasions elsewhere in the text, the chronicler infers that accepting a gift is paramount to taking a pledge

generosity"); and III:230–4 (on William, who seems to Orderic to have strangely mixed great cruelty and great generosity, even though he recognizes that William's savagery was widely reported (234–5) and that it helped William subdue potential enemies by image and reputation alone (306–9)).

of obedience, and accepting the authority of another over oneself.[30] The chronicle concludes Harold's visit with the ambiguous phrase, "after keeping his valued guest Harold with him for a while longer ("post moratum aliquandiu")" William sent him away "loaded with gifts" (77). The Latin phrase describing the stay suggests an extension beyond the normal limits of a visit – a kind of compulsory gift of hospitality forced upon Harold by William. The text then immediately launches into an attack on Harold for breaking his "sacrosanct oath" (77) when he later resisted William's claims to the throne.

The overall import of the passage is to portray Harold as somewhat bumbling and helpless, and clearly dependent on William. William's gifts and Harold's acceptance of them serves both to symbolize and reinforce this impression. The political relationship is enacted almost entirely in terms of gift-giving. William was clearly following an aggressive strategy of conquest both in general and on this particular occasion: the medieval historian Eadmer even considered that Harold's oath was sworn under duress.[31] The rescue from captivity and virtual payment of ransom, the gifts and the hospitality must be understood not only as gestures of friendship and alliance – which they were, in part – but also as essential elements of aggression and the creation of duress,[32] as Eadmer recognized. Like any ambitious medieval knight, William knew how to take advantage of an opponent's temporary weakness and to place that opponent in a position where his social standing – and thus ability to command the loyalty of potential allies – would be diminished.

Certainly on one level, William has established an abstract, "legalistic" basis for his later invasion. But he has also weakened Harold's ability to attract tangible support, through an attack on his integrity. Later, as the moment of invasion approaches, the chronicle notes that men came to William due to his "well-known liberality" in giving (103) as well as due to a sense of the rightness of his cause, while Harold obtains help by "buying" ("emere," 107). Of course, William also bought help, but the chronicle pointedly ignores this. Here, Harold's problem is not lack of money per se, since the chronicle notes that he has plenty of gold and silver. Rather, Harold is portrayed as lacking the integrity which would allow him to attract men and then give, rather than buy. He is in a position of need in relation to those whose help he buys, while conversely it is the knights who come to William, not he who goes shopping for them.

---

[30] See 9–11, where a rival is critiqued because he recieved many gifts but did not remain loyal; 21, where "sumptuous liberality" causes a vassal to be "bound" ("coniunctior") to William; 43, where clemency is presented as a gift and creator of debt, meant to "inspire" loyalty; 63, where a marriage is arranged "by his generosity, at great expense" in order to gain the right to additional inheritances; and in general, William's "gift" strategy for helping him control English lands after the conquest.

[31] Eadmer states this in *Eadmeri Historia Novorum in Anglia*, ed. M. Rule (1884), p. 7. The text is cited in Davis and Chibnall's edition of the *Gesta*, in a footnote to p. 70.

[32] William of Jumièges notes that Harold arrived in France specifically to swear fealty to William (159–61), and that after doing so, he was sent back "with many gifts" (161).

Harold's status represents in reverse what William Miller says about vengeance in medieval Iceland: that it was not necessarily vengeance per se which mattered, but rather "as long as [a man] could still elicit in others the *expectation and fear* that he would indeed avenge the next shame he suffered, he would still be counted a person of honor" (1993:117; my italics). Integrity is a social judgement granted by those around the individual, and a judgement about potential rather than necessarily about actual economic wealth. In very prosaic terms, the text depicts Harold as a "loser," from whom knights feel a need to get their money up front, since there's little chance there will be a victory to provide it later, while William is a "winner" from whom one can expect liberal gifts and rewards after his military success, and who incites envy. Having things to give is less important than being perceived as having the potential to continue to have things to give. Integrity symbolizes freedom from the relations of dependency which would compromise this potential.

Of course, William also *received* many gifts, but these essentially all came from those recognized as below him in rank. They are typically presented in the chronicle as repayments of previous gifts, as forms of symbolic supplication from inferior to superior which will be more than repaid (31, 59), or as adherences motivated by William's prior reputation for generous giving (103). Giving – and power – attracts more gifts, more service, and more power, but from below. Integrity is threatened primarily by gifts from above or from equals. While a gift from below could function as a challenge to integrity, the chronicler notes that William "took care also that his friends should owe him as much as possible" ("et procurabat semper ut sibi quamplurimum amici deberent," 16–17).[33] In his *Roman de Rou* (written between 1160 and 1174), the Norman poet Wace similarly notes of William's ancestor Rollo that he "bien prist autre don quant il le vout merir" (l. 1192) ("he accepted gifts from others whenever he was able to repay them," p. 33). Rollo, like William, clearly recognized the perils of an inability to reciprocate, and thus the need to be more giver than receiver. Here is the essence of William's sociopolitical strategy: gifts created debts, and established political control. "Friends" were the victims as much as anyone of gifts which carried an important component of aggression and constraint. As giving attracted additional gifts, which allowed more giving, the giver always stayed one step ahead of his receipts. In so doing, William obviously continually increased the economic burdens on himself. But at the same time, he acquired better means to defend the integrity of his lands, possessions and person; he acquired additional lands, resources and sources of revenue; he received various counter-gifts from those around him; and he acquired the forces needed to engage in warfare, with the rich sources of loot which it offered. Power, triumph and subsequent

---

[33] See Crouch 1988 for a similar study of the way in which William Marshall avoided "the levelling tendency in chivalrous society [which] was a danger to [his] dignity at the least, and to [his] person at the worst." Crouch stresses that "a prince or magnate needed to keep his followers at a distance" (1988:2).

largesse thus attracted the means to additional power, triumph and largesse.[34] William thus looks in many ways like a Melanesian "big man": while he may have the title of "count" or "duke," much of his effective power comes not simply from the inherent recognition that accrued to the title, or from any public source of authority, but from his aggressive strategies of giving. In this sense, he also broadly resembles the Germanic warlords of the early medieval period.[35] From a more theoretical perspective, Christopher Gregory notes that one key strategy for improving standing within a gift culture is to increase the rate of circulation of gifts (1982:60–1). This is essentially William's strategy – always getting more, in order to always give even more, constantly converting gifts to social obligations owed him, in an accelerating cycle. This strategy explains clearly why it was primarily the lower nobility who benefitted monetarily from such strategies.[36]

We also see that distinctions between antagonistic and non-antagonistic gifts become very tenuous where there are no clear-cut, *de jure* relationships of dependency or solidarity. William's gifts are to "friends" and thus do serve to create adherence and internal group solidarity. Yet they also serve to coerce and enforce these same values. And William, always one step ahead in the game, was clearly under no illusions about mutual solidarity – he clearly wanted indebtedness and the right to call on service or wealth from inferiors whenever he needed to convert the honor obtained from giving into material aid. Honor can thus be understood quite literally as symbolic capital.

Another example from a Norman context involves Robert Guiscard, a successful (and notorious) conqueror in southern Italy in the eleventh century, whose deeds were related by William of Apulia early in the twelfth century. Once he had obtained success, he was able to marry off his daughter, and on the occasion of her marriage "Sollicitat comites dux et quoscunque potentes,/ Dona petens, laeti quibus et vir et uxor abire/ Donati valeant" ("Went about among counts, the duke and other powerful men, demanding gifts so that the husband and wife would be happily married.") (William of Apulia, Book III, ll. 499–501). In response:

> Communiter illi
> Omnes tristantur, quasi vectigalia posci,
> A duce mirantes; sed non obstare valentes,
> Et mulos et equos diversaque munera praebant.
> His generum donans, addens sua, classe parata
> Ad sua cum magno patremque remisit honore.   (ll. 503–8)

[34] See Dunbabin 2000:202, 223, 226, 231.

[35] See for example Evans 1997, where he notes the many Anglo-Saxon words for lord of the type "ring-giver" "treasure-giver" and "ring-lord" (114), as well as the name of the lord's seat: the "gifstol" (109).

[36] See for example Verbruggen 1997:49 and Duby 1990:91 on the downward circulation of money in the medieval warrior economy.

> All were aggrieved by this, seeing it as virtually a form of tribute; but not withstanding they offered mules, horses and diverse presents, giving generously so that the father made off with great wealth aboard his ships.

While one might want to object that this scene is about compulsory tribute, not "gifts," my point is that gifts among the warrior aristocracy were virtually always at least in part about compulsion, as were counter-gifts. The passage mixes the vocabulary of tribute with that of "generosity" and "honor" and "giving" which typically applies to gifts, and without the first sentence would be indistinguishable from so many standard chronicle reports of "gifts."[37]

The exact degree of compulsion ascribable to Robert's official rank and position, and the degree ascribable to his military successes and lavish, previous gift-giving would be hard to separate here, but that is my point as well – strategies of giving and the benefits of rank were intimately connected. Robert gained his *de jure* rank of duke from the Pope only after successful military conquest and the acquisition of de facto power in competition with other counts: "Hic comitum solus concesso iure ducatus" ("to this count alone was awarded the title of duke") (Book II, l. 402). The fact that another "dux" was expected to give at his daughter's wedding suggests that it was less hierarchy than de facto power which motivated/compelled acquiescence. One encounters Robert later as well "Undique dona petens et supplementa" ("everywhere demanding gifts and support") (Book IV, l. 125). The phrase "dona petens" perfectly captures the link between gifts and the compulsion exercised by the powerful – especially through prior giving. Wace underlines even more powerfully the close link between affection, gifts and compulsion in the *Roman de Rou*. He notes that "envie out de Guillaume qui si ert haut monté,/ pesa li qu'il nel creint ne ne tient en chierté,/ vis li fu qu'il le tint par Franchoiz en vilté" (ll. 1388–90) ("it upset [Riulf] that William [Longsword] was not afraid of him and had no affections for him; he thought that William had contempt for him," p. 36). Riulf apparently felt that such fear and affection was intimately linked to a relationship of equality or even superiority for himself, because he revolted against William Longsword. William successfully put down the rebellion, however, and Wace notes that he was "proisiez et cremuz" (l. 1525) and that "mout le redoutoient et si l'amoient tuit" (l. 1547) ("praised and feared ... people feared him and everyone loved him," p. 39). Clearly love (and gratitude, one imagines) were not incompatible with fear, and in fact, for many subordinate warriors, the two were virtually equivalent. Power and authority was represented

---

[37] See William Miller's remark about medieval Iceland that "in the culture of honor, the prospect of violence inhered in virtually every social interaction between free men" (1993:85). The larger point is that solidarity and compulsion, violence and friendship, are largely inseparable. Likewise, "all saga conversation ... hovered on the edge of insult" (1993:85).

as a specific kind of public identity defined by the fear and gratitude that integrity could inspire.[38]

This is not to say that there was no difference in scale between more and less antagonistic gifts. But it is important to recognize the ways in which virtually all gifts worked to both enforce and strengthen the power inherent in formal, *de jure* social rank, and to allow the construction of more de facto forms of social power as well, in a delicate balance.[39] William the Conqueror was after all a bastard son of highly questionable *de jure* legitimacy, yet this did not prevent him from becoming a powerful king.

Giving and Performance

William the Conqueror and Robert Guiscard came from families which were already members of the warrior aristocracy: they were born with certain prerequisites necessary for the pursuit of power. But they largely "performed" their way to their final social positions, through military conquest certainly, but also through exchange practices which complemented and even enabled their military successes. Certainly one did not become a medieval nobleman purely through gift-giving in the way that a Melanesian "big man" owes his social position specifically to his ability to out-give his competitors. Nor was gift-giving technically necessary to maintain juridical noble status.[40] In the medieval context, giving often tended to express – rather than constitute – the superiority of the giver to the recipient, or conversely, to honor the recipient and recognize his superiority.[41] In relationships of dependency, gifts were often not directly aggressive since the social ranks were not open to competitive adjustment through gift-giving. Thus

[38] See William Miller's remark that honor could be thought of as "the ability to elicit envy in others" and "to extract from them a judgement of your superiority" (1993:125).

[39] In relation to this "balance," I should note that William of Poitiers at no point favors a pure "big man" society. Respect for broad categories of rank and public authority remained vital. The narrator's ethnographic sketch of the Bretons (73–5) reveals his horror at a society which, ironically, closely resembled the Viking war-lord society of William's ancestors. David Douglas shows that key elements of William's success as Duke depended on his ability to draw upon *de jure* forms of public power and authority which were better preserved in Normandy than elsewhere in France (Douglas 1969:133–58).

[40] See Gregory 1982:37–41 for an analysis of the gift in the context of clan-based and class-based societies, and the differences these two types of social organization entail for the role of the gift. Using his analysis, medieval western Europe appears as a "mixed" society. Testart (1993:87–90) argues for an anthropologically more restrictive understanding of the term "gift," and his analysis suggests that exchanges or transfers between juridically "bound" individuals in class-based societies should not be considered "gifts" at all, though I reject this personally.

[41] Such gifts – including official "fiefs" – became more and more common as legal and sacral notions of status and authority gained prominence, especially in France under the influence of Abbot Suger. See Poly and Bournazel 1991:202ff for a good analysis of the use of gifts in the service of this royal politics.

integrity was to a significant degree legally defined. But in the interstices of such relationships, gift-giving could clearly act not just to express, but to constitute and maintain social and political authority. This distinction between the expression of de jure authority and the constitution of de facto authority is fundamental to the concept of performed as opposed to juridical identity. And as William and Robert's lives suggest, the interstices open to the performative constitution of identity and power were sometimes quite large, and even socially dominant.

Gift-giving is most effective for (re)constituting and altering social status in societies which are most open to social movement, where individuals are least bound by juridical restrictions. In western European history, this corresponds to the era of the rise of so-called "banal lordship" in the tenth, eleventh and early twelfth centuries.[42] At this time, more and more de-facto power devolved to lower and lower levels of the warrior aristocracy, resulting ultimately in the virtual independence of neighboring aristocrats.[43] Adalbert of Laon noted in 1030 that although among the nobles there were only two overall lords, the king and the emperor, there were "others" whom "no power constrains" provided they avoid crimes of *lèse-majesté* (Carpentier and Le Mené 1996:74). This culminated, in extreme cases, in the quasi-independence of each single *chastellenie*. The devolution produced a significant leveling of the landscape of power in many parts of western Europe (Dunbabin 2000:223, 226).

In this context, more and more lords and castellans began to conceive of their place in the social order in terms of actual or potential sociopolitical integrity, and this integrity could be both constituted and later expressed in relationships of giving. Geoffrey Koziol's work on begging pardon and favor (in other words, seeking gifts from superiors) in western France is particularly illustrative. Koziol shows that the use of deferential language in charters spread farther and farther (socially lower and lower, in other words) in the area as comital hegemony declined (1992:250). But at the same time, sacral language of the type used to petition those seen as having clear-cut public authority disappeared (254). Koziol thus shows how a new model of political authority evolved, in which fluid social status and military strength replaced sacral authority (254–6). The word "strenuitas" appeared more and more in documents to denote the source of a lord's power (260) – the same word which is used on multiple occasions by William of Apulia to signal the uniqueness of the Norman lords whom he chronicled.[44] Most crucially, the authority which was formerly the basis for gift-giving, but

---

[42] See Georges Duby 1953 for a classic study of the Maconnaise region. For a good overview, see Jean Dunbabin 2000:145, 152, 162–4, 179 (for Aquitaine); 180–1 (for Burgundy); 189 (for Anjou); 209 (for Flanders); 218 (for Picardie); 219 (Berry and Auvergne); also 226, 235 on the general conditions.

[43] See Fossier 1982:969; Carpentier and Le Mené 1996:74; and Duby 1988a:81, 1988b:21–22, 164–6. Brown 2001:166ff documents fundamental shifts in the resolution of disputes already occurring in the period 836–854 within the Carolingian Empire, with charters showing "third-party authority" being replaced by "extrajudicial" modes of settlement.

[44] *La Geste Robert Guiscard*, Mathieu, ed.

which actually resided in forms of sacred and juridical power, became located *in* the act of giving itself (259–60), and identity was constituted fundamentally through performance. Although Koziol concentrates on strategies for creating solidarity, he also underlines that gift-giving and gift-beseeching were intimately connected to the perceived "autonomy" (307) of the lord addressed – including, most obviously, the implied autonomous ability to grant petitions, and to give.[45]

Certainly there was great variation across Europe in both the timing and extent of this devolution of power, and the argument here is not that rank among the aristocracy was ever unimportant.[46] But with rank greatly leveled, conditions came partially to replicate those of a classic "big man" society, in that all men of a certain basic nobility could pursue power and integrity on a roughly equal footing. The direct pursuit of autonomy was clearly through military means. But military power rested on the lord's ability to recruit sufficient followers and allies, and this recruitment itself depended on strategies of competitive giving.[47] The increasing size of seignorial households in the tenth and eleventh centuries no doubt reflected the increased opportunities for establishing local power through giving and taking, as well as of the social organization needed to take advantage of those opportunities.[48] As Robert Fossier notes, the goal was to "saisir sans mesure, mais ... aussi donner sans compter" (1982:804).[49] The widely noted increased demands on peasants by lords of the eleventh and twelfth centuries can also be understood as part of the intensified local competition for power made possible by the rise of banal lordships.[50] In his study of the expansion of Europe up to 1350, Robert Bartlett stresses the importance of this cycle of production and consumption through giving for aggressive aristocrats of the period, and places it in the context of the high rates of aristocratic turnover which marked much of this fluid era (Bartlett 1993:44–7). This is the sociohistorical context of antagonistic gift-giving, and it is the context which William and Robert took

---

[45] N.B. Aitchison documents a parallel process in medieval Ireland. There however, the quality of freedom was linked to sacredness, so sacredness itself was "perceived to permeate farther down the social hierarchy" (1994:66–7).

[46] See Reuter 1978:4–5 for a general discussion of the "open" (i.e. determined only by merit and achievement) "mixed" and "caste" (i.e. closed to new entry) models for the medieval aristocracy of this era. My argument is that a mixed model continued to prevail, but that society was more open than previously. A useful recent summary for twelfth-century France is Evergates 1995. See also Dunbabin 2000:145–6, 184–7 on the rise of castellans from the more general ranks of the warrior aristocracy.

[47] See Duby 1988a:126 on the importance of competitive giving in feudal courts.

[48] See Fossier 1982:438–9 on the increase in household sizes.

[49] See Duby 1973:190–1, where he mentions the vocation of "rapine" and the usage of "consommation" among the knights.

[50] See Fossier 1982:706–8 on the increased demands on peasants, as well as Duby 1973, 1988b. See Fossier 1982:774–83 on the increasing giving and conspicuous consumption by lords and its effects on the peasant classes.

advantage of in order to rise far beyond the wildest expectations offered by their births.[51]

Post-modern studies of identity typically critique the notion of "essential" or legalistic/juridical identities. Medieval historians, on the other hand, have traditionally devoted much energy to defining the exact nature of "legalistic" relationships, whether of kinship, vassalage, or nobility. More recently however, key studies have questioned the legalistic conception of institutions such as "feudalism."[52] Jean-Pierre Poly and Eric Bournazel (1991) and Susan Reynolds (1994) question the very existence of any clearly defined notion of the "vassal" and the "fief." Reynolds's earlier work (1984) points to the customary and performative nature of collective action in Europe throughout the period in question here. Work by Stephen White places legal strategies and practices of inheritance, judicial procedures and ordeals into the context of more open-ended, performative settings (White 1988, 1992, 1995, 1996).[53] This ongoing turn towards notions of performance invites a further reconsideration of the role of giving as a means of achieving integrity through performance.

Medieval Big Men

Georges Duby writes of the nobility of the eleventh and twelfth centuries:

> Parce que la dissolution de l'autorité monarchique a fini par établir tous ses membres dans une position d'indépendance et dans des attitudes mentales qui jadis avaient été celles des rois, elle n'accepte aucune contrainte, aucun service, sinon ceux qu'elle a librement choisi de rendre et qui, parce qu'ils ne prennent pas la forme de redevances matérielles, ne lui paraissent pas déshonorants. Elle refuse donc toute prestation qu'elle n'a pas consentie et n'accepte de se dépouiller de ses biens que par des dons gratuits et par des générosités mutuelles.
>
> (Duby 1973:190; see also 195)

Duby suggests that socioeconomic integrity was intimately linked to the socio-political world of the time.[54] The essence of high social status becomes now not

---

[51] See France 1999:188–9 on the social mobility characteristic of western Europe at this time, especially at the margins. See also Halsall 1998:31–2.

[52] The classic legalistic study of feudalism is Ganshof 1957. A recent general survey of the questions is Bouchard 1998, Ch. 1. She points to the emergent consensus that wealth and power were more important than noble birth for participation in the medieval aristocracy (6), and that legalistic self-definitions of a noble "class" arose only in the thirteenth century (25), while fief-holding remained during our period a very narrow phenomenon (35).

[53] See also Moore 1987:126–30, on the performative character of medieval ordeals, which would on first glance appear to be a clear example of transcendent judgement and authority.

[54] See Davis 1987's argument that the Mediterranean model of honor/shame, which is intimately related to the concept of integrity here, derived in areas peripheral to the state, as part of a kin-based alternative (or resistance) to central states.

simply the right to bear arms, but the right to be free from fiscal obligations (Duby 1973:195; 1988a:29), and indeed to be able to refuse even "prestations" freely. Power is epitomized in the ability to give "freely" of one's own will, to need nothing, and to face no obligations or debts. Free giving symbolizes lack of dependence. As Lévi-Strauss notes, "to be able to give is not to need" (1969:87).

We have already mentioned in passing the "big man" societies of Melanesia. In fact, it is interesting to compare the medieval social setting under discussion with Marshall Sahlins' analysis of the difference between hierarchical chieftainships (in Polynesia) and big-man cultures (in Melanesia) (Sahlins 1963). The comparison is far from exact, since the importance of hierarchical forms of power, and of blood nobility, always remained strong in western Europe. There were very few truly "new men" who rose to great power from totally obscure origins, although Robert Guiscard came close. But relatively speaking, the devolution of power functioned to open up increasing space within the ranks of the warrior aristocracy for the enactment of big-man-like modes of power. According to Sahlins, such power arises in "underdeveloped settings" and is of a highly personal nature. The big man functions as a type of hero who is able to act socially by establishing both renown for giving, and also "personal relations of compulsion" through giving, by "placing others in gratitude and obligation." His essential means to power is the production of followers through amassing and giving away goods, in such a way that he "create[s] and use[s] social relations which give him leverage on others." Sahlins notes that such power is comparatively unstable, needing continual reinforcement, and that it also tends to result ultimately in the "economic extortion" of the big man's sources of production. But at least for a while, the big man is able to "negate reciprocal obligations" by "substituting extraction for reciprocity." He thus establishes a form of integrity based on his "ability to give outsiders more than they can possibly reciprocate."

Sahlins's theories of identity formation can be further elaborated by turning to Marilyn Strathern's work on the gift. She argues that individuals should be conceived as the "composite site of the relationships that produced them" (1988:13), and that gift exchange is the essential producer of these relationships. "Identity is the outcome of interaction" (1988:127–8).[55] But for effective social action, individuals often need to emphasize or "maximize" a specific identity. In these cases, "internal ... differentiation must in turn be eliminated to produce the unitary individual" (1988:14). Occasions may also arise where group action can only occur subsequent to "a process of de-pluralization" which presents "an image of unity" (1988:13). But in either case, the exchange behaviors and ritual action which produce these new identities lead only to temporary, unstable states, and social life "consists in a constant movement from one state to another, from

---

[55] See Humphrey and Hugh-Jones 1992, Introduction (especially p. 13) for a similar view of personal identity as a product of exchange relations, but focusing more on barter.

one type of sociality to another" (1988:14). Strathern shows that intense investments of giving are required to achieve (and maintain) these states.

This situation recalls the social organization of the medieval warrior aristocracy. These aristocrats were notorious for their divided and multiple loyalties,
especially in relation to land tenure and expectations of service – this is, after all,
a central theme of many literary texts of the time. Even kings were at times the
vassal of another king. Aggressive giving as a recruitment tool served essentially
to "de-pluralize" relationships between a lord, his various followers, and their
other potential relationships, and to create and coerce the unity necessary for
action. Meanwhile, competitive giving also must be understood as an investment
which could suppress an individual's own plural relationships to equals and superiors, and constitute a single identity for that individual which formed the basis
of power, authority and action. As Strathern says, gift-giving can be as much
about doing things to oneself as it is doing things to or with others (1988:166).

The drive for integrity can thus be understood as a continual series of investments which serve to maintain over a long period of time otherwise fragile and
unstable unitary identities – a potentially endless series of inputs necessary to
prevent the decay of identity in an inherently entropic world. The individual literally suppresses plurality and creates unity and integrity through the process of
investments in gift-giving (and gift-refusing). The key difference from Melanesian big men is that William's sources of giving came as much or more from
military action as from exploitation of lands and dependents. Whatever degree of
authority or public power ("chieftainship") he may have inherited, it is clear he
was nearly always at war in the years between 1047 and 1060 (Douglas 1969:53ff)
trying to defend, extend, and fully realize that potential power through socioeconomic and military performance. And this activity occurred at a time and
place where "vassalage would seem impossible to define ... in terms characteristic of later feudal society" (Douglas 1969:96) and where "few [Norman char-
ters] use any of the terms of feudal status in anything like the precise sense they
subsequently acquired" (97). Thus even Normandy, a region often cited as an
exception to the devolution of authority in the post-Carolingian world, turns out
to be characteristically fluid and unstable in many ways.[56]

[56] Douglas does argue however that William's ultimate success was due in part to his
ability to take advantage of the remaining base of organization and power in Normandy, which
was indeed more intact than elsewhere in Europe (1969:133–52). The interplay of public
authority and performance was thus crucial in this instance.

2

The Symbolic Constitution of the Giving Subject: William the Conqueror and Robert Guiscard

Up to this point, we have been analyzing antagonistic giving and the integrity-drive with an economistic approach. The honor accruing to givers expresses an underlying socioeconomic power, which is banked in the form of honor. More precisely, honor from giving expresses social ties and social obligations ("debts") which are owed to the holder of the honor. The honor is convertible to goods and services which are the means of exercising power. Honor is thus a classic form of symbolic capital in the sense that Bourdieu uses the term in his economistic analysis of gift culture (1977, esp. Ch. 4).[1] More prosaically, honor is the currency of the warrior aristocracy. As economic anthropologist C.A. Gregory says, "gift production must be understood as the process of production of symbols" (1982:91). But there is more at stake in this notion of the symbol than just economics. The emphasis which Duby places on the will in his remarks cited in the previous chapter, as well as Wace's interest in the dual emotions of love and fear, allows the economic and political to bleed into the ethical and psychological domains, and reinforces the notion of identity elaborated by Strathern.[2] In this chapter, we will explore this second component of identity, honor, power and integrity more fully.

The importance of gratuity and spontaneity in gift-giving has been widely noted.[3] For this reason no doubt, charters recording gifts in the eleventh century often stressed that the gift was "spontaneous," and that any counter-gifts were provided purely out of "charity," and not as part of a negotiation (Tabuteau 1988:21–2). It was in fact "the gratuitous, wholly voluntary nature of a gift which earned the donor merit in heaven," to cite Emily Tabuteau's discussion of gifts to churches and monasteries (1988:27). But whether one is talking about heavenly or earthly merit, the absolute freedom (as well as ability) to give seems to represent the essence of integrity for the warrior aristocrat. Studies in Medi-

---

[1] For a recent critique of Bourdieu's economistic orientation, wherein symbolic capital ultimately converts always to economic capital, see Godbout 1998, especially pages 119ff.

[2] The ethical as well as political and economic versions of integrity all have classical analogues. See Aristotle's *Politics* and his notion of the "economy," to take just one example, and Horace's poem "Integer vitae scelerisque purus".

[3] On the connection of gifts and spontaneity more generally, see Godbout 1998:142; Godelier 1999:14; Miller 1993:6, 19; and Schwarz 1996:77. See also Barraud *et al.* 1994:41 on the same feature in a particular Melanesian society.

terranean anthropology since the 1980s have begun to focus not just on honor, but on "grace," recognizing that honor is not really the final goal of social actors, but rather a measure of their closeness to a more profound goal, that of "grace," which bears many similarities to our "integrity." In such studies, grace is repeatedly linked to "gratuity," which takes the form of "non-reciprocity" (Pitt-Rivers 1992:216, 222). Bourdieu also notes the "gratuitous" quality which is linked to "authority" and "charisma" (1977:193). Integrity enacted through gratuitous giving demonstrates not just economic but also psychological freedom from compulsion. This symbolic demonstration of integrity is what underlies the conspicuous spending and consumption so common in the Middle Ages (Duby 1973:189–201, 260–7), and more generally the "grandiose gestures of generosity" (Peristiany and Pitt-Rivers 1992:12) which are integral to both gift cultures and honor cultures. Returning to William of Apulia's accounts of Robert Guiscard, one sees a curious alternation of terror and cruelty on the one hand, and extraordinary generosity, unexpected even by the recipients, on the other, in his relations with captured or rebellious cities (Book II, ll. 335–59; Book III, ll. 149–62). But in fact, as Wace shows, the two stratagems complement each other. The exercise of terror reveals what Robert potentially could do to his enemies, and establishes a position of strength. If his gifts and generosity derived from a position of weakness and inability to defend himself, they would only invite more depredations (as occurs when the Greeks try to give to the Normans). But given from a position of strength, they further augment that position: they show Robert with such confidence in his position that he can forego terror for generosity, while rendering the citizens all the more obliged to him, since he has essentially "given" them their lives. Only great status and power can beget great generosity, and gratuitous generosity conveys that power.

An even clearer example of this dynamic occurs in another Norman source when a Greek envoy arrives at a Norman camp to determine whether the Normans wish to fight or withdraw in the face of a large Greek force. The envoy arrives on a "pulcherrimo equo" ("extremely fine horse") which a certain Norman named Ugo strikes on the neck and kills with his bare fist. The envoy is then sent back with "meliori equo" ("a better horse"), along with word that the Normans plan to fight. The gratuitously aggressive violence provides the occasion for an equally aggressive gift; the fact that the horse given by the Normans is better than the one on which the envoy arrives is clearly meant as a challenge and insult. It leaves the Greeks "admiratione et metu percussi" ("struck with astonishment and apprehension"), and they suppress the report among the larger army lest the troops be tempted to flee.[4]

Even more stupefying, apparently, was a gift reported by Wace to have been given by Richard III of Normandy. He relates that a certain youth arrived with a fine gift for Richard, in hopes of receiving permission to hold onto his deceased

---

[4]   Geoffrey Malaterra, *De rebus gestis Rogerii Calabriae et Siciliae Comitis*, Ernesto Pontieri, ed., 1. 9 (p. 12); the text was composed sometime in the early twelfth century.

father's lands. It was a vase, described as "mult bone e chiere,/ n'iert mie a achater legiere,/ tote iert d'or mult noblement faite" (ll. 2347–9) ("very fine and splendid; it would not have been easy to buy, as the whole thing was expertly made from gold," p. 117). Richard takes it, then turns to a cleric who happens to be sitting nearby and says "Dan clerc, pernez!/ La juste est vostre, recevez!" (ll. 2353–4) ("take this vase, the vase is yours, have it," p. 117). The cleric takes the vase, and then "estendei sei e si murut" (l. 2359) ("he fell prostrate and died," p. 117). Everyone then marvels at the occurrence. Whatever the exact cause of the cleric's death, the event no doubt produced a great deal of positive publicity for Richard's social identity and advertised his integrity, as of the event "en firent lunges grant paroles" (l. 2364) (It was "discussed ... at length," p. 117).

We should note in passing that this anecdote is a good illustration of the distinction between acts of honor, which occur in situations of reciprocity, and acts of integrity, which create situations of non-reciprocity or advertise already-existing situations of this type. According to classic honor theory, one should only engage in challenges and recognitions of honor with one's peers or those immediately above or below oneself. It is seen as dishonorable to become involved with those "not in the contest," so to speak (Pitt-Rivers 1966:31; Bourdieu 1966:197). Richard's act towards the cleric, from this perspective, is not an act of honor. But it is clearly an act of integrity, and the cleric's death is of course the perfect indicator of the impossibility of a reciprocal relationship with Richard.

Clearly, one's social identity involves a complex mix of economic, ethical and psychological components, which honor must account for in its measurements; and integrity produces a complex mix of economic, ethical and especially psychological effects on others, which all contribute to their willingness to adhere to and act for the individual in question and translate the individual's identity and integrity into power. It is illusory to try fully to separate these components. For example, the more freely one gives and the less one seems to care (psychologically) about the material things given, the more effective the gesture of giving will be as an (economic) recruitment tool for potential followers hoping for potential future gifts. But then what should one make of the most drastic social gesture – the refusal of the gift? Is it just a demonstration of self-sufficiency and a lack of dependency, or does it offer a clue to more fundamentally non-economic elements of the integrity drive? This act is the one which seems most closely tied to issues of psychology and personal identity. It is this subject which this study would like to examine more closely in thinking about the deeper implications of integrity for our understanding of the medieval aristocratic individual as he struggles to become the "original proprietor of [him]self" (Strathern 1988:135).

Symbolic Identity: Constituting the Self through the Gift

In the *Gesta Guillelmi*, after Harold's body is found on the field at Hastings, William refuses a generous gift offered for the body, suggesting that it would be "indignum" (140) for Harold to be buried while his dead followers lay on the field, sacrificed to Harold's greed. Harold is accused specifically of "cupiditatem" (here and previously). This is the code for a desire for "things themselves" within the discourse of gift culture, outside the framework of exchange and reciprocity. William's refusal of the gift for Harold, while it might initially seem to be simply another medieval example of aristocratic avoidance of buying, selling, and exchanging, has more profound consequences. His lack of interest in the gold offered for Harold's body is due primarily to the fact that the gold carries a negative symbolic value.

In fact, the symbolic element of the system of honor is presented in the discourse of William of Poitiers – and in the epic as well – as its central feature. That is, the ethico-psychological element is presented as superior to – and on occasion even opposed to – the materialistic or economistic character of honor as a resource. It should also be noted that material objects are dominated by this symbolic system as well. While the symbolic capital of honor accrued to givers, this honor was itself symbolized by the thing given. And while it is true that more highly ranked gift items provided more honor to the givers, that rank depended crucially on the honor symbolically embodied in the item itself due to its own specific history of ownership, use and exchange. Within the upper, prestige spheres of the exchange system of the warrior aristocracy, the value of a given material object, piece of land, service rendered, or even quantity of money always remained fundamentally symbolic – tied to the particular circumstances of a specific history, act of transfer, owner, and giver.[5] Things were thus themselves symbols of the primary symbolic capital of honor, and had to remain always subsidiary to that symbolic economy of giving, receiving and human relationships. People created symbols, and the symbols were subsidiary to the people.

In such a context, things per se thus have no real status – only a symbolic one. In a commodity economy, virtually everything is for sale, and has a value mediated by the universal measure of money within a single exchange system wherein everything is convertible to everything else. But gift cultures typically have many different categories of exchanges, and the same object can enter several different categories, and have radically different values due to both the type of exchange and the specific identity of the exchangers. Anthropologists have thus argued for the de-essentialization of the category of object in gift cultures,[6] and Strathern

---

[5] See Aafke Komter's suggestion that in social psychology the gift is an instrument to assign symbolic meaning to the fundamental dimensions of personal relationships (1996:8). See also Godbout's analysis of the character of primitive money as fundamentally symbolic in this sense (1998:113–15). And see Miller 1993:110, 119 on the importance of local context in giving.

[6] On the varying modes of exchange and the shifts in status which an object can undergo,

argues that objects do not have stable or essential properties in Melanesian gift culture (1988:134). Maurice Godelier suggests that the "'symbolic' dominates the imaginary and the real in these cultures" (1999:7).[7] While the validity of this statement actually depends on the particular sphere of exchange involved, it seems to become more true the more rarified the exchange sphere and the more highly ranked the participating individuals are.

Returning to the earlier point that gift objects are seen as inalienable extensions of the individual giver, bearing his or her identity, we can begin to appreciate the full sense of the symbolic nature of lands, services or material things in this culture.[8] The thing is the symbolic extension of the self, part of what Georg Simmel calls the "ideal sphere" which surrounds personal honor.[9] Roland's sword, Durendal, in the epic *The Song of Roland*, is a classic example of this phenomenon. (This text will be discussed more fully in Ch. 6. See the opening pages of that chapter for a plot summary.) The sword is so strongly identified with Roland that its loss would constitute an assault on his own personal integrity, the text implies.[10] As Roland lies near death after a climactic battle with the Saracen foe, an individual Saracen approaches, and "Rollant saisit e sun cors e ses armes" ("He seized Roland's body and his armour") (l. 2280). He says to himself that "... iceste espee porterai en Arabe" ("I shall take this sword to Arabia") (l. 2282). But he is killed by Roland, who uses his last dying bit of

---

see especially Appadurai 1986b. On the de-essentialization of the category of object, and more generally of the subject-object distinction, see Barraud *et al.* 1994, Introduction and pp. 102–3.

7   Godelier's terms here clearly echo the analytical categories of Lacan. However, his use of the term "symbolic" – and certainly mine – approaches more closely the meaning of that term in the work of Pierce, where "symbolic" contrasts with "semiotic" (see Godelier 1999:174). Here the symbolic is not a realm into which the individual enters, thus "losing" an essential part of the self, but rather a realm constructed and controlled by the individual, in reference to him- or herself. At least, this is how this symbolic realm is represented in the medieval texts. I will have occasion to question this at a later point.

8   The word "honor" itself referred to both the moral standing of an individual, and to the lands which that individual held – if in fact these two could be truly separated. Dominique Barthélemy has recently underlined the importance of the "integrité" of medieval "honor" and its indivisibility, suggesting that honor is to be identified specifically with inalienable lands (Barthélemy 1996:135–8). Thus lands functioned as symbolic extensions of the self.

9   Cited in Pitt-Rivers 1966:25. See also Gregory 1982:33–5 on the "personification of things" in gift cultures and the lack of distinction between person and thing, as well as Mauss 10, 18.

10   Peter Haidu's brief analysis of the sword, as integrally linked to the specific narrative of Roland – and thus as a classic symbolic product of specific circumstances – could be consulted in relation to this point (Haidu 1993:35). See also his study of the aesthetic fetishization of weaponry in the text (44–9), and his remark that "it is as if the weapons were the concretization of the warriors' value and contained their heroism as a precipitate. The weapons and their beauty are signifiers" (46). For philological analyses of the naming of the sword in medieval epics, see Wathelet-Willem 1966 and Lejeune 1951. More recent analyses of the sword's discursive role for the hero and for issues of identity are in Miller 2000:207–9 (the hero) and Warren 2000, esp. p. 18 (national identity and alterity), and in passing throughout.

energy to do so. Note that the narrator scarcely differentiates between name, body and weapon in the Saracen's grasping act, though he does indicate that the Saracen's interest is clearly in the sword, the great symbol of Roland's prowess. Roland clearly believes that the possession of the sword will be read symbolically as an indication of the Saracen's triumph over him, and that the Saracen is essentially trying circumvent the symbolic economy by obtaining the symbol without truly accomplishing the deed to which the symbol should refer. Roland both prevents this abuse of the rules of the symbolic economy, and also underlines their functioning in his reply to the Saracen: "cum fus unkes si os/ Que me saisis" ("how did you dare/ Grab hold of me?") (ll. 2292–3), he says to him. Seizing the sword means symbolically seizing Roland, the reply suggests, and he will not allow this symbolic fraud which might divest him of honor. The opposite corollary of the same situation would be that Roland would never take or accept any object whose symbolic content would threaten to diminish his own integrity. And a final point is that the symbolic objects which are linked to integral individuals – swords, horses, and so on – have a great deal invested in them, just as the individual's more abstract unitary identity does. More generally, one must recognize that gift objects, contrary to much classic gift theory (especially Mauss 1967 and Gregory 1982) are not necessarily personal: rather, individuals seek to personalize such objects as much as possible, and in particular to enhance the link between their own personality and that of the object. This is what gives the objects such value. Supplicatory gifts, however, to take one example, would be as likely to bear the personal mark of the receiver as the giver. The larger lesson is that unlike signs or everyday objects, neither integral persons nor symbolic objects come "ready made": their meanings must always be constructed – and reconstructed – through performance.[11] Ambitious individuals constantly seek to render heterogeneous ("personalized") a field of homogeneous social signifiers, to borrow a description from Antonio Callari (2002). In fact, Callari argues that the essence of the commodity is its homogeneity, whereas the essence of the gift is the personal heterogeneity it produces – a heterogeneity "embedded in a culture of ethical and political performativity" (2002:255).[12]

If we follow Callari's lead and reintroduce the gift/commodity opposition in this way, we can see that for the medieval case, commodification has nothing to do with markets, money, or consumer goods per se. Rather, a commodity is a socially-defined thing, whose meaning is generalized and homogenous across the culture – a standard sword is just a sword, a horse is just a horse. The things

[11] See the critiques in Strathern 1988 and Laidlaw 2002 of Gregory's notion of the "personal" character of the gift. Both critics attack Gregory's Marxist, metaphysical (and, they claim, ethnocentric) notions of the "individual," "identity," "property" and "value." See also Osteen 2002b on the tenuous and shifting conversion of what he calls "commodities" to personalized objects (and vice versa).

[12] Speaking specifically of the situation in western France, Geoffrey Koziol has likewise noted that symbolic action is commonly a "vehicle for competition as well as for consensus" (1992:305).

may signify knighthood, but they symbolize no particular individual identity. The commodity is simply the "social thing itself" as primary object, devoid of any secondary status as symbol of personal performance. And direct engagement with the thing itself represents for the unitary individual the potential dissolution of his carefully constructed personal identity in the faceless mass of more or less generalized social meanings.[13] In this context it is giving – or refusing to give – that constructs heterogeneity. But since this type of gift is also a form of violence, one could say that violence produces personal heterogeneity in the field of social homogeneity. The gift, violence and the symbol share a generalized opposition to the commodity qua sign and thing.

In such a system, William the Conqueror's accusation of greed against Harold works on two levels. William implies that Harold was dishonorable in having failed to recognize his debt of honor to William as his superior: he short-circuited the system of symbolic exchange by keeping the things exchanged while failing to respect the rules requiring reciprocation. But "greed" here also means that Harold wanted an office, land or thing "for itself": William implies that Harold was not interested in accomplishing the honorable deed of which the office, land or thing would be the secondary symbol. He thus rejected the very basis of the rules of the symbolic economy, converting gifts from symbols to simple objects. In other words, he engaged in an idolatry of the symbol, or if one wishes, of the thing itself, making him, in essence, unaristocratic and unworthy of respect.[14] His body will therefore be left on the field for the wolves and ravens, to be literally dis-integr-ated.[15] William's refusal of the gift underlines his own lack of "cupiditas," as well as his purely internal, honor-oriented motivation. The refusal underlines the essentially symbolic quality of wealth, and the need for it to be rejected when the symbolism of its acquisition would make it inappropriate to acquire. William's act thus goes beyond the bounds of economistic motivation, since it rejects the material for the symbolic. Studies of the anthropology of "grace" (that is to say, integrity) have stressed repeatedly that abstinence is a sign of grace (Campbell 1992:143–4), and that a general "ascetism" is linked to this quality (Bourdieu 1992:85–6). William's behavior enacts these moral categories in the most direct and concrete circumstances of (potential) material exchange.

William's strategy was a common medieval one, found in both historical sources and literary ones. The relative weight given to the economic motive of

[13] See Warren 2000:17 for a similar analysis of the threat of the material object, and in particular of the way in which its potential autonomy would challenge that of the autonomy of the warrior. See also Gurevich 1992:146ff for an analysis very similar to mine in terms of the issues of internality and externality, and the dependent, symbolic character of objects. Similar points are made in Gurevich 1985:211ff, with more emphasis on gift-giving.

[14] See Jamous 1992:171, where, in speaking of the Iqar'iyen Berbers of Morocco, he notes that "it would be difficult to speak of an exchange of women or of goods valued in themselves."

[15] Robert Guiscard likewise engages in the dismembering and metaphorical "devouring" of his enemies on the field of battle (Book II, ll. 196–256).

not wanting to be placed in debt through a gift as opposed to the psychological value of showing one's contempt for both the thing given and its giver varies, but in fact the two are virtually inseparable. Wace's account of the Normans' rise to power is full of examples of refused gifts, which are all part of their strategy to achieve full socioeconomic and political integrity. At one point, the king of France offers Rollo half his kingdom in gratitude for services rendered to him, but Rollo responds " 'Vostre tere,' dist il, 'vous rent...de vostre tere nulle rienz ne demant/ne de tout vostre avoir'" (ll. 664–6) ("I give you back your land … I ask for no part of your land and for none of your wealth," p. 24). He then calls for men willing to help him go and conquer land on his own. When the king offers his own men, Rollo again refuses (l. 673/p. 24). Later William Longsword reconquers a castle for one of his allies, and gives it back to him. The ally then says he cannot properly defend the castle for his own, and tries to give it back to William, but William refuses it, insisting on giving it back to the vassal along with a gift of all the extra resources needed to defend it (ll. 1864ff/p. 45).

This strategy suggests that there was a radical anti-materiality which characterized warrior-aristocratic culture. Depending on one's perspective, one could say that the materiality of the thing disappears, or one could say that the subject/object distinction vanishes into a dominant subject.[16] As a result of this system of medieval aristocratic thinking, material objects, and especially money, enter into a complex and subtle discourse. Texts often speak of material motivations for actions, and a desire for wealth. Yet such remarks need to be understood within the larger context of the symbolic economy. William of Apulia's account of Robert Guiscard in Italy again offers a relevant example. William states that the Normans were attracted to the region of southern Italy "Est adquirendi simul omnibus una libido" ("all of the same acquisitive desire") (Book I, l. 38; see also ll. 185–7). Yet at key moments in the text, the Normans refuse gifts and offers of money, and William often accuses their opponents – or rebellious Normans themselves – of cupidity and avarice (I, ll. 210–1; I, l. 325; see also IV, ll. 390–4).

Such paradoxes can be understood if one realizes that material wealth per se remains always symbolic of honor, and is acquired through actions that bring the honor which it symbolizes.[17] It must be rejected if it represents non-symbolic desires. Thus a group of Normans refuses to obey their chosen leaders and join up with an Italian noble. It is at this point that William of Apulia imputes to them negative motivations of material wealth:

> … quos forsitan ipse vel aurum
> Dando vel argentum, pacti mutare prioris
> Compulerat votum; quid non compellit inire

[16] See Thomas 1991 for a "deconstruction of the essentialist notion that the identity of material things is fixed in their structure and form" (28). Thomas studies in particular the "mutability of things in recontextualization" (28).

[17] Note that honorable actions, both in this text and in others such as the William of Orange cycle, can include clever ruse and trickery as well as military action.

Ambitio census? sanos evertere sensus
Haec valet, ac fidei rigidos dissolvere nexus.   (I, ll. 323–7)

... [that noble] must have convinced them, by giving either gold
or silver, to shift their sworn allegiance away from their previous
lord; is there anything that will not be undertaken out of desire for
gain? It is capable of rendering wise men foolish, and of causing
firm men to forswear their oaths.

Soon after this passage, the Normans are again offered the chance to betray a
leader for money. But this time they reply that they will follow a noble who
is "poor, but brave and generous" (I, l. 422), showing that generosity is more
of a psychological than an economic evaluation. They state that it is not gold
which interests them, but the noble himself, son of their great ally (ll. 425–6).
When he protests that he has nothing to give them (ll. 430–4), they reply that
"Nostrum te princeps nullus/ Pauper erit vel egens" ("with you as our leader,
no man will be poor or in need of anything") (ll. 435–6). The passage is virtually a moral lesson on what integrity really is about, and it explains why Harold
of England is described as having to buy troops, while William the Conqueror
has men flocking to him before his invasion of England without giving them a
penny. This noble is "brave and generous" – in other words, he has the potential
to obtain things to give away, if he has help, and once he gets the things, he will
surely give them away. He and his family have established a degree of symbolic
integrity in the past which inheres with him even when material wealth is gone,
while his opponent – like Harold – may have plenty of wealth, but he does not
have the requisite integrity. The Normans are able to underline their preference
for symbolic capital over material wealth, but in the end of course, they are victo-
rious and gain plenty of material wealth anyway – as a secondary byproduct of
the choice of the symbolic over the material. At various other points, the text is
also at pains to underline that it is loyalty and adherence to internalized codes
of honor, rather than desire for material gain, which are the key motivations
of the Normans, even when they do accept money (see I, ll. 512–9). They also
conspicuously refuse gifts on other occasions (see II, ll. 55–66), thereby refuting
suggestions by their enemies that they might be simply "prona ... ad avaritiam"
(II, ll. 44–5) – in other words, desirous of things themselves disembedded from
their symbolic connotations.[18]

In this context, the quest for integrity begins to look less and less like a prima-

---

[18] For another study of gift-giving as simultaneously "generosity and aggressiveness," see
Warren 1999. She looks specifically at the giving of a highly symbolic object in the context
of a series of lesser gifts. She shows how the entire set of exchanges can be seen as a series of
maneuvers which attempt to convert gifts to commodities and vice versa as part of a symbolic
competition for authority. Most importantly, she analyzes how the chronicler makes use of a
discourse of the gift in a unified, strategic fashion, such that the historiographical discourse
and the anthropological "facts" become inseparably melded in a more general "trope" of the
gift.

rily materialistic or economic drive, motivated by utilitarian calculations of symbolic capital conceived in a socioeconomic framework. It begins to appear more and more centered on a certain symbolic conception of individual identity and power. This identity and power is constructed and expressed through a symbolic economy in which spontaneous or free acts of giving – or refusing to give or receive – allow the assertion of the dominance of the individual's will and internal, self-directed motivations over external constraints, external temptations (material or otherwise), externalized social values, or social necessities or obligations.[19] Tellingly, even Harold's messengers try to pass off his attempts at buying his way out of William's sights in these terms. Wace reports that they told William before the Battle of Hastings that "por t'amor e por ta grace/ e sainz crieme de ta manace,/ te dorra quantque tu voldras,/ or e argent, deniers e dras" (ll. 6875–8) ("for love of you and your grace, and without fearing your threats, [Harold] will give you whatever you want, gold and silver, money and clothing," p. 168). Harold desperately tries to show that he is acting freely, without external compulsion. But William of course rejects him.

In an integrity model of identity, symbols also remain secondary to the individual – defined or created by him through performance, rather than determining him from the outside. Thus when William the Conqueror puts on his hauberk backward, as he prepares to attack Edward, he refuses to have himself be inscribed by this socially-accepted negative omen or sign, but instead laughs at it, thus converting the incident into a symbolic image of his own integrity, which was then picked up subsequently by at least two other narratives. The man is not subservient to signs; rather, he redefines them as personalized symbols.[20]

This is a classic, extreme example of what Douglas and Isherwood call "tak[ing] charge of the information" (1979:79). Their study of the communicative function of goods, like those of Baudrillard, Barthes, and others, focuses on the semiotic aspect of goods – the way they constitute a system of largely stable signs, which consumers use to access and produce meaning, just as they do with linguistic signs. For the most part, medieval language and medieval material objects worked the same way – carrying socially predetermined meanings which might be manipulated only slightly by users. But as Douglas, Isherwood, and students of the gift in general all recognize, gift economies feature discrete spheres of exchange. Moreover, the more elite the sphere of exchange, the more open to symbolic manipulation and personalization the items in it become. At the limit, medieval objects such as war horses, heraldic standards, or fine swords – which participated in a symbolic sphere of exchange incommensurable with everyday items – were less semiotic than symbolic. Their meanings did not come with them, socially determined for the user, but rather, the user created the

[19] See Campbell 1966, especially 155–9, for an example of the theorization of sexual and material desire as the primary threat to honor and integrity.

[20] This incident is reported by William of Poitiers (125), and picked up in the *Brevis relatio* and Wace's *Roman de Rou*, as noted on p. 125 of Davis and Chibnall's edition.

meanings.[21] This is what William the Conqueror does with signs (the omen of the hauberk), and what elite-level gift exchanges did with objects like Roland's Durendal. Rather than operating within an information system, William takes control of it and becomes the producer of the information. The production of symbols becomes itself indicative of the integrity of the producer in relation to the semiotic system around him. Since we are talking about sign systems, we might even say that integrity means acceding to the "Name of the Father," in Lacanian terms, and escaping the "lack" that characterizes entry into what he calls the symbolic, but what in our terms is more appropriately the semiotic. William's "refusal to transact" in relation to Harold must ultimately be seen, in this light, as similar to other anthropological examples of "refus[al] to be tempted ... by material considerations" (Douglas and Isherwood 1979:139). The material considerations would produce a transaction between hierarchically differentiated spheres, and most importantly between a symbolic and a semiotic (monetary) sphere. William would thus lose integrity by entering into the semiotic. His refusal deftly turns the dilemma on its head, for he converts money into a purely symbolic object – representing Harold's shame – and thus subverts the potential threat.

The phrase "taking charge of the information" cited above allows us to arrive at a better and fuller understanding of the relationship between personal identity, integrity, and power among the medieval warrior aristocracy. Earlier we defined power fairly traditionally as the effect in the world of others' evaluation of an individual's personal identity, with that identity being evaluated in relation to an idealized personal identity taking the form of integrity. But integrity is an example of what Foucault would call a "discipline," by which he means a system of social control.[22] For Foucault, power is exercised when the codes of a discipline are effectively imposed onto members of a society in such a way that their range of action and conception is effectively structured by this imposition. In the case of the medieval warrior aristocracy, we have seen numerous examples of the imposition of such codes onto individuals; in the language of medieval chronicles, the successful imposition is indicated by the use of terms such as "fear," "love," and "amazement" which are attributed to either witnesses or recepients of the imposing actions. Stephen White has shown how medieval emotions were socially constructed and coded, and how their effective use by individuals was part of a Foucauldian "technology of power" (White 1998). While he focuses on the use of anger by agents to impose power *onto* subjects, it is just as important to recognize that emotions such as fear or love experienced *by* such subjects were equally constructed and coded in relation to disciplines of authority. Foucault

---

[21] The one exception to this, at least in part, involves objects connected with the sacred, and specifically with relics. I will examine the relationship of performance to the sacred in detail in Ch. 3.

[22] Brief introductions to Foucault's thoughts on power are Foucault 1988:208–26 and his Afterword to Dreyfus and Rabinow 1988. Much of his later work on prisons and sexuality revolves around the general question of power and the individual.

argues that power is both a cause and an effect in the world, not just the latter as more traditional definitions suggest. This can be clearly seen among the warrior aristocracy: on the one hand the many nonpowerful men are the judges who must be impressed, and whose positive evaluation – and fear – must be earned, in order to exercise power. These people structure, enable, and constrain the powerful individual's actions, thoughts, and even conception of himself as an individual. But these people are also the victims of the powerful individual's imposition of the social discipline of integrity.

Yet this medieval era does not fully conform to Foucault's model of power, in that integrity was a very abstract and loosely defined discipline or code, at least in comparison to modern psychiatry and surveillance. As we have seen in the actions of William the Conqueror, it is performed or represented by highly individual acts which by definition resist being "encoded," and instead insist on their own quotient of uniqueness in relation to codes of behavior. To the extent that powerful individuals "take charge of the information," they impose personalized symbols and resist social codes.[23] In these moments, they thus escape the disciplines of power with which their society otherwise might contain and define them. As a result, power among the warrior aristocracy is less of a generalized social phenomenon than Foucault's analyses of other time periods suggest, and more of a piecemeal, individualized phenomenon – not just in the sense that power is linked to individuals, but more profoundly, in the sense that the code(s) and discipline(s) of social control must be understood as fragmented, variable, and very strongly the product of certain highly marked individual identities.

Integrity, Non-reciprocity and Selfhood

As noted briefly in Chapter 1, honor cultures have often been seen as having a very strong degree of social integration between the individual and his society, and thus as inimical to modern western notions of the individual. Yet it has been pointed out that this is not entirely the case. In particular, the code of honor is typically completely internalized by the individual of the culture, who is then often more concerned with being "faithful to himself" (Bourdieu 1966:211) than with directly worrying about the opinion of others. Such an individual must always measure himself against his own ideal image (Bourdieu 1966:211). His honor lies first in his own eyes, though as Pitt-Rivers points out, the key to completely realized honor is to be accepted by others at one's own evaluation (Pitt-Rivers 1966:22). Thus while the moral value system of the individual and society may by the same, and the individual may conceive of himself through the perspective of the larger, watching society, the value system itself is perceived as

---

[23] See N.B. Aitchison's remark that in medieval Ireland, [performative] "power" and "rank" [i.e. juridical status] were different modes of "communication" (1994:73), with the latter being based on generalized social models of authority, the former much less so.

freely accepted, not imposed, and the individual has a strong sense of individual identity in relation to that society – indeed, is always critically evaluating the potential distance between the society and his or her own self-image.

The temptations of the anti-symbolic, material world seem to offer a means of conceiving in microcosm the possibility of loss of the essential free choice which founds the individual as subject and symbol-maker, rather than will-less object of his honor and gift society. Each such temptation presents the possibility of failing to be faithful to oneself through a failure to be faithful to the logic of the (freely adopted, internalized) symbolic economy. This falling for the temptation of the external and semiotic is the real meaning of commodification in this context. Obviously, markets and money, with their potential to create (ethically) value-free, de-individualized semiotic systems, are powerful agents of commodification. But as seen here, commodification can be conceived of in quite different and more general terms as well.[24]

In contrast to this danger of disintegration, the free and spontaneous gift becomes a ritual *mise-en-abyme* of the symbolic constitution of the individual, whose identity is founded on the free embrace of the sociocultural order and engagement in free, symbol-making acts within it. In a similar vein, the act of refusing the gift marks a break from the supposed obligation to give, receive and reciprocate which Mauss offers as the essence of gift cultures. It again opens up a space for the willful individual, as an agent and actor in his or her culture rather than as simple enactor of a functionalist or structuralist paradigm.[25]

We are now in a position fully to grasp the meaning of integrity, following up on the definition offered in Ch. 1. Integrity is the opening up of a maximum – potentially limitless? – space between the individual and his society, both socioeconomically and psychologically. Integrity is reached, however, through the use of the exchange mechanisms of the society. Such a notion corresponds in part to analyses of the nature of medieval "autobiography," which tended to emphasize quantitative superiority over qualitative difference. In other words, medieval "great men" shared the same qualities as those around them, they just had "more" of them (Vitz 1989: Ch. 1). But as we have seen, the notion of integrity includes a generalized desire to exchange in only one direction, and in fact, in its purest form, to exchange not at all – to end the practice of reciprocity external to the subject and his or her dependents. In a similar manner, integrity finally represents not just the culmination of accumulated honors, but accession to a position where socially recognized honor, as granted by a group of peers, is no longer active

---

[24] The idea that gifts are central to development of the individual, and that commodification is a threat to that individuality, makes functionalist and structuralist views of gift-giving look all the more ironic in contrast. As seen earlier, gift-givers from that perspective, whether Trobriand Islanders or Old French knights, are supposedly products of the group, act always within the mental constraints of that group, and identify themselves only in terms of the group's identity. In this perspective, the rise of the "modern subject" has been linked to the rise of markets and commerce – to the end of the gift! (see Shell 1982, 1991; Stock 1983:74).

[25] For more on the "opening up of space" through such maneuvers, see Bourdieu, 1977.

as a term of evaluation or a measure of standing. This essentially constitutes a
transition from quantitative to qualitative difference, and offers the model of an
individual who would be, as Dumont describes it, "independent, autonomous,
and ... essentially non-social" (Dumont 1986:25).

Lévi-Strauss cites a myth from the Andaman Islands which expresses a supposedly universal fantasy: "a world in which one might keep to oneself" and avoid
the "law of exchange" (as Annette Weiner describes it (1992:6)).[26] In remarkably
similar terms, Duby writes of the medieval knight in the tournament,

> Thenceforth prowess was the virtue of an individual man, whose action
> of course remained entirely dependent on team solidarity but who looked
> upon his glory as his own property. ... Prowess liberated the individual
> from the real-life, necessary, constraining, at times suffocating, hold of
> lineage and friendship. It conferred the illusion of solitude, this glorious,
> exalting, imaginary solitude of vagabond Percevals and Gawains.
>
> (1990:97)

Lévi-Strauss famously locates the origin of culture itself in reciprocity. Although
we will have reason to question this claim later, we will follow his lead in
suggesting that in cultures where reciprocity is most clearly enacted through the
form of gift-giving, the practice of the gift is the key trope for thinking about both
reciprocity in general and the desires for integrity that seem often to underlie this
reciprocity.[27] Given the importance of the ethical component of the will and the
psychological identity of the individual in gift-giving, one could even say that the
gift and the integrity-drive were not just social practices. Rather they were both
tropes through which the medieval warrior aristocracy theorized the idea of the
subject, social and individual identity, the notions of interiority and exteriority,
as well as the more general bases of power in the fluid world of banal lords. And
clearly, that power was seen as fundamentally personalized.[28] But perhaps, given
the qualification of non-reciprocity as a fantasy, the gift may also be seen as the
theorization of the impossibility of the fully independent subject. This is a point
to which we will return in greater depth in later chapters.[29]

[26] "The future life will be but a repetition of the present, but all will then remain in the
prime of life, sickness and death will be unknown, and there will be no more marrying or
giving in marriage" (1969:457).

[27] Compare both the Biblical Garden of Eden, which presents paradise as a "pre-economic"
world without scarcities, and thus without the necessity of exchanges; and the various medieval
versions of the "Golden Age" such as in the *Romance of the Rose*, where money and markets
(the new, dominant form of exchange in the thirteenth century) do not exist (ed. Langlois, vv.
8355–9527).

[28] See Bourdieu 1977:185, 190 on the personal nature of power in performative social
systems.

[29] Scholars of the Middle Ages have pointed to various indigenously medieval discourses
of the subject or subject formation. For the most part, however, incipient subjects are linked to
either the rise of literacy and vernacular textuality, or to the various (literate) discourses of the
Church. See for example Morris 1972, Vitz 1975, Zink 1985.

Identity, Integrity, Honor, and Power

In this chapter, we have seen that gift-giving was a key source of honor among the warrior aristocracy, and that receiving of gifts could be a source of dishonor. Honor was itself the incremental measure of the approach of one's social identity towards the more fundamental quality of integrity, which served as the baseline for notions of giving, receiving, identity formation, and honor, even if complete integrity was only potentially – never actually – attainable. This entire system can be analyzed, it was suggested, from the perspective of symbolic capital. But we also moved towards a rejection of a strictly economistic analysis of identity formation, honor, and integrity. One's identity, honor – and ultimately integrity – were as much psycho-social as economistic qualities within the medieval warrior aristocracy. They centered on the strict control and inner-directedness of desires and motivations, and depended on a more generally symbolic relationship between the individual and the surrounding world, a relationship in which the material, external world remained always a subsidiary world of secondary symbols which referred back to the identity and honor of the individual. Economic, political and social power were all linked to an idealized notion of integral identity, whose symbolic expressions serve to anchor the larger social system that evolved around the individual. The production and concrete expression of these symbols took the form of gift-giving and gift-receiving – or not, as the case may be.

The non-economic nature of this system – even non-economic from the symbolic perspective of Bourdieu – will be revealed more fully in later chapters in the study of the epic hero. We can already begin to anticipate this issue however, by citing a remark made by Evelyn Vitz: she suggests that for Roland, heroism is a function of intention rather than results, and that desire is moral rather than causal for him (1989:187). This is simply another way of stating that the inner-directedness of integrity, when pushed to its logical conclusion, demands the rejection of all external calculations about results and success. The gratuity involved in demonstrating integrity is perhaps the most powerful revelation of this fact. In such circumstances, the line between wholeness and destruction – of self and/or group – becomes very fine. One symptom of that tenuousness is the related fragility of the distinction between gift and violence. But up to this point, we have looked only at the gift as a form of more-or-less sublimated violence. We need to now turn our attention from giving to violent "taking." The next chapter reveals how giving and taking are intimately connected in the same symbolic economy centered around the concept of integrity.

3

Violence and "Taking":
Towards a Generalized Symbolic Economy

In Geoffrey Malaterra's early twelfth-century chronicle of the Norman conquest of Sicily and southern Italy, he reports an encounter between the armies of Robert Guiscard and Peter of Tyre. Robert, seeing the great wealth of the opposing army and leaders, considers how he can obtain it. After consideration, he proposes a discussion in the open field between the two forces, involving only himself and Peter. All seems to go well, but then just as the two leaders arise to head back to their respective armies, Robert physically grabs Peter and "interdum portando, interdum volutando, interdum trahendo, usque ad suos perduxit" ("now carrying, now rolling, now dragging, brought him back to [Robert's] men," *De rebus gestis* 1.17). This amusing (for us) and outrageous (for Peter) event would seem to be a blatant breach of the rules of reciprocity and negotiation. The Normans are jubilant about the event, on the other hand ("gaudentes quasi de triompho," "exulting as if in a victory"). Peter is not killed however: in typical medieval fashion, he is held hostage. After a few days, he ultimately buys his freedom "pecuniam mirabilem persolvens" ("with an enormous ransom"). Robert's extraction of money, from this and other sources, goes immediately and "abundanter" to his military companions, strengthens his own position militarily, and quickly leads to the capitulation of various Calabrian cities and their agreement to pay tribute. The capitulation no doubt came all the easier not just because the Calabrians were made fearful by Robert's evident personal audacity and violence, but also due to his demonstration that he was willing to continue a sort of reciprocal relationship with the leaders of the cities: he would not kill or even remove them, and they would offer up wealth in return, with which he could further strengthen his military position. As Geoffrey notes regarding a similar event earlier in the chronicle (surely one of the more bizarre out-of-context citations of the Bible in medieval history): "Unde et illud evangelicum illis provenit, ubi dicitur: Date, et dabitur vobis: quanto enim ampliora largiebantur, tanto majora lucrabantur" ("As the Bible says, Give, and you will be given to: the more he gave away, the more he profited"). Geoffrey's remark could refer here either to Robert's gifts to his own troops, or to his subsequent "gifts" to Peter and the leaders of the other Calabrian towns of life and limited freedom. Escalating giving and taking, from a position of strength, produced even more escalating giving and taking for Robert, in his pursuit of integrity. For all their humor, these passages illustrate the two central themes of this chapter: first, the connection between taking by force, giving, and receiving, and secondly, the ways in which controlled, calculated violence can be understood as simply a more aggressive form of reciprocity.

Reciprocity and Violence

We saw in the previous chapter that the goal of the competitive individual to give, to give first, and to give the most or the best, as well as immediately to cancel counter-gifts with new, bigger ones, and even to try to avoid receiving initial gifts at all, poses an obvious problem – what resources can one rely on in order to continually give out more than one takes in? It has been noted that the gift-giving system of the medieval aristocracy benefitted primarily the lower nobility, at the expense of the upper, which means that those on the top of the gift-giving hierarchy faced a continual drain of material resources.[1] Anthropologically, one very common answer to this pressure is the increasing exploitation of one's own resources, whether it be the Melanesian clan and its agricultural plots, or a medieval lord's demesne. As already seen, such internal resources obtained from dependents do not count as things received in antagonistic gift-giving settings. But such resources may be insufficient, and they may also not provide certain key types of items which are most valuable as gifts. In the latter case, one can convert internal resources into money and purchase needed items. But another alternative – the opposite side of the gift – is exemplified in the complementary side of William the Conqueror's giving – his conquering and taking. As Richard Kaeuper notes, in speaking of medieval combat, "the great virtue of largess is enabled by the great virtue of prowess" (1999:198). From a more theoretical (and economic) perspective, C.A. Gregory proposes three strategies for dominance by "big men" in competitive cultures. The first, used by William the Conqueror, is the "finance strategy," which seeks to increase the velocity of gift circulation. The second, the "production strategy," seeks to increase internal production of resources – a phenomenon encountered in the preceding chapter as well. The third is the "destruction" strategy, which seeks to destroy the opponent's ability to reciprocate when receiving gifts, thus increasing his likelihood of falling into a relationship of dependence (Gregory 1982:60–1). This is the strategy of taking, and of pillage and destruction as well. Taking is even more effective in many ways than destruction, however, because it aids the first strategy as well. It is taking which is the focus of this chapter.

The importance of warfare and raiding as a source of gifts for the medieval aristocrat was mentioned in passing in Ch. 1. Among medieval societies, it has been most closely documented and examined in Anglo-Saxon Britain and Iceland, but was important throughout western Europe.[2] Especially in cultures

---

[1] Baldwin 2000:102; Verbruggen 1997:49.
[2] See Evans 1997:110–12, 126–9 on the Anglo-Saxons. On Iceland, see Miller 1986.

where the giving of antagonistic gifts plays a central role, the antagonistic taking of resources may often play a similar role. In the Iqar'iyen Berber society of Morocco, which is strongly motivated by honor, Jamous points out that honor must be continually actively sought (1994:19–20), and that the honor involves not just conspicuous giving, but violent display, and more particularly, violent attack – which, however, is simply a form of exchange; gift-giving and feuding are both antagonistic acts in the society (1994:20, 89). Obviously other means of obtaining resources do always exist for the Iqar'iyen – in particular, the exploitation of agricultural and pastoral resources to produce a surplus available for giving, often with the help of extended family networks maintained through non-antagonistic gift exchanges. In fact, in their case, it is not really the resources that are the central point of the violent attack and taking, but the act itself, as a source of honor. Anything taken is essentially the subsidiary product of this act of honor, and acts as a secondary symbol of the primary act.

A similar practice occurred in medieval Iceland. William Miller's analysis of the practice of "hostile taking" ("rán") suggests that the raider achieved honor very similar to that obtained from giving a gift, and that the victim was in debt just as if he had received a gift. In the case of gifts, a reciprocal gift was owed, while in the case of the raid, a reciprocal act of vengeance was "owed" to the raider (Miller 1986:24–8; see also 1993:16; 58). Thus gifts and raids were simply two different kinds of reciprocity, each hostile to a greater or lesser extent, with the first supported in part by the second.[3] In both this and the previous case, it is clear that the act of exchange is primary, and that honor and symbolic capital flow from the act itself. The reluctance to accept gifts of land portrayed in the *Landnamabok*, and the preference for seizing those lands by force, thus involves not just an avoidance of the debt accrued from accepting a gift, but also the honor associated with force and violence. The same refusal of land gifts and the preference for taking lands "the hard way" can be found in medieval epics such as *Doon de Maience* (vv. 6209ff) and *Le Charroi de Nîmes* (vv. 444–511).

As already seen, objects in exchanges are ranked, and greater symbolic capital accrues to exchanges – givings or takings – of objects of high rank. Raids offered the opportunity to obtain such high-rank objects for subsequent giving. Moreover, the violent taking of the object functioned to further increase the object's symbolic value or rank. In other words, a horse captured from a rival noble made a more valuable gift than a materially equivalent horse bought from a merchant. A captured sword symbolically carried enormous honor.[4] In fact, such a system occurred even with relics, which, as Patrick Geary's studies have suggested, were also subject to an economy of taking (Geary 1986:183ff).

---

[3]   The fundamental similarity of gift-giving and violence as alternate forms of reciprocity in societies dominated by honor and antagonistic giving has been widely noted. See Barraud *et al.* 1994:1, 19–22; and Bourdieu 1966:213–15 on the way in which all gifts are to at least some extent an aggressive challenge in Kabyle society.

[4]   See Pitt-Rivers 1966:24 on the idea that honor accrues according to the relative value of the one conquered.

Indeed, in some cultures, such objects are incommensurable with un-taken ones. Egyptian Bedouins must give, as a bridal gift, a camel which has been taken in a raid – a camel raised by the family, or purchased, is simply not acceptable (Abou-Zeid 1966:246).[5] Thus there are a number of symbolic parallels between general systems of giving and taking: the importance of the act over and above the object which symbolizes that act; the creation or adjustment of the symbolic value of the object in the process of exchange; and the way in which the exchanges produce debts and obligations, in the eyes of both the two direct participants and the larger society which witnesses the exchange; differing spheres of exchange; and the symbolic capital of honor that accrues to the actor/taker.

The Symbolics of Taking

Taking must be understood not just as a functional economic practice which provided a means to give – a way of getting otherwise unobtainable gift items, or getting items at a bargain price, so to speak. It was fundamentally part of the symbolic exchange process: a positively coded action which itself produced symbolic capital for the taker, as well as adding symbolic value to the thing taken, just like a gift ceremony.[6] As Bourdieu has noted, domination in symbolic economies can occur either through overt violence, such as taking, or symbolic violence, which would include giving (1977:191). But overt violence must be recognized as equally symbolic. In medieval antagonistic settings, many gifts, no matter how peaceful in intent they might seem, were simultaneously adver-tisements of prior force and violent taking; the gift could be seen as founded upon violent taking. And in these circumstances the gift not only advertised past violence, but carried the promise of potential future violent reciprocity should the less violent methods of the gift not be respected, as seen in the case of Robert Guiscard. As William Miller has noted, the issue of gift or overt violence is less important in aggressive honor societies than "the ability to instill fear in others, with the suggestion of ominousness and threat" (1993:64). Conversely, in both the Icelandic and Iqar'iyen cases one sees that, unlike Lévi-Strauss's famous distinction between gift/reciprocity on the one hand and violence on the other, not only can the gift itself be a form of aggressive violence, but violence can be a form of socially-regulated reciprocity. Indeed, violence itself can poten-tially be socially productive or constitutive in certain forms – though one would rush to agree with Peter Haidu that this was certainly not the case for the vast

---

[5] Note that the people studied by Dresch 1998, who sought to avoid commercial transac-tions, were totally dependent on taking for the things not produceable by a nomadic desert people; these taken items were without fail the most highly valued ones in the culture.

[6] See Haidu 1993:2–3 on violence as "positively coded" in the Middle Ages, as well as Bennett 1998:126–7 in Halsall 1998. On violence as a symbolic act, see especially Riches 1986, "Introduction." Kaeuper 1999:143–50 discusses the positive coding of aggressiveness within the chivalric world.

majority of innocent, non-aristocratic victims of this violence in the Middle Ages (Haidu 2004:16ff). But it does appear to have been the case among the aristocracy, who often carefully managed violence *among* themselves. This is a point which has been stressed recently by medieval historians, who have argued against the perception of the tenth and eleventh centuries in particular as times of feudal anarchy in which violence was "out of control" and uniformly disastrous, suggesting instead that violence could function as a form of social communication.[7] The same point has been made by anthropologists, especially in situations of institutionalized violence: it comes ultimately to resemble a ritual game, where the degree of damage is carefully controlled (Bourdieu 1966:201–2). Such was the case in the Middle Ages as well, where battles often produced very few aristocratic casualties, and where capture and ransom were far preferable to killing.[8] Thus either a gift or a raid could function as the opening, aggressive gambit to open power negotiations between rivals. These findings obviously point to a need to reconstrue certain forms of violence as practised in the Middle Ages, as well as the traditional dichotomy between gift and violence. Taking and giving must be seen as mutually dependent parts of the same symbolic economy. Of course, extreme forms of taking (which destroyed the system of reciprocity and sought to eliminate an opponent's ability to negotiate responses either through overt violence or more peaceful means), while certainly having important symbolic meanings, could not be considered as symbolic counterparts to gifts. The violence under consideration here was conducted within social constraints, according to certain customary rules and expectations, and generally allowed for a framework of response. Thus much of the violence of medieval society was not simply a regrettable element that could be removed, leaving the society peaceful but otherwise unchanged, as many writers and thinkers of the time seem to have imagined. Rather, the violence was at least partially constitutive of the society.[9]

In order to reconstrue giving and taking as potentially equivalent forms of reciprocity on a deep level, the theory of giving must be applied to the theory of taking in a thoroughgoing manner. Anthropological theory, so far as I have found, has not taken full account of the mirror relationship of taking with giving, as essentially symbolic acts of honor. Yet medieval epic culture suggests the intimate connection of giving and taking; studies of medieval history show that taking (war, the raid, the "guerra") was intimately connected to giving, both

[7]   See Dunbabin 2000:xx; Geary 1996; White 1995; Halsall 1998:11–21 contains an especially good overview of the concept of violence as reciprocity and communication, when contained within certain boundaries; see also Kagay and Villalon 1998:73–82 on the way in which the "défi" could serve as an opening for negotiations, thus resolving rather than heightening a crisis; and Miller 1993:82–5 on violence and social order in Iceland. Barton 1998 makes parallel arguments about anger in the Middle Ages, showing how rather than being the sign of a lack of individual control and restraint, it could serve to "open doors" to compromise (1998:153–4) and act as "a positive social force" (158) when carefully used.

[8]   See especially Duby 1990:107–10.

[9]   See also Fox 1994, Part 2 for a discussion of the parallel resistance of modern academic studies – particularly anthropology – to the idea of violence as socially constructive.

symbolically and materially. In medieval western Europe, two forms of taking seem to have predominated. One was direct (raids, ransoms, booty, and so forth, coming from direct violence) and the other was indirect (exploitation of agricultural resources by peasants and serfs, whose labor and tribute could be seen as an ordered, instituted form of taking, a sublimated form of violence – see Haidu 1993:50ff). We will concentrate here primarily on the place of war and raiding within the symbolic economy of giving and taking.

War and Symbolic Capital

The purely economic connections between giving and taking – as the twin bases of early medieval society – have been much more widely recognized than the symbolic, socio-psychological ones. Many scholars have noted that war was the central focus of early medieval society. Philippe Contamine notes that the barbarian Germanic tribes were "communities fundamentally organized for war" (1984:14). John Gillingham speaks of the "pillage economies" of the Scandinavians, Slavs and Celts (1999:68). Examples of violent seizure, followed by redistribution to followers, dependents and kin, are numerous from the Carolingian epoch as well. Indeed, they virtually formed the basis of the Carolingian economy: Charles Martel went on a military campaign every year, and Charlemagne did so nearly as often (Contamine 1984:22–5), and the warlord and warband remained the essential feature of Carolingian armies in the ninth century (Nelson 1998:95).

But the situation was not fundamentally different in the early parts of the second millennium. Georges Duby, most prominently, has argued that the entire European economy, into the eleventh century at least, was essentially driven by warfare, due both to the importance of loot taken (especially from border regions)[10] and to the degree to which both war's expense and the looting involved acted to stimulate the circulation of money and valuables and break up ecclesiastical and royal hoards and treasuries.[11] Page after page of the *Gesta Guillelmi* is occupied with recounting the massive gifts which William the Conqueror distributed throughout England, Normandy and France, to secular and religious recipients, following his conquest of England (see esp. 153–79). (Here is an important global example of the way in which internal violence could function

[10] See Dunbabin 2000:142 and 183 on the immense amounts of wealth entering France in the eleventh century from Spain thanks to raiding expeditions originating in Burgundy. More generally on the question of the border nature of much of the most valuable booty entering Europe, see Duby 1973:144, 185, 202 and France 1999:188–9.

[11] On the liquidation of treasuries, see in particular Duby 1973:136 Also Dunbabin 2000:141–2; Fossier 1982:295–6, and Gillingham 1999:68 in Keen 1999. See also Baldwin 2000:98ff, where he notes especially the devolution of the raid and redistribution economy from high nobles to even local lords in the eleventh and twelfth centuries. For more on predatory castellans, see Kagay and Villalon 1998:14–15 and the many references cited there.

as a socially productive form of reciprocity.) As late as the later twelfth century, armies of irregular warriors numbering in the thousands alternated between raid and pillage and mercenary activity on behalf of more stable authorities – service which itself often paid handsomely in terms of booty (Contamine 1984:243–7; Duby 1990:79–80).

Philippe Contamine goes farther than Duby, insisting on the "decisive place" of war in the Middle Ages as a whole, calling it "the product of a whole cultural, technical and economic environment" (1984:xii). Furthermore, while the Carolingian campaigns were largely external actions, the period following the dissolution of the Empire, from roughly the later 800s through the 1000s, witnessed such activity occurring on a small scale internally throughout Europe.[12] Thus, in a very real sense, the world of the warrior aristocracy of the tenth through twelfth centuries was a world founded upon violent taking, which then enabled the competitive giving on which power was based,[13] just as was the case for the earlier medieval period up through the ninth century. Amatus of Montecassino writes of one eleventh-century Norman aggressor that he "carried off everything he could and gave it away, keeping little ... in this way the land about was plundered and the number of his knights multiplied" (cited in Gillingham 1999:64). Like William, this lord successfully combined Gregory's first and third strategies – increased circulation of gifts, and destruction of the opponent's ability to reciprocate with counter-gifts or competitive gifts. This was in essence the general strategy of most medieval violence.[14] The Fourth Crusade's deviation to Constantinople in 1204 is simply the most notorious example of the fundamental linkage of military campaigning and looting for redistribution during this latter period.

Of course, the majority of life's necessities in the European economy were almost never obtained from taking, even among the Carolingians or the earlier Germanic war-bands.[15] The peasants plodding in the fields produced the basic foods, wine, cloth, wood and stone products – the essential items on which everyday life was based. The exploitation of these sources by lords, for gifts to various followers and allies, and for conversion to money for the purchase of items not produced locally, was central to the economy. This became ever more

[12] Contamine 1984:30–1; Reuter 1999:14–17, 30–1; Gillingham 1999:70. See Baldwin 2000:98ff and Fossier 1982:294ff for a discussion of the ways in which the devolution of power was related to the expansion of the process of taking.

[13] See Duby 1973. On the "raid and redistribution" economy, see esp. pp. 47–74 (600s and 700s); 89–90 (800–1050); 127–8 (Carolingian); 131 (European invaders); 161 (Spain); 182–5 (1000s). See also Fossier 1982:294–5; Duby 1990:77, 191; Halsall 1998:19. The more general recognition that war was often fought for profit – i.e. booty, is a commonplace of medieval studies. See for example France 1999:6; Verbruggen 1997:50; Duby 1990:105–6.

[14] See Reuter 1999:24 and Gillingham 1999:79–80 on this dual strategy, as well as Hanley 2003:63–5 and 158 on its appearance in chronicles and epics.

[15] See Riché 1993:315 on Carolingian income coming predominantly from the village. See Evans 1997:121–6 on the fundamental role of the "food render" for Anglo-Saxon warlords.

the case as such production increased in the late tenth and eleventh centuries (Duby 1988b:112; Duby 1973:204), while efforts to rein in internal raiding and plundering began to take effect. However, this exploitation itself could be seen as a form of institutionalized taking by the aristocracy. Peter Haidu has stressed the violent quality of medieval exploitation of the demesne,[16] and it has been widely noted that the function of the castle shifted in the eleventh century from a political one – protecting lands from invasion – to an economic one – enabling the more efficient plunder of neighboring territories, but also the plunder of one's own peasants.[17]

But if openly violent taking accounted for an ever-decreasing amount of the overall economic production of the western European economy, its importance remained paramount in a world where symbolic capital trumped economic capital. As we have seen, differing spheres of consumption are often incommensurable, and it is the upper, elite spheres, with their limited number of goods, which assure access to and control of power. One can find many examples of hunter-gatherer societies where the gathering of plant materials forms the caloric basis of the diet, but where the rarer and calorically less important acquisition and consumption of meat through hunting is central to social prestige (in important part due to the opportunities for redistribution, and thus social honor and prestige, which large game offers to the successful hunter). A similar phenomenon, it seems, occurred in western Europe in the tenth, eleventh and even twelfth centuries: the "gathering" produced through the increasingly intense exploitation of agricultural estates clearly was the central economic engine of the society, but honor and prestige remained focused on the practices of violent seizure and redistribution, though in increasingly sublimated forms (the tournament, for example, in the later twelfth century), and in increasingly external locations (the crusades, for example).[18] Richard Hodges, writing on pre-market economies, talks about "dispersal" and "withdrawal" systems which operate for prestige goods, and notes of the latter that its essence involves goods being ostentatiously taken out of circulation (1988:36), with combat being one such form of ostentatious action (1988:39). While studies have shown that from a purely fiscal standpoint, wars and tournaments may have been "a wash" (Fossier 1982:779–80), or even a net loss for most participants, even the winners (Duby 1973:257), the symbolic capital accrued in these privileged spheres of exchange was key. Lords were evidently willing to invest large amounts of monetary capital into warfare because the symbolic capital thus accrued was of higher value than initial monetary capital. Jean Dunbabin has argued, for example, that the Burgundian aristocracy may have owed what little cohesiveness it had to the military expeditions undertaken by the Counts of Burgundy in the eleventh and twelfth centuries,

[16] Haidu 1993. See also Reuter 1999.

[17] Dunbabin 2000:xxii, 144, 231. Fossier 1982:402–10.

[18] For an extreme example of the reliance of prestige entirely on "force of arms," see Baroja 1966, especially pp. 88–9, where he analyzes the case of medieval Spain.

which produced substantial rewards of loot (which were then distributed down-wards – Dunbabin 2000:183, 231). I would add that the costs of these wars can be seen as the ongoing "investment" required to maintain a coherent group identity in the face of threats of pluralism and entropy, as seen in the end of Chapter 1.

The main means of producing or acquiring symbolic capital thus remained the act of taking (and then giving).[19] Many, even most of the highest-value gift items – war horses, swords, armor, high-quality cloth goods, precious metals and gems (or the money to buy these!) – were in fact often obtained through violent taking, which was certainly preferable to purchasing these items with the proceeds of the demesne.[20] For certain key objects, the symbolic value invested in them through taking was such that they were more highly valued than huge quantities of hard cash.[21] Indeed, this symbolic value was incommensurable with cash, and fundamentally superior to it. The *Gesta Guillelmi* especially celebrates William's capture of Harold's "famous banner," whose symbolic value derived both from its fame itself and from its previous holder. This banner was sent to the Pope, allowing William to repay the debt incurred when the Pope sent him a papal banner. Objects of taking could be ranked just like objects of giving: their value was essentially an interdependent function of their inherent rarity, the fact that they were typically held by enemies of high honor, and the fact that they could only be acquired through taking from that enemy.[22] Despite the massive quantities of gold and silver which William also sent to the Pope after his victory, it is the banner which explicitly allowed his repayment ("an equal return," "par redderet," says the text). William thus established his integrity in relation to the Pope himself.

[19] See Duby 1988b:48–72 and Grierson 1959 (cited in Geary 1986) and Geary 1986:173 on the fact that gift-giving and "theft" were the key means of property transfers in general among the aristocracy of the early Middle Ages. Geary also comments on their higher prestige.

[20] See Dunbabin 2000:142 on Raymond III of Rouergue, who returned home in the late tenth century with great wealth from a Spanish raid and elected to keep an especially attractive Spanish saddle, which was no doubt unavailable at home. The *Gesta Guillelmi* notes the thoroughbred horses and knightly arms and equipment which were the great prize of William of Normandy's conquest of Maine (87). All of this was then given to his knights. Such was also the case for the Anglo-Saxons of the early Middle Ages (see Evans 1997:126–7). See also Kaeuper 1999:196–7 on the preference for warfare over manorial income for obtaining the sources of noble generosity, as well as Duby 1990:77 on war as the best way of acquiring cash. See Duggan 1989:24–5 on the extraordinary value of military items such as swords and horses in purely economic terms as well, and the difficulty of obtaining these purely through money generated by exploitation of the demesne.

[21] This enhancement of value through plunder has been analyzed in terms of the "diversion" of objects from their normal sphere of circulation. See Appadurai 1986b:26–8.

[22] Appadurai analyzes "luxury" goods in terms of the following characteristics: 1) restriction to elites; 2) complexity of acquisition; 3) signaling of complex social messages; 4) specialized knowledge necessary for their appropriate consumption (i.e. use or giving away); 5) a high degree of linkage to body, person and personality (1986b:38). Thus medieval objects of taking would constitute classic luxury items from a cross-cultural perspective, with the taking itself being a significant part of the creation of the luxury.

Combat, in the High Middle Ages, must thus be thought of as essentially concerned with symbolic capital – or at least, this is how it is presented in medieval texts.[23] Combat of the era involved a quest for money, and also for power, but these two things were embedded in the symbolic capital of honor.[24] And as a result, the acts of combat were themselves embedded in the formal apparatus of taking and giving, which constituted the realization of the abstract ideals of honor. Taking, or "prowess," always preceded symbolic reward, though that reward was vital as well, if always secondary.[25] This ordering of deed first, material symbol second is a crucial aspect of the discourse of the gift, to which we will return in detail later.

This is not to deny the presence of utilitarian considerations in knights' evaluation of their possessions. A well-made sword is better than a brittle and dull sword. But almost inevitably in epic literature, the most useful objects are also the objects which symbolize knighthood and status itself. (And indeed, the most useful object may be a symbolic one, even when no longer utilitarian.)[26] And even more importantly, the highest-quality objects are also owned by the most worthy of heroes and adversaries, and they rapidly acquire their own history, and their own particular symbolic status. The historic narrative of possession, and the honor it confers on the current owner, is typically more important than the purely utilitarian aspect of the object. When William of Orange worries about having his battle horse stolen by thieves in the *Moniage Guillaume*, he says first that "when you urge him on with the steel spurs,/ he moves so quickly over land and rocks,/ that no falcon or sparrow-hawk could catch him" (ll. 321–3). The horse is clearly highly useful, and thus valuable, but it is already evaluated in relation to other symbolic emblems of nobility (birds of prey). He then adds, "I won him from Aerofle, the fierce,/ when, with my sword, I cut off his head./ If they take him from me, I will go mad" (ll. 324–6). There may be other fast horses, but this one is irreplaceable as a symbol of Guillaume's particular victory over this foe, and in its inseparable connection to him as an individual.

The fundamental importance of taking and gift redistribution in the aristo-

---

[23] See Hanley 2003, especially 127–30, 139, 147–9, and 155 on the symbolic element in descriptions of combat in medieval epics, as well as the symbolic role of armor, weapons, women and relatives in relation to the hero in those descriptions.

[24] Duby 1990:95–6 notes the same thing for the tournament: money per se was scorned by the participants, while a purely symbolic top prize was sought at the end of the tournament. Behind this representation of course lies the fact that knights made their living off tournaments, and used them to pay the bills.

[25] Richard W. Kaeuper argues this point as well, noting that "any deep gulf between the acquisition of wealth and the practice of chivalry is a modern myth" but noting nevertheless that prowess was always the key ingredient, with land and wealth "assumed to *follow* naturally" (1999:132, my italics). As our symbolic analysis suggests, the wealth and violence were not just intimately connected, but necessarily so, within the same symbolic system. See also Geary 1986:173 on the symbolic character of taken property.

[26] See for example the rusty sword which the Earl Warenne used to warrant his lands (cited in Duggan 2000:10–11 and Clanchy 1993:36–8).

cratic ideology of war is underlined by the fact that even when armies began to be raised and paid with wages or grants of lands, great care was often taken to represent these transactions as gifts (Contamine 1984:90ff; Duby 1990:77–8). "Money gifts," or "donativa" was one term used to describe these wages (Contamine 90). The fief-rente, or money fief, was another instance of adopting the form of the gift for wages.[27] Contracts for fief-rentes often specified "free service" in exchange for the fief, by which was meant military service (Contamine 92–3): the idea of reciprocal counter-gifts was maintained. In fact, documentary sources suggest that the pay that knights received was probably not sufficient to actually cover their expenses for serving on many campaigns (Contamine 96–9), and thus it maintained a somewhat symbolic quality in relation to their services as well. Thus the vocabulary of the gift becomes the optic through which military organization is presented.[28]

The same emphasis on giving and taking explains the willingness on the part of chronicles of the era, as well as poets such as Bertran of Born, to describe in detail the looting and pillaging that surrounded warfare at the time. While in some cases, this was meant to condemn violence, in many others, the violence is frankly celebrated. While this fact has been adduced to demonstrate that the Peace of God and Chivalry failed fundamentally to transform the more "evil" side of medieval combat (Kaeuper 1999:176–85), it should rather be understood in the context of the symbolic capital that accrued to taking. In such a context, the looting, pillaging, and destruction of a rival's ability to fight back were exactly the features that one would want advertised to the world, as examples of taking (Gregory's gift strategy number 3).[29] The goods then of course became the object of giving – as opposed to "salaries" (Duby 1990:104–6). As seen earlier in relation to violence more generally, looting and pillaging were not simply unfortunate side effects of war, to be removed so that the battles could then go on as usual, but less harmfully – rather, they were essential aspects of the symbolic economy of taking and giving.[30] This fact explains why Chivalry – itself founded essentially on the symbolic economy of honor – failed to halt them. Had plunder been seen mainly as a necessary material evil to support medieval armies (which it certainly was, in part), then Chivalry could have at least halted the celebration

[27] Contamine 92; Duby 1988a:78; Lyon 1957 for a general study. See however Dunbabin 2000:231 for a note on the quite early appearance of the fief-rente.

[28] See Haidu 1993:55–9 on the ways that "economic value, in multiple forms, is normalized in the codes of the text [*Song of Roland*], without any derogation to the courage, the honor, the glory of ... the feudal system as a whole" (58). Haidu's analysis emphasizes the tensions of the "material" which always threaten to pierce the veil of the normalized codes.

[29] William Miller notes of medieval Iceland that being a "victimizer" was "status-enhancing" in many circumstances, and that such people had "inducements to claim themselves more violent than they may have been" (1993:58). Hanley 2003 notes the frank approval of such behavior in both chronicles (63–5) and epics (158).

[30] See Halsall 1998: "Introduction" for another analysis of the various ways in which forms of combat and aggression were integral to the medieval social order.

of the plunder, if not the fact. But it failed (at least initially) to do even this, since plunder was above all a form of glorious taking.[31]

Likewise, depictions of violence as the product of lack of self-restraint and control on the part of medieval warrior aristocrats (Spierenburg 1991:192ff), and as equivalent to anarchy, need to be re-evaluated. Once one begins to see the symbolic importance of violence, its use begins to look more and more rational within that context, and its users more and more controlled and calculating, at least as long as it remains within the limits of reciprocal negotiation. Such understanding is constrained by the fact that the huge majority of chroniclers and commentators on medieval life were monks or clerics who often represented the viewpoints of various segments of the Church, as opposed to the warrior aristocracy. But even in the chronicles, the symbolic rationale of violence can be found – typically in accounts of events, rather than in the rhetoric of the chroniclers themselves. As Robert Bartlett notes, the notoriously violent and aggressive Normans were quite "clear-headed about their own ... acquisitiveness" and violence, and used it in carefully controlled ways (1993:87). As Geoffrey Malaterra says, they were "gens astutissima" (1.3, p. 8) and avid specifically for "domination" (1.3, p. 8; 2.38, p. 48; 3.7, p. 60), rather than simply for material wealth or lands.[32] What they really wanted was the symbolic capital of honor, and the power (domination) which was its correlate.

In conclusion we return to the Normans, where Wace's *Roman de Rou* again illustrates the point well. He tells of the Normans that "Chevaulx quistrent et armes a la guise franchoise,/ qu'icelle lor semblot plus riche et plus cortoise;/ le gaaing qui ont grant les orgueille et envoise" (ll. 555–7) ("they sought their horses and arms in the French manner [i.e. by conquest and pillage], which seemed to them to be the most splendid and most appropriate. The great booty they acquired filled them with pride and joy," p. 22). Clearly, Wace suggests, the Normans may have had a choice of other modes of acquisition for war weapons. But they chose both the most dangerous and most glorious – and most symbolically profitable – method. In the following chapter, we will examine the career of the Cid in Spain from this same perspective.

[31] Housley 1999:132–3 discusses the many similarities between mercenaries and "chivalric" knights, despite the many claims for differences.

[32] All three passages cited here are noted by Bartlett. He also mentions Amatus of Montecassino's remark that the Normans "non firent second la costumance de molt ... liquel se metent á servir autre, mès...voilloient avoir toute gent en lor subjettion et en lor seignorie" ("did not follow the custom of many ... who commit themselves to the service of another, but ... wished to have all peoples subject to them and under their rule") (1.2, pl. 11).

4

Taking an Identity: *The Poem of the Cid*

An Epic of Aggressive Identity Formation

An appreciation of the symbolic capital which plunder represented helps to better understand an epic which has always seemed anomalous in its concern with money and quantification – *The Poem of the Cid*. This epic, which dates from the end of the twelfth century, is a classic story of the rise of an individual through the construction of de facto social power, as opposed to inherited, juridical or public power and authority, in a fluid social context which left large openings for performative success. The epic is rife with precise accounts of the capture and distribution of money and other material forms of wealth, especially war horses – accounts which are comparatively absent from many other European epics. Thus it appears strikingly bourgeois and commercial to many critics, and even anti-noble.[1] Yet the apparent anomaly is in fact simply a more explicit rendering of the same ethos which dominates all early medieval epics, that of symbolic giving and taking.

The Cid can be summarized as follows: the Cid is a lower-level noble, who despite great military success has been punished and ordered into exile by his king, apparently for withholding gift tributes owed the king from his own takings; he begins his adventures as an outsider whose only status lies in the minimum qualification of blood nobility which is necessary to enter the context of giving and taking. The Cid's nobility is emphasized throughout, even if that noble status is not especially elevated. He is called an "infanzón," meaning a petty noble. In the judicial scene that concludes the epic, one strategy used by his opponents is to explicitly question his noble status, but this strategy clearly fails. Thus, as Maria Lacarra has argued most forcefully, the epic does not ever question the natural hierarchy of nobility (1980:131ff). But blood is simply the lower defining limit of the playing field of performance, despite his rivals' protestations otherwise. The Cid then aggressively takes, and gives and takes and gives sequentially in order to recruit followers and elevate his status. Each new step upward is marked by an aggressive gift to his king, Alfonso, which is oriented as much towards the audience of potential followers as it is towards the king. Eventually, he is able

---

[1] See Lacarra 1980:113, 134 for further discussion and references to the supposed "anti-noble" aspects of the text. See Lacarra 1980:136, 201–7 on the supposed "pro-bourgeois" elements of the text. An example of this argument is Rodríguez-Puértolas 1977.

to give a gift which makes the king realize that a continued ban on the Cid will place the king's own followers in an either/or position in which they may choose the Cid rather than the king, and he therefore begins to reaccept the Cid into the society (tir. 82). As the Cid then begins to defeat not just other nobles, but other kings, his own king must eventually give him a full pardon (tir. 102). Seeing the potential of the Cid to rise to a position where he may ultimately attain the integrity of sacred kingship for his own family, the king welcomes the interest of a pair of high nobles – the Infantes – in the Cid's daughters, in order to waylay his further advance. The Cid is disappointed in such a marriage (tir. 102), but is forced to accept given his status relative to the king. But he partially parries the king's aggressive gift of the marriage by insisting that it is the king, not he, who is giving the daughters – and who will bear the shame should the marriage turn out less than advantageously for the Cid and his family (tir. 104–5; 133). When this does occur, due to the Infantes' abysmal behavior towards his daughters, the Cid is quite happy, since it offers him the chance to advance higher by breaking his relationship with the Infantes and making better marriages for the daughters (ll. 2830–4). Once the Cid and his followers prove the dishonor of the Infantes in a court case, the king finds himself in a position where he can only accept the proposal that the Cid's daughters marry the princes of Navarre and Aragon, so that the Cid's family attains a sacred status equivalent to that of the king.

The text's language consistently couches the aggression and defense described above behind a rhetoric of loyalty and honorific exchange. But confrontations of varying subtlety between the Cid and the king over giving first, best and most occur commonly throughout the text,[2] and as we will see in this and the next chapter, the text is fundamentally about the *conquest* of integrity. The Cid's strategy is conceived and represented in the epic in terms of a symbolic economy of honor, just as in so many other medieval texts.[3] Thus, at the most basic level, the ideology presented in *The Cid* does not differ substantially from that seen in French or German epics. It is particularly fascinating, however, in the way that it foregrounds not only an example of the performative construction of identity, social status and power, but also in the way that it presents an alternative model of identity and status, and the tensions between the two in late twelfth- and early thirteenth-century Spain.

---

[2] For two lesser but highly revealing examples, see tir. 104 and the issue of who will be host and who will be guest among the Cid and the king, or tir. 135, where the Cid's aggressive display of excessive loyalty and subjugation embarasses the king, who recognizes – and refuses – the excessive gift which would place him in an awkward position before the onlookers.

[3] By far the most complete analysis of the economic aspects of *The Cid* is Duggan 1989. He focuses closely on the various aspects of gift culture, especially in his third chapter, using primarily the ideas of Mauss, as subsequently adopted by Duby.

Integral Motivations and Secondary Symbols

The Cid essentially follows a giving strategy centered on increasing the rate of circulation of gifts, similar to that of William the Conqueror. Throughout the epic, he conquers towns, cities and armies, seizes their wealth, and redistributes it to his followers. The news of these exploits then spreads – the emphasis on "news" or "rumor" in the epic underlines the symbolic capital of honor which such deeds represent.[4] This news of taking and giving then allows the recruitment of additional followers, allowing larger amounts of taking and giving, on and on. At one point, the text underlines that "qui en un logar mora siempre lo so puede menguar" ("Whoever remains in one spot stands to lose") (l. 948), and this perfectly captures the Cid's logic of "evermore," recalling the consumptive spiral of ethnograpic big men.[5] The Cid himself is fundamentally uninterested in material wealth per se, since it is only something to be given away in order to enhance his social identity and honor, and thereby attain true power. Thus it is not only booty which is quantified, but the Cid's power, which is expressed in the increasing number of his followers.[6] Likewise, the symbolic nature of his taking is underlined in the three objects which are of most value to him, and most closely associated with him – and which not surprisingly, are personalized by means of naming. These are his horse Bavieça and his two swords, Colada and Tizón, all of which are specifically taken or won (tir. 86 for the horse, tir. 137 for the swords).

The followers, unlike the Cid, seem more interested in the material wealth itself: "al sabor de la ganançia non lo quieren detardar" ("And all who scented plunder came in haste") (l. 1198). Certainly, promises of such wealth are used as a motivational tool by the Cid even while underlining his own interests in honor or religious motivations:

> Por Aragon e por Navarra pregon mando echar,
> a tierras de Castiella enbio sus menssajes:
> 'Quien quiere perder cueta e venir a rritad
> viniesse a mio Çid que a sabor de cavalgar;
> ¡çercar quiere a Valençia por a christianos la dar!'   (ll. 1187–91)

He sent messengers through Navarre and Aragon and to the land of Castile to proclaim that anyone who was eager to exchange poverty

---

[4]   See tir. 28, 32, 40, 53, 54, 55, 65, 68, 74, 76, 78, etc. See Duggan 1989:26–7 on the intimate correlation of fame and wealth in the poem.

[5]   See Douglas and Isherwood 1979:137 (on the Yurok Tribe of northwest California), on the idea of consumptive battle (between individuals competing for power). They note the virtual necessity of such spirals of aggressive action.

[6]   See tir. 17 (115 men); 18 (l. 304, 395 men); 21 (now 300 men); 74, 77 (now 3600); 83, etc. In tir. 77, the Cid comments with pleasure on the increase of followers, and then immediately states "agora avemos riquiza, mas avremos adelant" ("We are rich now, and in the future shall be richer still") (l. 1269). For a more detailed analysis of these increasing numbers, see Cordoba 1967:162. The overall increase is from 60 (l. 16) to around 4000.

> for riches should come to the Cid, who had a mind to ride out to
> besiege Valencia and restore it to the Christians.

Yet even in these cases, the representations function within the context of a symbolic economy. This is especially true for all named followers of the Cid, as opposed to the unnamed masses. If one pays close attention to the moments where explicit motivation for action is cited, virtually never is the motivation of money and loot alone used. Typical motivations are: defense of lands; anger at offense by others; desire for honor and glory; desire for battle itself; and religious motivation. Thus either defense of honor, regaining honor through vengeance, desire to increase honor, or religious faith (clearly an internal motivation) are the overwhelming choice of motives. All could be seen as oriented towards integrity. Characters also typically mention their loyalty to someone else, and often go out of their way to stress their lack of interest in monetary rewards per se. Martín Antolínez, the citizen of Burgos, decides to accompany the Cid even though he has won nothing yet, and exclaims "quanto dexo ¡no lo preçio un figo!" ("I don't care a fig for all that I am leaving behind!") (l. 77). After a battle, "sos cavalleros legan con la ganançia,/ dexan la a mio Çid, todo esto non preçia nada." ("His knights then arrived with the loot they had collected and handed it over to the Cid as if it meant nothing to them") (ll. 474–5). The most notable example is that of Alvar Fanez, who refuses a gift from the Cid which he feels he has not merited:

> Yo vos la suelt[o] e avello quitado.
> A Dios lo prometo, a aquel que esta en alto:
> fata que yo me page sobre mio buen cavallo
> lidiando con moros en el campo,
> que enpleye la lança e al espada meta mano
> e por el cobdo ayuso la sangre destelando
> ante Rui Diaz el lidiador contado,
> non prendre de vos quanto vale un dinero malo.   (ll. 496–503)

> I hand it back to you to have again freely, and I swear in God's
> name that until, on my good horse, fighting Moors in the field, I
> use my lance and my sword till the blood drips down to my elbow
> in the presence of the great warrior Ruy Díaz, I shall not take a
> penny piece from you.

(Note in passing that in this passage, blood is not a guarantor of social position, as the Infantes will attempt to claim, but rather a secondary symbol of performance).

In its focus on pure motivations, *The Cid*, despite its extraordinary interest in taken wealth, reflects the same ideological world-view as many texts arising from the Crusades. Those texts also stressed over and over the fundamentally nonmaterial, religious motivations of the participants, while nevertheless allowing that there was great wealth to be won (France 1999:205–6; Verbruggen 1997:50–1). While there was clearly a threat (indeed, a reality for some or even many) that the potential wealth was the reason for going crusading, this wealth was not seen as inimical to the crusading spirit. In the examples of monetary motivation cited by J.F. Verbruggen in his survey of the knightly literature of the First Crusade, there are always key qualifiers to the wealth motivation which indicate its secondary nature: one will become rich "if God wills" (*Gesta Francorum*); one can become rich and "improve his status" (*Chanson d'Antioche*); those who were poor "became rich here through God's favor" (Fulcher of Chartres). Given the symbolism of wealth in relation to taking, this is not surprising, though here one also sees the influence of specifically Christian ideas on symbolic reward, which are overlaid on more strictly aristocratic conceptions of taking. In this context, it is unsurprising that hostage-taking and ransom – tactics which might seem strange to modern exponents of total war – continued to be practised (France 1999:228). They provided material wealth which was the secondary, after-the-fact symbolic reward of honorable deeds.

The Cid expresses this same point in the temporal structure of the scenes of gift-giving and redistribution which occur so frequently. When the Cid himself gives gifts, they are virtually always presented as occurring after loyalty, bravery and service are displayed, not before. Thus for the individual recipient involved, the gift can be seen as secondary to the honorable action – a symbolic reward.[7] The Cid, likewise, is seen as symbolically recognizing honorable loyalty, rather than offering money in advance for help, which would suggest a purchase on his part, and consequently a dependency and lack of integrity.[8] He states at one point: "¡Hy[a] Avengalvon amigol sodes sin fall! / Si Dios me legare al Çid e lo vea con el alma/ desto que avedes fecho vos non perderedes nada" ("You are a loyal friend to the Cid, Abengalbón. If God spares me to return and see him, you will not be the loser for what you have done here") (ll. 1528–30).[9]

Even the vocabulary of the text inscribes this economy of symbolic reward – of gift after deed. The most common word for loot or booty is "ganancias," which derives from the word "ganar," meaning "to win." Thus the loot is liter-

[7] Tir. 25, 31–2, 40, 56, 59, 61, 63, 68, 74, 75, 87, 95, 96, 118, 119, 121.

[8] Two corollaries: when money is presented as the primary motivation, this is to be read implicitly as a negative character judgement, though typically the text underlines this explicitly. The only key characters in the epic to be labelled as acting out of purely monetary interests are the Jews and the Infantes, both of whom are portrayed negatively. Secondly, when someone is offered money or gifts prior to their service, this is as an implicit negative commentary on their honor, moral value and integrity, even when the text does not explicitly make this point. The degree of negative judgement varies greatly, but is always there. This is really just a logical consequence of the idea that one should always give first, and that such giving places one in a superior position to the recipient. Thus the common medieval admonition to kings to always give generously in order to ensure loyal followers carries with it the promise of an exaltation of the king and a diminution of those around him. The greatest of knights serve loyally without hope of reward, after all – as in the case of William of Orange in *The Coronation of Louis*. The only exception to this rule is when gifts before deeds are given as a way of suggesting that the recipient is so internally honor- and integrity-driven that the appearance of acting due to the inspiration of the thing itself is impossible. (Evans 1997:109–12, as well as Duby 1990:78).

[9] Tir. 5, 11, 23, 41, 76, 77, 79, 84, 87, 95, 183.

ally the product of military victory – the most "honorable" of accomplishments. The word "crecer" meaning "increase" is used indistinguishably for both material wealth and honor. The word "pagar" has two senses in the text, one being to satisfy a debt, the other being to render someone else content.[10] Yet the two senses often blur, and "paying" often refers more generally to "symbolically rewarding." Michael Harney has noted the importance of the word "amor" as a standard term used to describe relations between men and their motivations: things are done out of "love" (Harney 1993:90–2). While Harney stresses that this word points to the "amity" which underlies the action of the Cid's war-group, it seems more fundamentally to be related to the notion of integrity: it indicates an internal, self-directed motivation for action on the part of leaders and vassals, and thus refuses the notion of motivation based simply on material gains. The word typically occurs as an indicator of (supposedly) selfless generosity, rather than of desire (see l. 1811), and the verb "to love" is virtually a synonym of "give" in many cases: when asking a favor, a vassal says "si este amor non feches yo de vos me quiero quitar" ("If you do not grant me this favour I shall leave you and go my way") (l. 2379).[11] Vassals act for "amor" of the Cid (ll. 1240, 2658, 2883) and then give him their winnings to redistribute. As Harney says, love is a "prestation" (1993:92), but the prestation is intimately tied to notions of integrity.

The epic is thus the story of the Cid's conquest of integrity[12] – his construction of an "integral" identity, one could also say – and his freeing himself of the dependency represented by his forced monetary transaction earlier in the text (tir. 11). But even this transaction – a loan contracted with Jewish lenders – could be seen as a taking, since the deceptive collateral given by the Cid is only a box of sand, and since the Jews are presented later in the text as still unrepaid. It is notable that in the text the Cid often takes and often gives, but is never shown receiving gifts from others of equal or higher status, the text even explicitly stating at one point that he has taken, not received some war horses (ll. 2010–11). What he receives is loyalty from recruits and tribute from the conquered. His integrity is underlined in other ways as well using the discourse of giving and taking. Most particularly, the law codes of medieval Spain, or *fueros*, specified that the king was entitled to a one-fifth share of all booty (Lacarra 1980:32–7). In the epic, however, it is the Cid who receives this one-fifth share. This underlines the Cid's political and economic independence in relation to the king.[13] The three increasingly large gifts which the Cid sends to his king are far less than a one-fifth share, and oscillate between gifts recognizing the honor of the king as superior, with the ultimate power to reintegrate the Cid fully into Spanish society,

10 See Escobedo 1993:180, 255–6.

11 See also ll. 1247–48: "el amor" is indicated by the fact that vassals are "pagados."

12 Duggan 1989:35 uses the same term in a similar context, though without developing a theoretical framework around it.

13 See Lacarra 1980:43. Note also that the Cid bestows the bishopric of Valencia – something only the king can in theory do.

and aggressive challenges to the king, which virtually force him to respond with political favor.[14] The Cid's concluding marriage of his daughters to the kings of Aragon and Navarre, which is presented as a horizontal exchange, also validates his claim to kinglike integrity.

The Poem of the Cid clearly lends itself to an ultimately economistic analysis, even if this orientation in the text is embedded in a symbolic economy of honor. But in fact, the notion of embeddedness, which is often used for discussing economics in gift economies, seems misleading. It suggests that sociopolitical or moral elements of the culture dominate economic ones, which could however be disembedded in order to see the truly economistic aspects of the culture. This can easily cross over into a tendency to see the economic as a suppressed aspect of the culture, maintaining a status of signified in relation to the signifier of symbolic capital. But the evidence in Chapters 3 and 4 of this book, particularly the discussion concerning *The Cid*, suggests that the economic elements such as quantified amounts of money can just as often be the signifier – of symbolic capital. The economic orientations of a culture need not be suppressed or subsidiary to the sociopolitical or moral ones – rather, they can maintain a symbolic relationship to each other. But the key to this relationship lies in its specifically symbolic character. And, as already seen, the symbolic character here is key for the question of the identity of the aristocratic individual as well, since that identity is created and expressed fundamentally in terms of symbolic acts and symbolic possessions.

Performance, Ritual, and the Meaning of "Honor"

Beyond the emphasis on sociopolitical and economic integrity, *The Cid* is concerned with the construction of an identity embodied in willful action, and more specifically in internally-derived motivations which establish the integrity of the body and identity of the Cid himself. Images of the integrity of the body itself include his famous beard, which remains uncut and unplucked, unlike that of a defeated enemy (tir. 137, 140 in particular). The Cid's story could be read, in this context, as the enactment – or performance – of an internally derived image of his own integrity. Geoffrey West (1977:205) has suggested that *The Cid* is the story of an individual who is uniquely faithful to himself. That is, his social identity at the beginning of the text is quite low, but his personal vision of that identity is very high. The Cid then forces the world to accede to his own vision of himself and his identity: the hero forces the world to change, while he does not (see also Hart 1977; Montgomery 1987:204). This is the essence of what Susan Gal calls "symbolic domination": the "ability to make others accept and enact one's representation of the world" (Gal 2001:424). The text thus resembles the

---

[14] Lacarra 1980:131–2 notes that the gifts are also aggressive challenges (indirectly) to the Cid's other principal enemy in the text, Garcia Ordonez.

children's game where one throws a rock, then tries to leap to that point, with the proviso that the farthest throw – and successful leap to that point – wins (Pitt-Rivers 1966:24). The Cid's own self-image of his identity is never verbalized or depicted in the text, but it could be reduced to the single word "integrity," with the "leap" to this point accomplished by taking and giving. The goal need not be pronounced explicitly ahead of time, since the culture provides the aspiration ready made. The giving and taking thus constitute a performance in the world which eventually enables the constitution of the Cid as integral subject: action fulfills potential (with of course the proviso in mind that reaching the potential means passing beyond the realm of performative giving and taking which got one to that point, as seen in Chapters 1 and 2). This is the deeper sense that underlies such prosaic epic compliments as in the following: "miedo iva aviendo que Mio Çid se repintra,/ lo que non ferie el caboso por quanto en el mundo ha/ – una deslea[l]tança – ca non la fizo alguandre" ("... for fear that the Cid should change his mind – a thing [which] that famous man would not do for anything in the world, for never in his life had he gone back on his word") (ll.1079–81). Once the word is "thrown out," the only option is to force the world to corre-spond to it. This concept of performance is best represented in the text by the word "lidiar," which means both "to fight" and "to prove the truth of a statement through combat." This is essentially what the Cid does in the course of the text, if the statement is taken as a vision of integrity.[15]

The word "lidiar" is actually used primarily at the end of the text, in the context of the judicial scene, and eventual judicial combat, in which the Cid and his allies hope to prove that the Infantes did wrong in beating and abandoning the Cid's daughters after marrying them. Such scenes are common in medieval literature, and function like the child's game mentioned above: one "throws out" verbally a potential truth, as does an opponent, and then one seeks to perform in the world (in combat) in such a way as to allow the potential truth to become "true." In such a worldview, nothing is verbally true in and of itself – things are made true through performance. The final judicial combat can thus be seen as a *mise-en-abyme* of the entire epic, and as an explicit rendering of the process of identity formation through performance. The ritualized give-and-take of the judicial combat echos all that has preceded it. With the victory of the Cid and his allies, the performative nature of honor is finally validated – through a perform-ance, fittingly enough.

The final judicial scene functions on another level as well, however. Metaphor-ically, the meaning of the word "honor" itself has been "thrown out" in two vari-

---

[15] This situation is a microcosm of the more general medieval motivation for warfare, which, when not to gain wealth, was intended to "translate claimed authority into real power" (Reuter 1999:31). War was a performance. For an additional analysis of warfare as a perfor-mance and negotiation of social order see Halsall 1998:21–2. See also Haidu 1993:72, where he suggests that the epic insult amounts to a splitting of the subject – between the subject's own self-representation and that of the insulter. The warrior must then performatively re-integrate himself in combat, by proving the insult wrong, and his own self-conception right.

ants in the text as the scene begins.[16] One variant – that of the Cid – suggests that honor derives from performance. Due to this performance, the Cid suggests, his social status is the equal of, and indeed superior to, that of the Infantes. Behind this suggestion is the belief that social rank is fundamentally open within the nobility, and that this rank is constructed de facto through the specific perform- ance of taking and giving.

The Infantes, on the other hand, suggest that honor derives "de natura," as they say on several occasions. Honor is thus an essential quality of lineage and of the blood (tir. 124).[17] As such it can never be gained by an individual, only lost and then recouped. When the Infantes state that, "¡esto lidiare a tod el mas ardido;/ que por que las dexamos ondrados somos nos!" ("I shall defend this against the best champion: that by deserting them [the Cid's daughters] we gained honour") (ll. 3359–60), they are talking of honor lost through association with those of low blood rank. For them, rank within the nobility is fundamentally closed. No amount of performance can change one's status, for honor is not based on performance, but essence. Thus it is not surprising that the Infantes are never depicted as giving gifts in the text. Their self-identity is not based on such a practice.

In this context, the poem can be read as a forum for the negotiation or debate of the meaning of the word "honor" itself, and thus as a "performance" in the sense elaborated by Victor Turner (1986), Dell Hymes (1981), Richard Bauman (1977, 1986, 1989), and others. Up to now in this book, the term "performance" has been used fairly broadly, focusing on the distinction between de jure and de facto bases of identity and authority. But as defined by the scholars above, it focuses more specifically on ritualistic, socially-defined genres of activities which feature a heightened focus on performer competence, a heightened metalinguistic and metasocial awareness of the performance itself, and a strong interaction between performer, audience and context, all of which serve to open up the topic of the performance, and the society more generally, to reflection, debate, reformation, or renewed, strengthened adherence to its mores. This is what I will call "ritual- ized performance." From this perspective, The Cid indirectly underlines the fact that language, in the epic context, has no essential meaning, any more than the specific word "honor" does. Epic language is the product of a ritualized perform- ance setting, in the literal sense that the specific meanings of specific words in an

[16] Peristiany and Pitt-Rivers 1992:4 discusses the more general tendency of the term "honor" to function in strongly performative cultures as a site around which larger social debates coalesce. It becomes a "conceptual field" on which different social groups can dispute both the meaning of the term and more complex views of social organization.

[17] This claim became increasingly common in later epics of the thirteenth century, such as the Old French Hervis de Mes and Les Enfances Vivien. In both cases, aristocrats raised as bourgeois act inherently as aristocrats once the chance arises, despite their upbringing – nature and blood trump nurture. The position taken by the Infantes can from this perspective be seen as the more radical position, with the Cid representing a fundamentally conservative posi- tion.

epic are the product of a series of oral, public, ritual performances elaborated over the course of many years within a specific literary performance tradition (Foley 1995), which can always reopen the meaning of those words when it wishes, and in fact does so to at least some extent with each succeeding ritual performance in its particular setting. More metaphorically, words are "filled with truth" through social performance. It is only fitting that honor be the specific nexus of the debate here, because honor is the fundamental quality of the nobility, and the image of nobility presented by the text is a fundamentally performance-based one, as opposed to an essentialist one.[18] Part of the genius of this particular epic is the way in which it portrays the integration of social performativity – as the basis of identity and authority – with ritualized, linguistic performativity. Both depend on an awareness of – and open embrace of – the "fluidity" of authority, whether one means sociopolitical authority or the "authority" of linguistic meaning. The text thus indirectly posits the epic as the perfect generic exemplar of the warrior aristocracy.

One begins to see now how gift-giving, taking, language, and identity are intimately connected. Individual identity and stature, class identity, social power, judicial truth, and language more generally are all constructed through projections requiring performative validation. Symbolic forms of action within ritual contexts such as combat or judicial trials – especially giving and taking (whether verbally or physically in fighting) – are the keys to this validation, since they are the primary means of producing symbolic capital. It is this capital which "pays off," satisfies, or validates the projection. This is in fact the fundamental sense of the word "pagar" in the epic. It is only fitting therefore that this epic itself was most likely a specifically oral, public, ritualized social performance, whose specific meanings and status were products of an interactive construction of the text between *juglar*, audience and sociopolitical context. Such interactive constuctions revolve crucially around satisfying an audience through ritualized, artistic performance.[19]

The coherence of the text's compositional and receptive form – if the present argument about that form is accepted here – with the form of its social milieu as represented by the text is striking.[20] Michael Harney has argued that the social

---

[18] See Resina 1984:424–5 on the Cid's violation of certain explicit rules of nobility. Such a violation is ultimately irrelevant, since his performance rewrites those rules. See Deyermond 1982 for an analysis of the originality of the Cid poet within the context of traditional rules of epic composition – his "performative originality" in other words, like that of the hero, the Cid.

[19] On the orality of *The Cid*, see in particular Duggan 1989 and Webber 1986. Performative views of solidarity are to be contrasted with more traditional, rhetorical views of solidarity, where the construction of solidarity is a one-way function of the author, and where little or no room is left for social analysis or negotiation. For a good example of the latter view of the poem, see Montgomery 1987.

[20] The most recent and accurate descriptions of the poem's oral character are those of Duggan 1989 (which is virtually an explicit reply to Smith 1983) and Webber 1986 (which also replies specifically to Smith). Neither critic accepts the neo-traditionalist viewpoint of

setting of the text needs to be seen fundamentally in terms of the anthropology of kinship: an arena prior to the formation of the state, in which modern legalism and respect for the textualism which accompanies such legalism is absent (1997:88). This arena of kinship and customary law corresponds closely to that of oral performance. This coherence makes the claims of some critics that the epic is the product of individual, written composition all the more problematic. Such a need for a creative founder of the textual tradition, who invested the poem once and for all with a series of meanings which were then closed to any future, oral, public renegotiation through subsequent performances recalls the essentialist position of the Infantes. Colin Smith, for example, argues strongly for this point, yet the supposedly brilliant author, who he insists was worthy of his own statue next to the Cid on the bridge at Burgos (1983:207), is a strangely limited and uncreative figure. Smith argues that the imbalances in the recounting of some episodes in the poem, as well as various other inconsistencies, were the result of imbalances in the available written source materials which the author relied on, as if this author were himself bound by the timeless, unchanging, essential version of events found in writing, unable to invent anew (Smith 1983:208–9).[21] Such a view of medieval composition as a slavish obedience to sources does not reflect even the typical procedures of literate writers. It certainly fails to reflect the larger world of *The Poem of the Cid* as the text presents it – a world highly open to mobility, re-invention and performative reconstruction of status, rank and meaning.[22] Instead, in Smith's analysis, the written sources become a kind of blood nobility for the poet, without which he can do little, and which he must constantly obey.

Returning to the poem in the light of this discussion, one can see that it is the competing stances on the value of social performance which make the meaning of the marriage between the Infantes and the Cid's daughters fundamentally different for the two sides. The Cid clearly reads his daughters as gifts who are symbolic of bonds established between his family and that of the Infantes. These bonds serve more abstractly to underline symbolically the Cid's new social status – his past performance will now allow the blood of his family to mix with that of the Infantes (in the next generation).

For the Infantes, however, there is no gift, only a commercial exchange or bartering of their words for the Cid's money and daughters. Since there is no gift, they do not perceive any relationship to have been established between the

Menendez-Pidal: both are influenced by more recent studies of oral performance, including those of Foley cited above.

[21] See Montgomery 1983 for a brief, incisive response to Smith on the question of the individual, learned author.

[22] See for example West 1977 on the variations in overall attitude between the twelfth-century Latin *Historia Roderici* and *The Poem of the Cid*, (not to mention those with the Latin *Carmen Campidoctoris*). West does not discuss whether the poet of *The Cid* knew these works, but the variations do suggest that this poet felt free to re-invent broadly in relation to the previous tradition, or at least the evidence we have for it today. See also Deyermond 1982.

larger families. Likewise, the Cid's daughters are not symbols, but merely things in themselves who accompany the bride-wealth which is the main object of the Infantes' interest. Since the daughters are not gifts, and not symbolic, they are also not seen as inalienably linked to their father, but rather as material objects permanently transferred – and disposable – as the result of an exchange roughly equivalent to barter.[23] In this barter, the Infantes give their word freely since words too for them are just things in themselves which seemingly have no need of performative reinforcement, any more than their noble status does. As long as the words are accepted in the exchange, their function is fulfilled, for the exchange is a one-time event, not the formation of an ongoing relationship.[24] Thus the harsh treatment the Infantes mete out to the daughters of the Cid, while perhaps socially unlikely and melodramatic, is theoretically consonant with their view of the marriage, and more generally with their view of social status as embodied in essence rather than performance. Indeed, nothing they might do will change that status, but a mingling of their blood with the Cid's through reproduction would change it, so the abandonment makes perfect sense within a logic of essential nobility carried to its absurd extreme. Likewise, essential nobility has no need to produce symbols performatively – it can just adopt the time-honored, socially institutionalized signs of nobility.

Thus we begin to see why this epic, unlike so many others, places so much stress on marriage. The marriage and subsequent court scene are ritual forums for a debate on the meaning of that most quintessential of epic qualities, honor, and more generally on the means of production and circulation of honor within the symbolic economy of the warrior aristocracy. *The Poem of the Cid* can thus be read most fundamentally as a debate about the social bases of power, rank and identity. The Infantes are clearly straw figures representing the *reductio ad absurdum* of the opposing side in their total failure to understand the workings of a performance-based symbolic economy embodied in giving and taking (Duggan 1989:38–9). While the Infantes argue for the equivalence of blood and rank within the nobility, the Cid accepts blood as simply the lower limit of the noble class, above which all depends on performance. The text clearly argues for social mobility within the framework of the nobility (Lacarra 1980:114–16, 160–3; Duggan 1989:43ff), and for this social mobility to be attained through violent strategies of taking and giving, in a society which was still fundamentally based on pillage and redistribution (Lacarra 1980:48). Such mobility would have made participation in the frontier wars of conquest around the turn of the thirteenth century all the more appealing to Spaniards of the time, and this has

[23] The Cid's concern with his two prized swords, which he makes sure to retrieve from the Infantes during the trial, could be read as an effort to re-symbolify these objects, which the Infantes have effectively deviated into the sphere of barter exchange.

[24] The Infantes' fundamental misunderstanding of the nature of wealth in their culture has been remarked on by many scholars, though not typically in relation to gift culture in particular. Most obviously, they keep things, but throw away people, in the case of the Cid's daughters and the accompanying wedding gifts (tir. 128).

been suggested as the key ideological aim of the text (Duggan 1989:20, Lacarra 1980:168–71).

The Menace of the Commodity

Despite the text's efforts to bring the debate to a satisfactory conclusion, it is riven by the tensions. The issue of blood, on the lower bounds of the performative competition, is clear. But even more important is the sacred status of the king, on the upper boundary of the competition. He seems to stand above any potential performative threat, since the Cid always continues to recognize his authority (even if that recognition comes in the form of aggressive challenges: the king is after all apparently the only person to merit such challenges). We will leave these tensions unresolved for the moment before returning to them in the context of the following chapter. For the moment, we will to return to the issue of the particularity of *The Cid* within the epic corpus.

The menace of the thing itself and of the idolatry of the symbol always shadowed the symbolic economy, and that shadow only became more imminent as material wealth increased in the twelfth and thirteenth centuries, while opportunities for gaining honor through violent taking declined.[25] The extraordinary explicitness with which *The Cid* underlines non-economic motivations, and places the gift symbolically after the deed motivated by honor, is perhaps a reflection of this increasing tension, and can be seen in other texts such as the *Life of William Marshall*. As such, it could be read as an effort to reinforce the validity of the ideology of the gift and the symbolic economy more generally in the face of competing discourses about reciprocity and social organization, as well as competing modes of identity construction and the related pursuit of power (in a way similar to that seen in Chapter 6 in the discussion of the smile in gift charters). It is a general rule that social structures and ideologies are most explicitly represented, theorized, or brought into consciousness when an opposing structure and ideology gains sufficient power to threaten the dominant one. The competitor calls forth certain features of the original social form (of the gift), and leads to the neglect or even suppression of others. We will return to this idea of suppression in the concluding two chapters. For the moment, let us focus on the tendency towards highlighting certain features of the gift.

This seems to be clearly what is occurring in another famous story of a spectacular rise to power, that of William Marshall, who rose from quite low origins to become regent of England in the early thirteenth century. His biography, the *Life of William Marshall,* written around 1226, offers – performs, one could say

---

[25] See Godelier 1999:57–77 for a discussion of the run-away object, and the way that this phenomenon occurred in the potlatch of late-nineteenth-century Native American societies. He bases his analysis on the understanding that new economic pressures related to colonization by Europeans had deformed the basic social mechanism (76ff).

– a representation of a certain kind of warrior-aristocratic culture which seems quite conservative and even anachronistic in the context of its place and date of composition. It is clear however, independently of the biography, that William Marshall himself engaged in the same kind of conservatively-oriented perform-ance, particularly in his gift-giving and religious practices.[26] The biography often seems to go out of its way to stress the non-monetary, integral quality of William's motivations. Early in his career, after he has helped conquer a village, his martial virtues are praised, but the account notes that "ne tendi pas al gaeing-nier,/ Fors a bien delivrer la vile" ("he was not interested in profit, but only in freeing the town") (ll.1140–1). The other knights, who have noticed this, ask him mockingly for a nice necklace (ll. 1147–8). When he responds that he has none, they mock his failure to procure booty after his brave deeds (ll. 1153–60). The joke actually works on multiple levels. On the one hand, the other knights mock William's apparent lack of understanding of the symbolics of booty and reward and the entire propriety of seizing goods that would symbolize his brave deeds. But in the context of the rest of the text, the joke also underlines the integrity of William's actions, so that the joke is ultimately on those around him. While they sell off their own king "par coveitise d'aveir/ E par traïson" ("out of covetousness and treason") (ll. 2710–11), William

> Unques al gaaing n'entendi,
> Mais al bien faire tant tendi
> Que del gaaing ne li chalut.
> Il gaainna qui mielz valut,
> Quer molt fait cil riche bargainne
> Qui onor conquert e gaainne.   (ll. 3007–12)

> Never sought out profit, but looked to act well since profit did not interest him. He won that which is more valuable, for he achieves a good bargain who conquers and gains honor.

The text continually attacks fallen "chevalerie" of which William is the only true example (ll. 2103, 4304–6, 5095–116), and it does so specifically in the context of an opposition between "envy" (l. 5127, for another example) and "honor." William ostentatiously refuses offers of money (ll. 6148–78 – where he follows his "volonté" rather than accept gifts for service; ll. 6260–84, repeating the story of the previous occasion) and continually disdains "gain" (ll. 10,631–4), giving his wealth away as fast as he gets it (ll. 11,969–80). He "out le cuer entier e pur" ("had a pure and whole heart") (l. 15,123) while all those around him desert the king once his wealth runs out (ll. 15,117–21). Yet at the same time, the biography constantly chronicles William's rising wealth and prestige, his winnings at tour-naments, the great booty gained in combat, and concludes with a celebration of

---

[26] See Crouch 1990:188–92 on William's unusual and "old-fashioned" choices of reli-gious orders to support, and also 1990:3 on his illiteracy and heavy focus on the military side of his life.

his ability to give massively to all around him as he lies on his deathbed. If one examines his life in the light of other sources, he also turns out to have been an important champion of mercantile commerce and an able fiscal administrator of the realm (Painter 1933:167, 242; Crouch 1990:168–70). Not only did he know how to get wealth, he knew how to promote it and manage it carefully.

One might be tempted to conclude that the discourse of honor and integrity is a pure imposture in this text, given the course of William's life. Certainly, the explicit resistance to commodification suggests an intense awareness of its temptations in the context of an increasingly monetized economy. These socio-economic changes must have produced a reaction in the form of a discourse of the gift which highlighted its opposition to such temptations. The greater the pressure from the competing discourse, the more the components of gift culture which were most clearly in opposition to that discourse would have come to the fore. We could even recall Lévi-Strauss's idea, cited in the Introduction, that the indigenous Melanesians were the true authors of the theory of reciprocity.[27] The theory of the gift was in fact first authored in the West by texts such as *The Cid* and *The Life of William Marshall*. Faced with increasing commodification, the medieval aristocracy began to author a theory of the gift which responded to that threat very explicitly, and which has since been taken as the theory of the gift, due to the rhetorical prominence that this discourse enjoyed, especially as the Middle Ages advanced.

But in this discourse, commodification was simply brought more clearly to the surface and highlighted as a danger. In fact, the threat was always present. "Commodification," understood as in the earlier chapters to mean the temptation of the thing itself and the rejection of the symbolic quality of money, objects, people and lands for their material component, is not the same thing as moneti-zation and markets. The danger of commodification understood in this broader sense is really the deeper danger of a loss of self in a world of independent, material existences which no longer respond or refer symbolically to particular individuals. Certainly money and markets intensified and clarified this menace very powerfully, and their increasing prominence in the twelfth and thirteenth centuries did produce a shift in the oppositional axis of the gift – from violence to commodification. But the danger of the material thing both preceded and always exceeds the danger of markets as objectifying, materializing phenomena. Both *The Cid* and *The Life of William Marshall* – and William of Poitier's chronicle of William the Conqueror – seem to speak from a time where money, markets, and commodities in the market had not yet become fused (as they since have) with the more fundamental phenomenon of what we have been calling commodifi-cation, but which could also be considered a special form of reification. This

[27] See also Thomas 1991, Ch. 5, on what he calls the "discovery of the gift." The discovery is of the explicit notion of the "gift" by indigenous peoples who resist western monetized economies: structures of opposition and resistance give rise to an explicit discourse and theo-rization of "the gift" only in such circumstances, he suggests.

fusion – which occurs in medieval texts quite commonly already in the thirteenth century – has produced the two fundamental modern misconceptions of the gift. First, it has, as already seen, obscured the gift/violence axis of opposition, as opposed to the axis of gift/commodity. But secondly, it has obscured the opposition of symbolic and anti-material gift versus reified object behind the simpler, and more historically and geographically particular notion of "gift versus market commodity." As James Boon has argued, our own economism prevents us from appreciating the true "extravagance" of forms which commodities can take across cultures in all their multiplicity (Boon 1999:251). Once this deeper opposition is seen, one can better appreciate that the discourse of the gift in *The Life of William Marshall* is more different from modern conceptions of gifts and commodities than might first have been apparent, and more conservative as well.[28]

In a similar sense, much of the symbolic structure of giving and taking in *The Cid* echoes quite closely that found in much earlier texts, where issues of commerce and market economies were not an issue. In the literature of Anglo-Saxon England, the same concern with the distribution of booty after the fact, as symbolic recognition of internally-motivated loyalty and service by the follower, was a central point (Evans 1997:111–13, 116). The public recognition of honor embodied in the public ceremonies of redistribution was in fact apparently more highly valued than the material items themselves. This is not surprising, given that the poetic acclaim of the court poets, the ceremony itself, and the wealth, were all symbolic forms. When in Beowulf the narrator notes of one such ceremony with regard to Beowulf that "there was no shame in those sumptuous gifts before the assembly" (ll. 1025–6), he clearly indicates that wealth per se, in the absence of preceding deeds worthy of it, was not only worthless, but actually harmful or shameful, representing a loss of symbolic capital even if it represented a gain of (obviously less important) economic capital. This same literature also included minute descriptions of the fine craftsmanship of the luxury goods seized by warriors (Evans 1997:125–6), much like *The Cid*'s long focus on the details of booty. Thus in many ways, the symbolic economy of *The Cid* scarcely differs from that of Beowulf.

---

[28] David Crouch examines the charters which document William's gift-giving, and he notes a number of episodes where virtual duels of gift exchanges occurred between William and King John as they fought for power, influence and control (see 1990:82–4, 92, 98). The tense, competitive and aggressive nature of these exchanges in an unstable political environment reveals the continuing importance of the gift/violence axis in understanding William's life. This component of gift-giving is underplayed or even suppressed in the *Life*. Thus although the discourse of reification is in its essence conservative, the relative emphasis given to this axis of the gift over the axis of violence does represent clear trends in the oppositional evolution of the discourse of the gift.

The Violent Self

Our examination of taking in this chapter points finally to the valorization of aggressive violence – either by means of giving or taking – in the earlier Middle Ages, as a mode of gaining honor, and as a form of identity construction. The implications of such attitudes – and the reasons why they are not often recognized as positively valenced by modern readers – must be considered in the context of more general modern ideas regarding violence and the individual. Such ideas fall into three general categories in current theory. One category sees violence and identity formation as always connected, and necessarily so, due to the very nature of social and semiotic systems. Such theories, however, typically view the individual as the victim of such violence.[29] For example, one may see the "entry into the symbolic order," as Lacan would put it, as a moment of violence and loss inflicted on the subject. Or, in more classically Freudian terms, the world does violence to the individual as he or she is in the process of acquiring a social identity, or the individual is even forced to do violence to him- or herself through the mechanism of repression. A second category of theories views the formation of identity in similar ways, with the subject as victim, but suggests that the violence is the product of particular social forms, which are open to revision and improvement, or which at least can evolve in potentially more favorable directions. Michel Foucault argues in *Discipline and Punish* (1975) that individual identity is largely the product of socially-elaborated psychological categories which are assigned to the individual by a state apparatus. Critics of capitalism have often suggested that individual identity is simply a by-product of consumer purchasing behavior – the acquisition of ready-made and typically repressive identities (see especially Baudrillard 1968, 1972), and theorists such as Adorno, Horkheimer, or Gramsci have pointed to the hegemonic operations of capitalist ideology on the subject.

The third key category is especially characteristic of those who look at identity formation within specific, subaltern social groups, based on specific genders, races, classes, ethnicities or other criteria – that is to say those inspired by post-colonial studies. These scholars and theorists have argued that violence is in fact a fundamental element of modern western society, and they do focus on *individual* violence as a component of identity formation.[30] The hegemonic individual (whether this be Western, White, Male, Heterosexual, or any of a number of others) is viewed as constructing individual, subjective identity by a more-or-less violent appropriation of the identity of the Other. Conversely, the subaltern's individual, subjective identity is the product of various forms of real and subli-

---

[29] See for example René Girard's work in this area, particularly on violence and the sacred (1972).

[30] See Haidu 1993 concerning the violence of the Middle Ages, the suppressed violence of the modern capitalist West, and the ways that these two interact. For two very different theoretical approaches to the question of how violence on the individual leads to identity formation and social order, see Foucault, *Discipline and Punish*, and Girard, *Violence and the Sacred*.

mated violence inflicted on him from without.[31] Here again, the focus of interest – the subaltern subject – is the victim of systemic violence inflicted from without. Individualized violence is perpetrated on another as part of identity formation, unlike in the other two categories, but typically the aggressive, hegemonic identity is primarily a group identity shared by an aggregate of individuals, not a specifically individual one; the focus is on intergroup confrontation, not intergroup and personal identity formation. Violence is a phenomenon of the group, the structure, the larger system, and the dynamics of unequal relationships of power.

Even where representations of individual violence as constitutive of identity do occur, such as in the English Renaissance as analyzed by Stephen Greenblatt, the valence of the violence remains negative. In his reading of Christopher Marlowe's dramas, especially *Tamerlane*, he shows how the Renaissance individual engaged in self-fashioning by means of "casual, unexplained violence" (1980:193–4, 217) and how such individuals could be characterized by an enormous appetite, will, and desire (194–5, 212–13, 218–19). Greenblatt specifically discusses violence and identity formation (197–8), and also shows how such violent self-fashioners sought to open up what in Chapter 2 we called "qualitative distances" between themselves and their societies (203, 213). All of this sounds like an ambitious medieval warrior aristocrat, especially since the violence is directed internally to the society. Yet such dramatizations ultimately served as a critique of the contemporary society and its own, more sublimated forms of commercial and colonialist violence, Greenblatt argues (205–9, 215). The violence of the individual only actualizes more clearly the violence inherent in the social order. Greenblatt thus reads Marlowe from the perspective of our categories two and three: Marlowe is dramatizing society-internal (commercial, mercantile) hegemonic violence, and society-external (colonialist) hegemonic violence. To the extent that Tamerlane or any of Marlowe's other violent characters are appealing, it is in their quality as the rebel who turns systemic violence against itself in a fundamentally critical or defensive maneuver. They anticipate the modern revolutionary, anarchist, or third-world liberation fighter. In sum, all three modern categories treat violence as fundamentally social, in such a way that the subject is typically the victim of violence. They also see individual violence, in the context of questions of personal and social identity, as either condemnable and criminal, or else as resistant and defensive in relation to primary social violence.[32]

The modernist attitude towards violence and the individual reveals itself among medievalists in their interpretations of the conduct of perhaps the most famous medieval hero, Roland (who will be examined in more detail in Ch. 6).

---

[31] Young 1990:1–20 offers an excellent overview of the critique of violent western identity formation at the expense of the other: Chs. 7–9 cover Edward Said, Homi Bhabha and Gayatri Spivak. Bhabha 1994 is perhaps the central text on this topic.

[32] See Fox 1994, Part 2 (on violence and aggression) for an interesting discussion of the resistance of academic anthropology to the concept of violence as socially inherent, much less as socially admirable.

The overwhelming majority of scholars, confronted with his repeated calls for war over peace in the battles between the Franks and the Saracens, and his refusal to call for reinforcements in the face of enemies who will ultimately massacre the entire Frankish army, see him in one of two ways. One view is that he is acting violently on behalf of the group. Such interpretations view Roland either positively – because he acts for his society as a whole as a culture hero – or at least as no worse than the society as a whole, which is seen as inherently violent. The other interpretation views Roland as acting violently primarily on behalf of himself. He is thus hubristic, guilty of "démesure," and seen in a negative light.[33] In other words, Roland may be excused as the product of a violent society, and even admired as the exemplar of such a society, but individual violence as a means of identity-formation cannot seem to be condoned: individuals who act violently apart from or against their own societies or parts of those societies cannot be conceived of positively. As William Miller has argued, modern western culture as a whole has inherited a dominant paradigm of nature and culture, in which violence is an aspect of nature, and thus "anti-culture" (Miller 1993:78–9). But could one read Roland's violence as both positively-valued in his culture, yet also fundamentally self-oriented? And if so, how could the individualistically-oriented violence be read in terms of any functional social benefit? Even those western theorists of identity formation who most willingly accept the necessity of violence in the process (Hegel, Nietzsche, René Girard) tend to see the violence as necessarily directed against either an outsider/other of some sort, or against a fundamentally corrupt society (in Nietszche's case). But Roland is the quintessential insider, and he is his own society's hero. In contrast, the notion of the violent rebel is quintessentially modern – it separates the Renaissance, and even the courtly romance, from the warrior aristocracy. It is notable that Marlowe's hero's attempts at violent self-fashioning ultimately fail,

---

[33] A good overview of the historical debate on whether Roland is guilty of "démesure" in relation to the values of his culture, or whether he is simply acting out the imperatives of the culture, can be found in Cook 1987, especially Part 2, Ch. 2, "Demesure and Choice." The central argument of the entire book is that Roland knowingly and willingly – as opposed to blindly – acts out cultural imperatives, but Cook carefully discusses and weighs the many opposing arguments from nearly a century of *Roland* criticism. Among work after 1987, Haidu 1993 is perhaps the strongest proponent of the "cultural imperatives" viewpoint, which has become the dominant one for the moment. The shift away from focus on Roland the (hubristic) individual hero to Roland as (faithful) exemplar of a whole culture, which has occurred especially since the 1960s, is representative of the larger trend in medieval studies towards a cultural and anthropological perspective, and also the more general trend in literary studies towards theoretical approaches such as structuralism and post-structuralism which diminish the centrality of individual subjects. In contrast, many earlier critics have tended to view Roland more in terms of individual psychology – and the text as the product of an individual, controlling, poet-genius. Classic examples are Bédier 1914, Le Gentil 1969, and Aebischer 1972. See Cook 1987:x (note no. 3) for many additional references. One important exception to this trend is that those critics who read the text as the product of strongly religious inspiration often see Roland as a Christian hero of the culture hero type. See Brault 1978, most prominently, and Cook 1987: xi (note no. 4) for many additional references.

primarily since "violence has no discourse" at the time, according to Greenblatt (198). In contrast, William the Conqueror and the Cid succeed at exactly the same enterprise specifically because violence does have a discourse during their time. Since the discourse is available, they have a channel within which to enact their appetites, desires and wills successfully within their societies.

It is perhaps tempting to see William the Conqueror, the Cid, Robert Guiscard, or Roland as colonizing figures. They are already powerful individuals, and they inflict that power onto sociocultural others in an effort to expand their territorial holdings as well as their personal power. They seem to establish their identity by exporting violence outside the group, and consuming others militarily. But once the ways in which giving and taking operate within social groups are understood, one begins to recognize that these figures engage in a great deal of real or sublimated violence internally within their own social groups as well. For the historical figures, William and Robert, this is sometimes quite subtle, but it becomes clearer once the symbolic economy of reciprocity is understood. In the poetic texts, such issues come to the forefront: some or all of the most dramatic conflicts in *The Song of Roland* and *The Poem of the Cid* are social-internal – between Roland and Ganelon, the Cid and the Infantes – and in *Roland* in particular, the conflicts lead to catastrophic internal consequences. But as *Roland* makes clearest, internal violence is not the work of the rebel; it is the product of the socially admired hero. Yet the hero acts fundamentally for himself, not for the society, it turns out. Violence is individual, yet admired.[34] The dynamic of exported violence and internal solidarity is false.

We will return to *Roland*, for it is an especially interesting if problematic case. But such a reading is essentially what is here proposed for *The Cid* as well. The Cid is driven by the desire to construct a subjective identity in terms of integrity – the identity with the highest status and the greatest correlative of power available in his society. And he does this through violent taking and aggressive (to a greater or lesser degree) giving. Solidarity, for the Cid, essentially works in one direction – the dependence of others on him. The text ends with his followers paying off the "debdo que les mando so señor" ("the obligation laid on them by their lord") (l. 3703), and however much the Cid's followers may be recipients of his "amor" and be motivated by the same "amor" for him, that text reveals at one point that they are not truly free to do as they wish: indeed, an improper departure can result in death (ll. 1249–54).

Of course, these obligations must be understood performatively. The Cid has no *de jure* power which would allow him to coerce action by his followers – he depends essentially on their voluntary adherence. Clearly, the obligation of self-interest is central to this adherence. But on a deeper level, the Cid's integrity, with its (eventually fulfilled) promise of sacred purity, seems to be a source of desire for his followers. It is the wholeness which they lack. And thus the term

---

[34] Peter Haidu argues similarly that violence carried a positive valence in the Middle Ages, which it lost after that time (1993:3).

"amor" comes to carry two contradictory senses. It marks the voluntary nature of giving and loyalty, as seen earlier. But it also captures the sense of wholeness which the Cid powerfully impresses upon all around him – overt enemies and followers alike – as aggressively as possible, and the powerful desire which this seems to evoke in his followers.[35] This image of integrity in fact seems to lie at the base of the power of recruitment shown by the historical Norman figures we have discussed, just as it does for the Cid.

The word "amor" thus captures the dual nature of the gift as both instrument of solidarity and instrument of violence. The "amor" of the Cid's vassals depends on his continued investment in his symbolic integrity (at least until he attains some juridical, unassailable status), and the "amor" of the Cid for those vassals depends on their demonstration of their own integral motivations. Solidarity, desire, self-interest, and sublimated or threatened violence all intermingle. Michael Harney's extremely interesting, anthropologically inspired readings of *The Cid* have made similar points: he argues that the text focuses on the phenomenon of the "charismatic leader" (whose symbolic identity is founded on "liberty" and "free will," 1992:85). He notes that such leaders are intimately associated with the social margins, and that they have a liminal character which includes both "dark" and "light" sides (1992:71–2; see also 1997:85 on the close linkage of rivalry and camaraderie). He also stresses the unstable nature of their authority (1992:86), as well as the tendency of their own group to collapse into internal discord (1992:88–9).[36] A key counter to this tendency, he argues, is the leader's redistribution of resources to followers (1992:90–2).[37]

In such a setting, the boundaries between internally- and externally-directed

---

[35] The word "amor" is used to indicate desire explicitly when talking of the Infantes (v. 2703), but they seem to be simply the limit case of a form of desire which lies below the actions of all those who encircle the Cid.

[36] Sarah Kay makes a similar point about the hero in medieval French epic: his allies are often outsiders, and his enemies are often within the social group (1995:176–7).

[37] Given Harney's discussion of these issues, and his broader recognition of the ambiguous nature of the gift (1993:79, 85–7, 219), it is puzzling that he claims that the text argues for a vision of the Cid's war group – and the larger Spanish Christian society – as based essentially on "amity" (89–92), "idealized teamwork" and "solidarity" (83–4), "co-operation" (204–5), "egalitarianism" (208) and "bilateral deference" (220). It is in a sense true that the text works to repress the true forms of desire which underlie the symbolic dynamics of the society, behind a discourse of honor, loyalty and solidarity (a tendency which will be addressed specifically in Chs. 8 and 9). But in many cases, it is our own theoretical tendency to repress a full understanding of the violence of the gift which stands in the way of seeing the true dynamics. Harney at one point seems to evoke the nostalgic desire for solidarity, which has traditionally been found among primitive societies (94). His reading of the world of the Cid as a kinship-based world of amity transfers such an image to the text. Yet it seems to be far more a celebration of the Cid's individual rise to pure integrity, and the fear and desire which this rise evokes around him, than a celebration of community solidarity. Even if we leave aside this issue of the gift's internal violence, Harney's reading seems problematic: *The Cid* is a story of armies of thousands fighting across entire regions, founding new kingdoms – not the story of a small clan of outlaws operating in the remote hill country of the eastern Mediterranean in the mid-twentieth century. It is also emblematic of a world of extremely aggressive warriors,

violence can be very tenuous. The often socially externalized violence of taking and the often socially internalized violence of giving are intimately connected, and as the Cid's conflicts with the king and the Infantes show, the one can easily become entangled with the other. As much as it is a Christian/Saracen conflict, *The Cid* is the story of a social-internal feud, with the Saracens simply serving as the instrumental victims which the competing parties attempt to use to resolve their group-internal conflicts. Indeed, the categories of Self, In-Group, and Other/Out-Group become difficult to disentangle in both *The Cid* and *Roland*. (The historical Cid allied himself with Muslims against Christians on occasion, and the literary Cid has a faithful Muslim friend, Abengalbón).[38] As a corollary to this, the violence that one looks to associate with intergroup conflict repeatedly turns up group-internally, and the individually-initiated internal conflict that one wants to see as the product of criminals and traitors is repeatedly the product of the admirable hero.

This is the reason why it was suggested earlier, in Chapter 1, that medieval warrior society offers fundamental challenges to classic anthropological notions of "honor," particularly in the Mediterranean context – and why one must be very careful in applying "honor" as an analytic category from contemporary anthropology to the study of the medieval warrior aristocracy, just as one must be equally careful in using studies of gift cultures. Rather than being a small-scale society peripheral to modern states, the medieval warrior society was a large-scale, dominant one. In this society, honor was not a matter of rough equality; rather, pursuit of honor was often closely linked to the creation of greater and greater inequalities between certain individuals and the rest of the group, leading ultimately to integrity. Furthermore, such a pursuit by an individual was not uniformly seen as excessive or hubristic, but admirable – though clearly dangerous as well, for all concerned. Moreover, rather than a strict in-group/out-group distinction, *The Cid* shows that the individual pursuit of honor could override such distinctions, blurring them considerably, with greater or lesser amounts of violence and agression directed towards both groups by the seeker of honor. And finally, the dictates of the honor system clearly did not serve simply as a means of social integration for individuals, which tended to suppress individuality and reflexivity.

Of course, more recent trends in the study of honor systems – like those of gift economies – have recognized other possibilities. Most interestingly, Maria di Bella suggests that codes of honor are in fact ways for societies to obtain self-awareness and gain control over events. They are "conscious strategies" used for thinking about alternatives and ordering social action (di Bella 1992:155–6). Of course, honor systems are not the focus of this book; for the medieval warrior aristocracy, "honor" is not the goal or central value of the culture. Rather, it is

whose loyalties constantly shifted, and who sought not bilateral deference, but the establishment of hierachical, unequal forms of reciprocity.

[38] See also Norman Daniel's remark (1975:82) that the two groups in the epic (Spanish and Saracen) are morally equivalent (and therefore nearly interchangeable), like "two rival football teams."

simply the symbolic currency which expresses the value of one's identity. Giving and taking are the central mechanisms used to construct that identity, as well as to think about it; and it is integrity which is the ideal identity-form which one seeks to obtain. *The Cid*, particularly in its intense focus on patterns of generalized, symbolic reciprocity, begins to look more and more like a very complex and subtle medieval effort to think through (recall Douglas and Isherwood's suggestion that goods – and gifts – are for "thinking") the questions of the individual, the group, the Other, and especially their interrelationship – in other words, the question of solidarity, violence and their intimate connection – in the context of a world of performative identities.

5

The Sacred Kept

Keeping and Transcendence

In the preceding chapters we have come upon instances in which the central goal of an individual seems to be not to give, (or to take), but to keep – recall Roland's concern with his sword Durendal. The importance of inalienable lands – technically the "honor" of a lord – was also mentioned. In these cases, the individuals are not interested in giving these items away, despite the honor that accrues to giving. It is better to keep than to give. And the violence that centers around these objects is for once less about aggressive taking than defensive protection.

Indeed, from a long-term viewpoint, the exploits of William the Conqueror, Robert Guiscard, or the poetic version of the Cid, could be seen as centering on taking and giving, but all in the ultimate pursuit of integrity: an integrity which would allow an end to dependency and even horizontal reciprocity. More prosaically, these individuals want political independence in the form of a heritable, "keepable" title and a crown.

Of course, heritable titles and lands are the antithesis of the fluid social settings where performative identity can be easily established. It seems initially quite ironic that each of these exemplars of performance should manage in one form or another to solidify his positions through the acquisition of a sacred status which is ultimately no longer given or taken, but simply kept. But in fact, the fundamental desire of the warrior aristocracy was exactly that: a freedom from performance, and a permanent essentializing of social status such that it would be unassailable, without need of the giving and taking required to defend it in more socially fluid and open settings. After all, in a purely performative social setting, even integrity is only temporary and contextual. The dream is to make it permanent and transcendental. Such appears to be the explanation for the numerous Scandinavian hoards which have been found buried throughout northern Europe by archaeologists.[1] Many have supposed that the wealth contained in these hoards was buried to protect it from momentary danger. But it has been argued that the wealth was never intended to be used – this is the symbolic import of its burial. The kept wealth pointed symbolically to the owner's absolute self-sufficiency – it was not

---

[1]   See Gurevich 1968:131 on the symbolic quality of wealth among the Scandinavians and its expression through the practice of hoarding.

even needed for his or her maintenance. Aron Gurevich suggests that the hoard constituted for the Scandinavians a "transcendent treasure" (1968:133).

Such a view corresponds closely to that of anthropologists who have begun recently to explore the role of "keeping" in traditional gift cultures. The power of the "kept" has been forcefully underlined in the work of Annette Weiner and Maurice Godelier, though with differing orientations.[2] Weiner argues that the key to understanding traditional societies lies in recognizing the "deep social priority" of "keeping-while-giving" (1992:ix). What she means by this is that gift-giving is actually a secondary phenomenon, not a primary one: one gives in order to be able *not* to give the most valuable and precious things, whatever they may be in a specific society (1992:xi). The goal of individuals and groups in traditional society is to keep certain things out of circulation. It is these things, finally, which are the foundations of authority in such societies: the royal crown, the exceptional Samoan fine mat, the Native American Sacred Pipe, the medieval family's patrimonial land (1992:34; Godelier 1999:8). Thus a Samoan family might engage in numerous exchanges in order to insure that it had the resources to reciprocate with something other than its exceptional fine mat if it were to receive an especially fine (and aggressive) gift from another family. It is easy to perceive that taking could be viewed in the same context: one takes in order to facilitate the giving that facilitates the keeping, or more directly, one might take in order to disarm a rival whose aggressive taking or giving might threaten one's kept possessions.

The things which are kept provide what Weiner calls "cosmological authenti-fication" (1992:4), and function as the form of the sacred, according to Godelier (1999:xx), or at least to connect the social with the sacred, according to Weiner (1992:4). They serve to motivate, anchor and rationalize the entire system of exchanges within the culture. If Weiner and Godelier are right, then Levi-Strauss's Andaman "fantasy" of escaping giving and reciprocity must be reinterpreted as something much more: it becomes the conceptual model upon which the social orders of exchange are premised and founded.[3] Weiner argues, based on work in the Pacific, that the inalienable marks a desire for "permanence" (8) and a possi-bility of "transcendence" (7, 37; Godelier 1999:33), which is the essence of the idea of pure, stable integrity as examined in this study.

Weiner does not argue that the kept item is equivalent to the possession of pure transcendence, however; the idea that the inalienable would not even need to be "defended" through defensive forms of reciprocity remains a fantasy (1992:65). But the kept exists in relation to a potential transcendence, while also functioning to provide a substitute for that transcendence, in the form of privileged access to the sacred. In other words, the system of giving and taking in a society is

[2]   See Weiner 1992 and Godelier 1999. More generally, many scholars have noted that the focus of honor in Mediterranean societies lies precisely in the "kept" or in "forbidden" domains – particularly inalienable lands and women.

[3]   See Weiner 1992:28–33 for her general critique of Levi-Strauss's argument that society is founded upon reciprocity.

anchored on two different levels: first, by specific, kept material items or lands, which are defended by giving and taking other items and services of lesser rank or value; and secondly, by a more abstract conception of transcendence or integrity wherein perfect essentializing would remove the kept item and its possessor from the spheres of exchange entirely.[4] It is this abstract conception, which both Weiner and Godelier link to the sacred, which underpins the status of the specific, kept material objects.

The project of Weiner and Godelier is finally to challenge the structuralist model of social organization. Following on the work of scholars such as Pierre Bourdieu and Victor Turner, their work emphasizes the specific, circumstantial, particularistic and contingent nature of social organization. In contrast to a world governed by semiotic exchanges based on classically structuralist, stable signs shared by the community, they imagine a world of symbols negotiated anew in each successive, individual exchange: symbols as products of performances. This corresponds closely to the world of the medieval warrior aristocracy as analyzed up to now. But these symbols necessarily represent transitory vehicles. The hope of the symbolic actor is to exchange or convert these event- and person-specific symbols, the temporal efficacy of which is limited by the timing of the next challenge and exchange, into items which are seen as timeless, trans-social, permanent markers of identity and sources of power. Clearly any individual whose social identity includes a general recognition of his privileged access to the sacred is someone who has extraordinary resources to offer to those loyal to him. As a consequence, that person can be extraordinarily successful in attracting adherents, and thus extraordinarily powerful. The uniquely defined "inalienables" which offer such privileged access are the elements which anchor the system of structural reciprocities found in society (Weiner 1992:10).[5] For the Middle Ages, Patrick Geary's work on traffic in relics reveals one classic example of giving and taking (or theft!) as subsidiary elements centered around keeping of theoretically inalienable, sacred material objects (Geary 1986).

Weiner in particular recognizes that the actual meaning and status of these seemingly transcendent inalienables itself shifts through time (1992:7–8). Thus from an outsider's, analytical perspective, neither she nor Godelier suggest that these inalienables represent true forms of "transcendency." From this perspective, they are best thought of as somewhat analogous to the "supplement" of post-

---

4   See for example Kopytoff 1986 on the process of "singularization" of objects, their removal from circulation, and its connection to the sacred (1986:73). Sarah Kay's analysis of the epic quest for "singularity" likewise points to the "anchoring" of singularity in marriage bonds, and the "vesting of identity in the uncontested control of territory" – both of which involve removal of women and lands from contestation and thus potential circulation (1998–2003:18).

5   As anchor, these inalienables both spur giving and taking so that they may be kept, and also attract giving and taking by others who might want to obtain them (43, 46–7). Parallel to Weiner, but using a different discursive vocabulary, Godelier argues that the imaginary dominates the symbolic; the imaginary must however be materialized in symbols (1999:8–9, 26–7), but it does not allow those symbols to dominate society, *contra* Lévi-Strauss.

structuralist thought, which is defined as the perceptual anchor of "structures" (Godelier 1999:28–36).[6] The inalienables are simultaneously the completion of the structures of giving and taking, without which these actions would not be comprehensible, but at the same time, the inalienables stand by definition outside the structures of reciprocity represented by giving and taking. What Weiner and Godelier's analyses have to offer is a way of thinking much more deeply about the interrelationship between notions of sacred kingship, blood nobility and juridical status (the kept) on the one hand, and the nature of performative identity (constructed through giving and taking) on the other.

The Sacred

For the moment, it is important to focus more carefully on Weiner and Godelier's allied ideas regarding the kept and the sacred.[7] As noted above, key kept objects are seen as offering a privileged access to the sacred. It is thus not surprising that true power in society should rest with those who have access to these objects, and thus to the resources of the sacred. As Godelier notes, regarding Melanesia, the "big man" is ultimately less powerful than the "great man," who controls such access to the sacred, kept object (1999:8). Likewise, in the Plains Indian cultures of North America, it is the keeper of the Sacred Pipe who is the ultimate locus of authority in the tribe, not the wealthiest and most generous giver, or the bravest and most successful taker. In a medieval context, Irish kings gained power through performance, but then "assumed a sacred mantle that was central to the legitimization of their rank" (Aitchison 1994:70). More specifically, they were "seeking to formalize and render less challengeable the possession of rank" (Aitchison 1994:73). The efforts of the French monarchy to establish its privileged access to sacred power – especially healing power – as incarnated in the possession of sacred objects such as relics and the crown itself are emblematic of this fact.

Access to sacred power marks the ultimate in vertical exchange. It represents not the vertical exchanges downwards between lord and dependents, however, but a vertical exchange upwards between God or gods and those who have access to these exchanges. Such power clearly trumps any possible advantages deriving from horizontal exchanges within the society, and thus allows the recipient a form of integrity which literally transcends the bonds of reciprocity between human individuals and groups. Anyone familiar with the thirst for relics exhibited by medieval society will recognize the validity of these ideas. Familial lands

---

6   Note however that Weiner suggests that such inalienables, though physically "immobile," offer only an illusion of permanence (7–8), since their symbolic valence is actually continually redefined by each hereditary or successive possessor, so that "problems of keeping nurture seeds of change" (8). See also 42.

7   For another anthropological perspective, see Alain Testart's analysis of Australian Aboriginal religions and the role of the sacred object (Testart 1993).

represented a similar phenomenon in the Middle Ages: these inalienable, kept lands were in fact occasionally alienated and given away, but usually in only one instance – as gifts to churches and monasteries, which were clearly understood by the donors as providing privileged access to the sacred. Indeed, inalienable lands were the preferred source of such gifts – lands bought or even taken were rarely used in this way, since they lacked the sacred component of the kept (White 1988). Of course, inalienable lands could sometimes be lost, as could relics, but this represented a devastating and often fatal blow to the institution or persons involved. Harold's loss of his banner to William the Conqueror obviously represented one such disastrous event, as did the theft of relics from a medieval church.

Integrity and Vertical Exchange

In light of this analysis, one might wonder what was the ultimate goal of individuals who pursued strategies of giving and taking in order to attain the ideal of pure integrity. In fact, evidence from other societies where such goals are pursued suggests that the attainment of integrity can be seen as a form of access to the sacred, or even, in the extreme case, as the sacralization of an individual and his or her key, kept possessions, so that they become incommensurable with all spheres of human exchange, and thus permanently beyond threat, beyond need of protection through giving and taking, and transcendent (see Weiner 1992:132–3, 149–50; Osteen 2002b).[8] William the Conqueror's conquest of kingship is one example of this strategy, for in the medieval ideology of kingship, it gave him access to certain privileged, sacred forms of power and authority.[9] The best medieval poetic example of this, to be explored more fully in Chapter 6, is Roland. Remember that the "kept" sword Durendal is a veritable museum of relics, and Roland himself, at the moment of death, is apotheosized, as the angel Gabriel comes personally to take him to Heaven. The Cid's desire to marry his daughters off to kings who share in this sacrality is another example, to which we will soon return.

Writing of the use of the aggressive, unreciprocable gift as a strategy for attaining what we are calling integrity, Jacques Godbout writes, "the law of evermore, manifested in the [Maori concept of] *hau*, reflects the desire to attain a position of mastery akin to that of the ancients, the elders, or [sacred] parents, for whom the gift of transmission – a gift with no reply – requires no reciprocation." Godbout suggests that this is the desire of turning the horizontal gift into the

---

[8] Studies of honor and grace stress that the ultimate goal of individuals in Mediterranean "honor" societies is to "convert … honor into grace and thus render [one]self impregnable" (Pitt-Rivers 1992:243).

[9] For a recent anthropological analysis of medieval kingship, in terms of the sacred, the kept and the vertical gift (termed "grace" in the analysis) see Lafages 1992, as well as comments on this article in Peristiany and Pitt-Rivers 1992:8–10.

vertical gift (Godbout 1998:140). A key aspect of the sacred, vertical gift within
anthropological theory is in fact its unreciprocability – the gift both requiring no
return, but also being unreturnable (Godelier 1999). Thus the quest on the part
of the ambitious seeker of integrity to give the overwhelming, unreturnable gift
and thereby to establish permanent dominance which can never be challenged by
a counter-gift replicates the very form of true, sacred gifts, and places that giver
in a position equivalent to those of the gods, sacred elders and ancestors.

A key point that emerges from the work of Weiner and Godelier, however,
is that the sacred is very often "already there," and that it is fundamentally a
"social" possession. Relics, sacred pipes and crown jewels may have recognized origins, but those origins are typically embedded in sacred and miracu-
lous genesis – they just don't make those things any more, one might say. It
is in fact possible to create such things, by permanently removing an object
from the different spheres of circulation which characterize a gift economy. But
this removal must be accomplished through symbolic manipulations or deeds
which make the object fundamentally incommensurable with the other, circula-
tory, spheres of objects (Weiner 1992:130).[10] The hoard of the Scandinavians
is an example. It was wealth which was removed from the system of reciprocal
exchange. Its quasi-sacred character is revealed by the fact that the wealth was
typically buried with the individual as well, when it was not buried in a hoard.

In addition, these items are often collective possessions, of nations, tribes, or
clans. Individuals are not allowed access to the sacred *qua* individuals – only as
representatives of the group. As Jacques Godbout noted in the citation above,
only the gods or the sacred ancestors are truly in a position to give the unreciprocable, vertical gift that marks true integrity. In fact, this gift is typically
seen as the only truly creative gift for the culture, and such founding, renewing,
life-giving gifts always come from outside the realm of the human. As Godelier
argues, "indebtedness to gods" lies at the beginning of social exchange (1999:30,
172). In the European context, it can be compared to the Grace of God, and
recent anthropological studies have also turned to the idea of grace as a necessary component for understanding the dynamics of honor-based societies, recognizing that the vertical component of grace crucially complements the dynamics
of honor (Peristiany and Pitt-Rivers 1992). Thus integrity and sacrality must be
denied to human individuals, for they would then be only a parody of their truer
versions. Put more prosaically, desires for integrity and transcendence on the part
of individuals are almost uniformly seen as potential threats to the social order, to
be carefully managed by the society, and ultimately frustrated. As will be seen in
more detail in Chapter 7, desires for integrity enacted through giving and taking
often focus, at their most extreme, on attempts to take the kept of other nations,
tribes or clans, and thus constitute the most severe of threats to social order and
reproduction (Jamous 1992:168; Weiner 1992:48).

[10] See also Kopytoff 1986:73 on the process of "singularization" which produces the
perfect anti-commodity, which is then marked as "sacred."

Group versus Individual: The Menaces of Integrity

As a result, societies in which such tendencies exist (i.e. those with more open access to power and status, and ultimately the sacred) typically have social rituals designed to reduce or eliminate the threats that ambitious individuals pose to the society. In Melanesia, the "big men" of many cultures there accumulate large amounts of wealth, which becomes a symbolic measure of their renown, but that wealth exists only momentarily before being given away in events so economically destructive that usually only twice in a lifetime can one manage such a "give-away" (Barraud 1994:42–4). The tendency to hoarding and social transcendence is countered by ceremonies which memorialize that momentary state while at the same time eliminating it by converting it to a more socially acceptable form of honor. Subsequently, the big man re-enters the social sphere of reciprocity. The 'Ane'ane society of Melanesia specifically recognizes the potentially socially destructive aspects of the accumulation practised by the big men, despite the fact that this accumulation is also the form par excellence of honor and prestige: according to Barraud, in the give-away ceremonies, the big man's accumulated wealth is seen to represent murder victims, and he becomes a caricature of the ancestors, whose sacred status he dared to seek.[11] The ceremony finally illustrates the ruination involved in his attempt, and re-encompasses the big man into society (1994:44–6).

Among the Iqar'iyen Berbers of Morocco, Jamous notes the predominant urge in that society towards being a "great man" and obtaining maximal honor, specifically through the means of violent exchanges (whether antagonistic gifts, oratorical contests, or physical violence and takings). This desire can be of a virtually suicidal nature, he reveals. But the society has various sacrally-based ways of preventing this tendency which risks not only individual suicide, but group suicide as well (Barraud 1994:91–6). The sacred, represented in the form of "sherif" wielded by holy men, is used to intervene in the violent exchanges and temporarily put an end to their cycle – an irresistible, unreciprocable vertical transfer puts an end to the aggressive horizontal ones, and brings social renewal.[12] In fact, Weiner argues that the inalienable is the "governor" which prevents giving and taking from spinning out of control (1992:6), suggesting that it should control excessive individual givings and takings. One could interpret this analysis slightly differently by saying that it is the separation of the sacred and the social which are at stake: individuals who seek to attain a form of supra-social integrity which would pretend to the status of the sacred are prevented from doing so by

---

[11] Compare this idea to Kantorowicz's idea of the king's two bodies in western Europe, one immortal, one mortal. Peristiany and Pitt-Rivers (1992:9) note the connection with Freud's idea of the king as killer of his successor, but destined to be killed in turn. The mortal body of the king resembles the body of the Melanesian big man in this regard, while his immortal body represents his sacred quality. The king thus mediates between the human and divine worlds, whereas the big man can only aspire to such mediation, having only a human body.

[12] Jamous 1994:20–2, 95–6; 1992:180.

the deployment of sacred-based forms of "anti-violence" against them. Likewise, the 'Ane'ane employ forms of mockery which evoke the sacred vertical gifts of the ancestors in order to reveal the lack of such among the big men. As Jacques Godbout writes:

> It is by tracking down, mercilessly, anything in their midst that risks breaking free – such as uncontrollable power or wealth so great that it threatens to accumulate while avoiding the imposition of reversibility – that they [traditional cultures] prohibit anyone laying hands on the nomos and making it his own by shifting it from its symbolic pole to that of the real. (1998:143).

Godbout's evocation of the tension between the symbolic and the real in this passage takes us back to previous chapters, where we saw the stress placed on the symbolic status of things, and on the symbolic economy more generally, in the discourse of the warrior aristocracy. Commodities can be seen as a threat from a form of "real" to the symbolic, since these phenomena can lead to a desire for the "thing in itself," the materiality of which threatens the basis of the symbolic economy. Moreover, the threat to the symbolic economy is a threat to the identity of the aristocratic individual, since this identity is constructed through symbolic manipulations. As Godelier says, the symbolic must be kept under the control of the imaginary (1999:26–7). But Godbout's remark suggests ironically that the very processes of identity construction and acquisition of power by means of symbolic exchanges and manipulation of symbolic objects can themselves be a threat to the symbolic economy. In other words, the symbolic system can be turned upon itself: individuals could use the symbols as part of an attempt to attain a supra-symbolic, iconic status. The evocation of the concept of the "supplement" earlier already suggests the form of this threat, since the hero's aspirations for the sacred essentially place him in a relation of supplementarity to his own society. As such, he completes – is the perfection of – his society's own internal logic. But he is also then the "excess," with all the dangers and disruptions posed by such excesses incarnated within him.[13] Note also that the individual hero's attempt to occupy a role which should remain quintessentially social recalls Lévi-Strauss notion of "social incest" (1969:58, 489), wherein the individual tries to accomplish what should be done by groups – in other words, to show his lack of need for group help, cooperation and support, thus withdrawing from the social system of exchange. The refusal to exchange is the core of the

---

[13]   Joel Grisward's study of the medieval epic in terms of tri-partite Indo-European models indirectly evokes much of what is discussed here. The three functions of worker, warrior and sacred correspond roughly to giver, taker and keeper (1981:57–8). He also notes that the hero partakes of all three of the functions (173), unlike the warrior. There is really nothing particularly Indo-European about this model – it is common to performative, pre-state, non-bureaucratic societies characterized by a well-developed internal system of hierarchicalization which is nevertheless not established purely *de jure*.

transgression of incest for Lévi-Strauss. It is thus interesting to note the incestuousness surrounding various medieval heroes – Roland for example, in the *Karlamagnus Saga*, as well as Tristan and Isold, in another context.

Revisiting *The Poem of the Cid*: From Performance to Sacred Essence

In the first cantar of *The Cid*, the hero pursues a strategy of giving and taking in order to enhance his social identity and acquire symbolic capital, which culminates in his (temporary) integrity even in relation to the king, as seen in the preceding chapter – he grants bishoprics, and receives the royal fifth of booty. But in the second cantar, the Cid immediately finds himself in the position of having to defend what he has taken, in order to be able to continue to give and thereby maintain his new status. Faced with the dilemma of this endless defense, the Cid eventually succeeds in marrying his daughters to kings-to-be. The marriages – which are only possible due to the Cid's (temporary) integrity – give him indirect access to the socially sacred, in the form of the sacral character of medieval kingship. This allows him to convert an unstable form of integrity, existing within a performative context, into a permanent form of transcendence for his family. The Cid, unlike some of the medieval heroes to be examined in the following chapter, never challenges the fundamentally social nature of the sacred, never tries to achieve a form of individual sacralization. He never challenges the sacred nature of medieval kingship, and in particular, stresses his continued loyalty to Alfonso at all times, even as he tries to coerce access to the sacred with his series of aggressive gifts to the king. This loyalty is clearly voluntary in the end, given the Cid's status in the world – the voluntariness itself underlines the essential integrity which he enjoys, and his ability to give of his loyalty freely and spontaneously. But the Cid's integrity within the human world of horizontal exchanges never crosses over into a violation of his respect for the sacred world of the vertical exchange.

His decision to turn to the royal courts to resolve his dispute with the Infantes is virtually a replication of the North African reliance on the holy men and the sacred quality of "sherif" to overcome the social strife occurring around the struggles for human "baraka" or honor which Jamous describes (1994). The fundamentally destructive quality of "baraka," and of medieval honor as well from a metaphysical standpoint, is underlined by the fact that the Cid's daughters are left beaten and abandoned by the Infantes due to the Infantes concern for their own honor. On the other hand, the socially renewing and reproductive nature of the sacred – of the "sherif" and of the divine sanction accorded the court – is revealed by the subsequent chance of the daughters to marry happily and presumably (certainly historically) productively. Given the performative, non-legalistic nature of the court's proceedings, based not on judicial texts, but on combat, the court scenes are perhaps best seen as a turn to the socially sacred – and not to the state, as most critics have argued – for a resolution of the dilemmas of honor, giving and taking.[14] While we considered the judicial scenes a performative *mise-en-abyme* of the epic in the previous chapter, it is possible to enlarge that view and see both the scenes and the epic as a whole as re-institutions of the proper relationship between the performative and the sacred. Without the sacred, the truth arrived at performatively in the trials has no social efficacy; and, to use Weiner's idea, without a respect for the sacred anchor of the society, the Cid's pursuit of giving and taking would have no goal or rationale, and would be simply an endless pursuit of the impossible. Thus just as blood fixes the lower boundaries of the performative arena, the sacred fixes its upper boundaries, defining a workable arena of competition.

With this framework established, we can also revisit the transgression of the Infantes. On one level, their confusion of people and things – keeping the symbolic things (money and wealth) given while neglecting or abusing the people who are central to the exchange act – is a form of commodification which undermines the symbolic order. If anyone could be called "bourgeois" in the text, it is them, as they show a fundamentally market-based, impersonal view of transactions. But more importantly, the Infantes attempt to collapse the playing field of performance by linking its lower boundary of blood with its upper boundary of the sacred. They claim that blood essentializes all status, even within the nobility, in a way that only the sacred can do, according to the text. And they attempt to elide the reality that access to the sacred must first be earned through performance. Whereas *The Cid* (text and hero) suggests that the sacred maintains a liminal or supplemental relationship to the system of performance (to use a post-structuralist concept), the Infantes attempt a metaphysical gesture which would incorporate the sacred directly into the hierarchies of the aristocratic social system. Thus it is they, rather than the Cid, who attempt to "lay hands on the nomos" so to speak, and thus threaten the coherence of the symbolic order.

The only true essential or metaphysical element in the text is sacred kingship, however. Though the Cid has obtained his social status performatively, and taken possession of Valencia as a kept item, he soon finds himself entertaining the fantasy that Annette Weiner suggests – the fantasy of not having to defend the kept. But the poem actually offers the realization of the fantasy, for it posits the sacrality of kingship as a form of essential identity which need not be defended. Thus the Cid, the quintessential performative individual, is able to render his status heritable and permanent through his daughters' marriages.

The notion of mediated access to the sacred is crucial to the organization of the warrior aristocracy. *The Cid* underlines that for the non-royal man, access to the sacred is always indirect. More particularly, it always occurs through a

---

[14] At this time, it is true, European states were increasingly attempting to sacralize their existence – most famously in the case of the French court perhaps and its involvement with St. Denis. But to the extent that *The Cid* is about the rise of proto-state ideology at all, we are witnessing more the state's adoption of the vocabulary of kinship and performance, and its appropriation of the social category of the sacred as linked to those institutions, rather than the beginnings of an imposition of an ideology of the modern state.

woman, by means of marriage or birth. The Cid himself has this status because his daughters marry the kings of Aragon and Navarre, while his son, if he should have one (he did, historically) will have it thanks to his mother, since royal men do not literally give birth. Thus while one may want to think of the daughters as gift objects, it is clear that they have a power of sacred access which the Cid lacks – a power over him in a sense, and on which he remains dependent.

The sacred, symbolically kept status of women in gift cultures, as sources of authority rather than simply objects used by men for expressing power relationships between themselves, has been stressed by Annette Weiner as part of her analysis of the kept (1992). She argues that women are not given in marriage at all, but rather banked in many cases. In the classic concept of giving women, the woman remains a symbolic object who refers back to the more fundamental relationship between men, which is established by the gift. In such a view, it is the political alliances of the two families and their male patriarchs that predominate. But banking suggests that the woman is seen as fundamentally still a part of her original family. In such cases, the woman's association with her marriage family transfers the honor of that family back to the birth family, and it is the wife's relationship to both her new husband and her old family which is fundamental, not the relationship between the two patriarchs directly. Here, I turn to the important distinction which Maurice Godelier has established between the "alienable given" the "inalienable given" (1999:46ff). Unlike earlier gift theorists, who consider the given to be always inalienable, Godelier suggests that this is only sometimes – in fact, rarely – the case. While every gift item may symbolically bear the memory of previous possessors and givers as part of its social history, certain things, though given, are seen to remain fundamentally linked to the honor of the giver. In this case, the fate befalling these things – or people – concerns not the honor of the physical possessor, but that of the giver. Thus such items are transitional between the given and the purely kept as Weiner and Godelier analyze this category. For example, in Egyptian Bedouin societies, the disgrace – for example, rape – of a wife falls not upon the husband, but upon her birth family (Abou-Zeid 1966).

The Cid clearly sees his daughters' marriages in this way: he has no interest in any political or personal alliance with the family of the Infantes, and also sees them as not particularly noble in his performance-based evaluation. He thus initially opposes the marriage. Once it occurs however, he hopes desperately that the Infantes will perform admirably, since their performative status will then reflect onto their wives, and thus indirectly onto the Cid. Thus when the Infantes briefly seem to have actually done this, the Cid is ecstatic:

> ¡Grado a Christus que del mundo es señor
> quando veo lo que avia sabor,
> que lidiaron comigo in campo mios yernos amos a dos!
> Mandados buenos iran dellos a Carrion
> commo son ondrados e aver [n]os [an] grant pro!   (ll. 2477–81)

> "Thanks be to Christ, Lord of this world," he said, "I have seen my desire fulfilled! My sons-in-law have both fought in battle by my side; good news of them will go to Carrión, for they have won honour for themselves and will hereafter be a great help to us."

It is the news that will be spread of the honor that they have won which pleases the Cid, much as he tries in the text to spread the news of his own honor as far as possible. Likewise, the ill treatment of his daughters represents dishonor for the Cid and the king (who officially gave them in marriage), not the Infantes:

> Hya vos sabedes la ondra que es cuntida a nos,
> cuemo nos han abiltados ifantes de Carrion;
> mal majaron sus fijas del Çid Campeador.   (ll. 2941–3)

> Now you know what honour has befallen us and how the Infantes of Carrión have disgraced us by their ill-treatment of the Cid's daughters ...

The Infantes of course fail to perceive the inalienable link between the Cid and his daughters, treating them as mere objects in their possession.

The key point to recognize here is that the women do not function symbolically, but essentially. The marriages with the princes are not gift exchanges wherein the exchange act dominates and determines the symbolic value of the things exchanged. Rather, the essential nature of the women themselves allows the transaction to occur, and they are the direct parties to the relationship. In the absence of the daughters, there is no other object or person which the Cid could exchange with the kings of Aragon and Navarre in order to establish a sacral relationship with them which would cement his own access to the sacred. His daughters – specifically as women – are incommensurable with any other thing or object. Unlike any other transferable elements of the culture, they are more important for what they are than for whom they are exchanged with. They thus partake of an element of essential being which is absent from the various other exchanged objects in the text.

This is not to say that the Cid's daughters are not subject to symbolic manipulation. Ironically, it is the Cid's own performative giving and taking which have vested his (dependent) daughters with the symbolic status required for the marriage to occur. But once it does occur, the reversal of the symbolic relationship makes it clear that the marriage cannot be considered a "giving" at all, in the usual sense, by the Cid to the kings. The daughters' connection to the (essential) sacred is in fact hinted at throughout the text. During the events of the first cantar, they are protected in a monastery, despite the king's condemnations. John Walsh has pointed out that the daughters' fate in the woods of Corpes recalls early Hispanic images of virgin martyrdom (Walsh 1970–1): the motif of two sisters; specific graphic details of torture; threat by wild beasts and birds of prey; and rapid, magical cures. The daughters themselves call upon their tormentors to use their swords upon them so that "¡cortando las cabeças, martires seremos nos!" ("Cut off our heads and make martyrs of us") (l. 2728). The daughters thus clearly invoke images of mediation between the secular and the sacred. The Cid, in his desire for a stable identity for himself and his descendants, vertically transfers his hard-won but unstable performance-based integrity and identity for a relationship to the sacrality of kingship through the medium of his daughters, who function in parallel to the gift of inalienable lands to the Church – they are banked as sacred.

Conclusions, and an Introduction

For the moment, by way of conclusion to this chapter, let us identify a number of the lingering problems of methodology which underlie the preceding chapters, and also point to the ways that the analysis just completed here suggests the way out of these issues.

First, there is the question of the hero: the remainder of this book will focus on this particular medieval character. The literary hero is the example par excellence of the individual in quest of permanent integrity and of social transcendence. The hero incarnates the values of giving, taking and keeping that are characteristic of the warrior aristocracy. But the hero – with the exception of the Cid – does not remain satisfied with a pursuit of integrity which would allow for socially mediated access to the sacred. Rather, heroes seek to claim a form of sacrality for themselves. This is not socially acceptable, even if it is socially logical in the context of the heroic culture of the warrior aristocracy. More particularly, it represents a form of "excess as perfection." As mentioned above, the hero is supplement. In consequence, Roland, Siegfried, and Raoul of Cambrai all come to fatal ends, along with most of the armies and individuals around them. This supplementarity explains the fact that the two most common readings of medieval heroes are first, as hubristic individual exceeding the constraints of proper social conduct (as excess), and secondly, as culture hero perfectly incarnating the key aspects of his society (as completion). Indeed, readings of medieval epic could virtually all be reduced to an argument over this question and its indirect implications and corollaries. The argument here is obviously that both of these views are incomplete, though they can be reconciled in an anthropologically nuanced notion of the supplement.

The notion of the supplement also allows us to address a second key tendency of readings of medieval heroes, for it suggests a model for understanding how the medieval epic served to establish sites of reflection about the social order and individual identity. Most readings of the epic assume that the hero is essentially unreflexive, and thus that his problems are fundamentally imbricated with the problems of the epic world of the warrior aristocracy. If the hero is read as hubristic, then he incarnates the way that unreflexive individuals can destroy societies which do not have ways of dealing reflexively with those individuals' impulses. If he is read as a culture hero, then his lack of reflexivity parallels that of the society directly. In either case, the society is essentially just as unreflexive as the hero. The epic then becomes a witness to the tragic fall of the warrior aristocracy, either due to the excessive hubris of its heroes, due to weaknesses of the society's own internally solid and unreflexive order, or due to the ways in which new, external social formations – markets, the romance genre – trouble the stable, but defenseless world of signs which is supposedly characteristic of the epic. The world of the epic and the warrior aristocracy – like most portrayals of colonized worlds until recently – is a world of victims unable to help themselves.

But what if the epic is not the witness to problems, but rather a reflection on them which also serves to contain them within the structure of the epic itself and thus at least partially resolve them? In fact, the epic will turn out to be the medieval version of the Melanesian and North African ritual ceremonies which call upon a social sacred in order to control and repress – in the everyday, real world – that which they examine in the context of ritual (and literature) – the hero. The epic portrays the drama of a fundamentally performative culture, fully aware of the non-transcendent nature of performed identity and power. It uses the literary trope of the hero to examine the complex relationships between the culture and the individual, as well as between the performative and the sacred kept. We will see how the literary hero – for the hero is essentially a literary, not a social figure – could act in some cases to reconstitute mythically the order of the sacred and of the unreciprocable gift, even in death and "defeat." We have already seen how in *The Cid*, the title character acts ritually to demonstrate and thus reestablish the legitimacy of the socially ordering sacred which governs human performance.

But in addition to the hero, there is the Other. Though the Cid acts to resolve certain social-internal tensions between group and individual, as well as between performance and essence, he also complicates matters by blurring the lines between in-group and out-group. Up to this point, we have largely elided such questions in favor of a closer look at the relation of the individual to his own group. But virtually all earlier medieval epics are border texts, which feature intergroup conflict. It is against the Other – classically, the Saracen – that the hero constitutes his identity. Yet the hero fights Saracens as much to distinguish himself from his fellow warriors and elevate himself above them as to help defend them. The hero and the enemy thus maintain an ambivalent relationship with respect to the hero's own social group, and hero and enemy Other become ambiguous terms indeed at times. If epics are obsessed with conflict on the borders, it is not simply because such conflicts raise important issues of group social identity. It is also because individual identity within the warrior aristocracy was often established on these same borders – both literally and in a deeper theoretical sense.

The epic will thus offer an analysis of the problematic nature of performative, symbolic social order – a problem of which the epic seems to have been quite aware, and one which is theorized in terms of giving, taking and keeping. At the end of the Chapter 2, I suggested that the gift was a trope for theorizing perhaps the notion of the subject, but perhaps also, the impossibility of the integral subject. It is now apparent that this impossibility is in a sense a necessity for the continuity of the aristocracy itself. We will follow up on these suggestions to see how the problem of individual identity is replicated in the problems of social order and group identity, with their own "impossible" status. As part of this examination, we will see that the simplistic definition of the Other suggested by the prototypical "hero versus Saracen" confrontation breaks down, so that the Other becomes a very ambiguous category indeed.

6

The Hero, Gratuity and Alterity: *The Song of Roland*

The Song of Roland and the Death of Reciprocity

In one of the most familiar scenes of medieval literature, Roland is nominated by his enemy Ganelon to be head of Charlemagne's rearguard as the French army returns victoriously from Spain through the pass of Roncesvalles in the Pyrenees in *The Song of Roland*. This nomination leads to an escalating confrontation which sets up Roland's eventual death and the destruction of the rearguard. Most importantly for us, the scene enacts a dynamic of reciprocity and its refusal which is crucial to understanding the nature of the epic hero. But the scene is merely the culmination of a growing conflict between Roland and Ganelon which centers on issues of giving and taking.

The epic, which dates from perhaps the end of the eleventh century, opens in Spain, where Charlemagne has defeated all the Saracens except for those of Saragossa. The desperate Saracens promise to offer Charlemagne gifts and hostages in exchange for his return to Spain, at which point they will follow him there and convert to Christianity. The baron Ganelon urges that the offer be accepted in order to avoid further war, while Charlemagne's nephew Roland mocks him for this espousal of peace over war. Ganelon's advice is taken, however. Then, when an ambassador must be selected to go to the Saracens (the last ones having been treacherously murdered by them), Roland suggests Ganelon, and then mocks him once again, this time for his hesitation to undertake the dangerous mission.

In response, Ganelon plots with the Saracens to destroy Roland. Upon returning, he nominates Roland to lead the French rearguard – to which Roland eagerly assents despite the misgivings of Charlemagne. As the armies go through the pass, the Saracens attack, and kill the entire rearguard. Roland is left alive on the field, having driven off the enemy, but dies of self-inflicted wounds; he bursts the blood vessels in his temples when he calls on his horn Oliphant for Charlemagne's army to return and avenge him. An angel arrives to take him directly to Heaven. The armies return, defeat an even larger Saracen force in an "epic" contest of Christian versus Muslim, and Ganelon is then tried, convicted, and executed.

The scene of the Saracen's peace offer can clearly be situated within a logic of taking and giving. Given the momentum of Frankish victories, the two sides cannot be seen as equals – the Franks are clearly in the superior position. The Saracens then offer an enormous number of gifts to the Franks in exchange for an end to hostilities. Receiving such gifts would not lead to a relationship of debt for the Franks; the gift could be seen rather as a form of tribute from a subsidiary, or even as a form of taking – a violently coerced gift. But such a taking, in its nego-tiated, contractual form, would still constitute a form of reciprocity. Ganelon, in campaigning for peace, promotes this reciprocity. Roland, on the other hand, proposes a continuation of the war against the Saracens, and thus a continuation of a more extreme and direct form of taking which, in this context of Christian and Saracen, Self and Other, must be seen as a rejection of reciprocity itself. In fact, within the context of the warrior aristocracy, the Other can be defined as the one with whom one does not engage in reciprocity of any kind – even controlled violence. Where the Cid was satisfied with tribute, Roland wants the glory of battle, to the death if necessary. Forms of exchange classify forms of relation-ship, and Roland's advocacy of the most extreme form of taking suggests an equal advocacy of extreme non-identity with the Saracens.

Although the discussion appears to be about issues of group identity and rela-tions, Roland's initial mockery of Ganelon during the discussion over whether to accept the Saracen's gifts can also be seen in the context of a competitive game of honor specifically between the two individuals, translated into action through giving and taking. In particular, each party offers or throws out a proposal, to which he will have to live up subsequently. Meeting the wager results in increased honor, as seen in *The Cid*. Of course, the more daring the wager, the more honor accrues in meeting it. This is true not just of the meeting of the wager however, but even of the placing of it. Roland has clearly placed the higher wager, with his promise of more violent taking, and thus dishonored Ganelon, even before the action begins. The issue of status and identity among Christians and Saracens is fatally entangled with the issue of status and honorable identity among the two Christian competitors – the forms of taking which classify the social relation-ships also work to define a hierarchy of individual relationships.

Almost immediately after this discussion, the second prelude to the final confrontation of the two men occurs. Roland nominates Ganelon for the ambas-sadorship in a context where it is clearly recognized by all that this position does not represent a job of high honor or status, thus suggesting to Ganelon that his own self-image is in fact inflated in relation to his real honor-status in the society – another crushing blow for Ganelon.[1] Then, when Ganelon expresses dismay at this insult, Roland laughs mockingly, suggesting that it is Ganelon's cowardice which is the cause of his anger at the assignment.

The importance of this double assault on Roland's part is that it suggests what will become increasingly clear: Roland is interested in rejecting the concept of reciprocity not just in relation to the Saracens, but in relation to Ganelon as well, and ultimately, in relation to the Franks. In an honor society founded on "chal-

---

[1]   See Pitt-Rivers 1966:22 on the fact that the key to honor in an honor/shame culture is to be "accepted at [one's] own evaluation," with the corollary that a gap between one's high view of oneself and the socially accepted view leads to "ridicule or contempt."

lenge and riposte" (Bourdieu 1966:197), Roland has already won the first round. Now he once more challenges successfully, then immediately challenges again, without awaiting a reciprocal challenge from Ganelon. The reciprocal game of honor competition is replaced by a laughing mockery which suggests that Ganelon is unworthy even to engage in the reciprocity.[2] In response, Ganelon swears vengeance on Roland, and engages in treacherous negotiations with the enemy. Then Roland has a perilous duty thrust upon him by Ganelon, who tries desperately to reinsert himself into the game. Ganelon nominates Roland to lead the rearguard as it returns through the narrow passes.

But Roland again crushes Ganelon. He eagerly accepts the challenge offered, in a way designed to underline his difference from Ganelon's previous distress, thus successfully riposting, or "giving as good as he gets."[3] But he also gives back "with interest," in a manner typical of antagonistic gift cultures. In particular, his counterchallenge not only meets that of Ganelon, but increases the stakes, again placing Ganelon in debt. Specifically, Roland goes beyond the call of duty and promises not simply that the army will get safely through the passes, but that not even the lowliest pack mule will be lost unless it is "bought with the sword":

> N'i perdrat Carles, li reis ki France tient,
> Men escïentre, palefreid ne destrer,
> Ne mul ne mule que deiet chevalcher,
> Ne n'i perdrat ne runcin ne sumer
> Que as espees ne seit einz eslegiet.   (ll. 755–9)

> Charles, the king who holds France, will not lose, I warrant, a single palfrey or war-horse, nor mule or jenny, which is fit to ride, and he will not lose a single pack-horse or sumpter without its first being purchased by the sword.

Roland clearly promises active, all-out combat – as opposed to a strategic willingness to lose a little in order to save a lot – at the slightest provocation. And his reasons here are purely personal, let us note.

This act of raising the stakes in the game of honor also broadens the field of the competition, however. It is not just Roland and Ganelon's honor which is at stake: Roland is upping the ante in relation to Charlemagne and his council of peers. At this point, Charlemagne attempts to intervene in the escalating game of honor, which threatens to spin out of control. He does this by making an offer – a gift – to Roland, thus attempting to reestablish a basis of reciprocity. More importantly, given Charlemagne's sacred character as king, this could be thought of as a vertical gift, intervening in a potentially harmful series of horizontal

[2]   In Bourdieu's analysis of Kabyle honor contests (1966:206), he notes that one indicates one's willingness to take up a challenge – continue an exchange by riposting – by outbidding the challenger. Roland leaves Ganelon no opportunity to do this.

[3]   See Bourdieu's analysis of the Kabyle society of Morocco in terms of honor and the honor-duel of "challenge and riposte" (Bourdieu 1966).

exchanges. He offers him half his army for the rearguard. If Roland accepts this offer, he accedes to a relationship of indebtedness to Charlemagne, and is thus clearly reintegrated into the network of reciprocity which holds the Franks together, though of course he will also now be in a relationship of debt in relation to Charlemagne and the Franks more generally.

Roland, however, refuses (1. 787), and chooses to pursue absolute integrity. In so doing, he breaks the relationship of reciprocity not just with Ganelon, or with Charlemagne personally, but with the Frankish army as a whole.[4] As we have seen, in a gift culture, to refuse a gift is to declare oneself the enemy, the Other, at least in the context of the particular, contextual moment of (refusal to) exchange, if not permanently. To accept an ambassadorship, or the leadership of the rearguard, is to fulfill a duty in a perfectly honorable way, to give back in service what one has first received in obligation. It means to operate within the logic of reciprocity. One may operate competitively, giving back more than the obligation. Even such an aggressive counter-gift would still recognize the reciprocal right of the recipient to reply.

But Roland refuses the gift that would save his life (as he already well knows, since Ganelon has openly promised vengeance); and moreover, because of this, his Otherness will not be just temporary, but permanent. His refusal of the gift that would save his life marks simultaneously his transcendent integrity, his gratuity, his heroic stature, his death, and the imminent disaster which will befall the warriors whose culture he epitomizes. The subsequent ambush, the battle between Christians and Saracens, Roland's refusal to blow the horn, the defeat of the rearguard, and Roland's death all arise from Roland's going out of his way, even with the knowledge of impending treachery, to make his own task all the harder and more dangerous. While it could be argued that Roland's honor would have been compromised in accepting half of Charlemagne's army, the risk which produced this offer was brought about by Roland's very aggressive challenging – "egging on," one might say – of Ganelon, as well as his promise to protect every last mule of the army. He himself engineered the circumstances that led to the offer in the first place. Had Roland been reasonable or prudent or "sage," the epic events would never have occurred. Roland thus gratuitously engineers the situation that will make the highest possible demands on his bravery and strength, and will lead to his apotheosis at the moment of greatest defeat and triumph – his death.

Yet however much Roland's death may be read as a triumphant apotheosis, that triumph is in terms of personal heroism, personal integrity and the symbolism

---

[4] Perhaps the closest previous reading to the one presented here is Jones 1963. Focusing on the issue of honor in particular, Jones argues that Roland is presented as primarily motivated not by duty, but by a desire "to indulge his self-esteem" (1963:94–5). Jones means "self-esteem" to be taken not in a modern, psychological sense, but a medieval, socio-psychological one. Of course, as Jones points out, the esteem is based on the judgement of those around him (95). This is another way of stating the claim made in this chapter – the logic of individual integrity is inseparably connected to the logic of the culture as a group.

of purely personally-driven, internal motivation. For the Franks the event was a political disaster. The pathos of the epic clearly echoes this same viewpoint. And since Roland precipitated this disaster through his pursuit of pure integrity, his moment of gratuity marks his passage into a form not just of absolute integrity, but of alterity in relation to his fellow Franks. He refuses a reciprocal relationship with the Franks, and thus becomes Other. In the intervening moments between his gratuitous promises and his death, he invokes loyalty to Charlemagne, or to his lineage – but on his terms – and he ends the day alone, on a hill above and in front of the largely nameless army which supported him, having come to blows even with his greatest friend Oliver at one point. Within the text of collective struggle is the more fundamental tale of the pursuit and construction of purely individual identity which forever separates Roland from the Franks.

But Roland is not a Saracen hero; he is a Frankish one. Indeed, he is a culture hero, whose conduct perfectly exemplifies the fundamental logic of his culture. Yet what began as a competition of challenge and riposte within the logic of giving and taking evolves into a moment where Roland, in pursuing the goal of integrity to its ultimate conclusion, shatters that logic itself even as he perfects it.[5] As is stated in the text itself, "Vostre proëcce, Rollant, mar la veïmes!" ("Roland, we can only rue your prowess") (l. 1731). Roland stands as a form of supplement to the ethos of honor – completion and excess simultaneously. The pursuit of integrity is what mobilizes the culture, but obtaining the integrity contradicts the logic of reciprocity through which the pursuit occurs. Roland becomes a supplement in relation to ethno-cultural identity as well. He is both the perfect Frank, and Other, at the same time: the exemplar of the Frankish warrior ethos, but also the destroyer of the Frankish warriors.

Roland has most commonly been read as an example of "démesure," as an individual whose pride or hubris leads to the destruction of both himself and the rearguard.[6] The opposite argument sees him as simply doing his duty bravely in the context of feudal vassalage, honor and loyalty.[7] The first view seems difficult to accept, given Roland's apotheosis: this person guilty of blind and foolish pride is clearly admired by the text that tells his story. The response is that Roland "repents," but this repentance is very difficult to find in the text, and the notion seems like a thirteenth-century anachronism. The second viewpoint seems equally difficult to accept: Robert Francis Cook suggests that Roland reveals

[5] Peter Haidu also notes the ways in which the hero's bravery leads to social disaster, and more specifically that the disaster comes from the hero's carrying of his culture's values to their extreme perfection or logical conclusion (1993:32–5; 80–3). He suggests that the "tragedy" of the battle of Roncesvalles is not a tragedy of flaw or failure, but a tragedy produced by the very success of the hero in carrying out his and his culture's aspirations.

[6] See Cook 1987 for an extensive analysis of the "démesure" interpretation, with numerous references.

[7] This is the argument in Cook 1987. See also the "Preface" (xii) for a summary of other similar arguments which attempt to rehabilitate Roland.

the necessity of following the generally applicable rules of his culture, no matter what the situation, rather than succumbing to the temptations of situational logic – and potentially fleeing. He thus tries to rescue Roland from blind pride and stupidity and to turn him into a culture hero who knowingly and willingly sacrifices himself for the values of his culture.

This argument seems flawed on two important grounds. First, it still leaves Roland – and by implication, all medieval warriors – trapped in a non-reflexive and inflexible bind. Surely medieval warriors – whose profession it was, ultimately, to stay alive and win – could react to the specifics of a situation and evaluate the differences between normal rules and expectations and the demands of the moment. Indeed, Roland was part of a performative, situationally-oriented culture which typically refused to be bound by absolutes. We have already seen the same performative flexibility at work – even valorized – in *The Poem of the Cid* as well, where legalistic and absolute rules – indeed all essentialist tendencies – were abjured except for the sacred anchor itself. And secondly, Roland does not simply do his duty, but actively sets up a situation that is beyond duty. Roland manipulates the situation in a performative and responsive manner, and would apparently have been perfectly capable of continuing to respond in the same manner and save himself and the army if he had wanted.

More recently, Peter Haidu has also argued that Roland essentially does his duty culturally, but that he is not so much a testament to self-sacrifice for the sake of the values of his culture as an implicit emblem of the failure of those values in a new world (1993). Of course, there must certainly have arisen situations where choosing or negotiating correct action and responses became difficult, but the problematic situation in our text – the ambush – would seem to be the exact opposite: a classic, common military situation, and the very reason for having a rearguard. More generally, it is unclear what this "new world" would be, since the central dilemma of the poem – the conflict of individual goals and social ones – would appear to be a timeless, universal constant.

From various perspectives, all of these interpretations have an element of truth. In fact, they are simply two sides of the same "fact." J. G. Peristiany relates that in a Greek Cypriot village, a man volunteered to serve in the Second World War, and died in combat. He was praised as a model of the ideal behavior, and a monument was put up. But then, due to "envy," people began to criticize the same man for "vaingloriously" sacrificing his wife and children's well-being (Peristiany 1992:124). The village dispute over reading a "hero" recapitulates the scholarly debate over Roland. In reality, the ultimate liminal moment – death – reveals the liminal nature of ideals themselves. Like the Greek Cypriot, Roland does in fact, as Cook and Haidu argue, follow the logic of his culture, as a culture hero. But that logic has an internal structure which means that anyone who follows it faithfully to its end must almost inevitably also "go too far," as Roland does. Yet the "excess" is not of a psychological nature, of the type of hubris, but rather is a result of social psychology; that is to say, the text examines the type of individual produced by this specific culture, as a cultural product. In his perfecting of the logic of integrity, Roland serves as the measure of his own culture – indeed, as a measure of the culture's potential for "démesure."

But this "measuring" of the culture is not finally a tragedy or even a critique of the culture either, it turns out. Rather, it is an exploration both of the logic of the culture and of the functions of the epic itself as a form of mediation which works to circumscribe the logical perfection of the culture within the space of the epic itself, as a literary space which explicitly works to prevent this same disastrous perfection in the social space. Indeed, the epic "formally" presents itself as a form of reciprocity which mediates between these two spaces themselves – that of epic content and that of the world at large. Alfred Adler argues in *Epische Spekulanten* that the epic itself is a form of speculation on the extremes and limits of its world (1975:21–2), and that the hero is emblematic of the personage who goes both to the limit and too far at the same time (1975:38–48). Pure gratuity – which is symbolic of both integrity and the break with reciprocity – is essentially the symbolic doorway into this speculative literary space: it is the "once upon a time" which separates ritual from transparent social portrayal.

In the remainder of this chapter, we will explore further the moment of gratuity – of things done "the hard way," or "for no reason," but more specifically understood as the moment which essentially defines an individual as a hero.[8] In contrast, the gratuitous act as seen in medieval epic culture is not an act of resistance, but an act which is simultaneously a perfecting and a "going beyond"; the acts must be understood not as resistance, but as the extreme affirmation of a system which they nevertheless also potentially destroy. Roland reveals the perfect consonance of his "excess" with his own culture, and unlike in "hubristic" heroes, his social psychology is perfectly consonant with his culture. Most generally, the moment of gratuity typically leads to the hero's death, because death is itself a moment which underlines the hero's absolute, integral unconcern with any of the temptations of horizontal reciprocity. Instead, by definition, it severs the possibility of such reciprocity, though it opens up the possibility of vertical forms of reciprocity. As already seen in the previous chapter, these vertical exchanges give

---

[8] Gratuity may be characteristic of all cultures in some form or another. Literature itself, especially from structuralist, formalist and post-modernist perspectives, is often seen as a form of gratuity: art for art's sake, the pure joy of language use, refusal of referentiality, play, the game. Socially, gratuity has been proposed by critics from Georges Bataille to Fredric Jameson as a refuge from the capitalist, the functionalist, the utilitarian. It is the unproductive expenditure, the refusal to enter an otherwise "homogeneous" system, to borrow from Bataille.

Of course, for both Bataille and Jameson (1991:131ff, 260ff), gratuity has a specific political meaning in relation to the systems it resists. The acts they evoke are gratuitous specifically in the eyes of the systems which the acts of gratuity oppose. Bataille's discussion of homogeneity and heterogeneity, in terms of "production" as opposed to "unproductive expenditure," clearly situates the gratuitous or surplus against the discourse of capitalism. In this sense, one is talking less of gratuity than affirmation of the possibility of other value systems, systems which would in fact see the gratuitous act as specifically not gratuitous, but as "valuable." Bataille thus argues in *La part maudite* that unproductive expenditure is in fact crucial to social reproduction, which capitalism threatens to impede (1988:19ff).

access to a transcendent sacred. The hero thus occupies the borders of Nation and Other, and Performance and the Sacred, simultaneously.

The Gift, Reciprocity, Gratuity and Alterity among the Warrior Aristocracy

The relationship between the breaking or refusing of reciprocity and the creation of alterity is a fundamental tenet of anthropological studies of gift-giving and exchange. It has been widely recognized that various types of reciprocity (and non-reciprocity) can be arranged on a rough scale, which serves to classify (as well as establish) the relationships involved.[9] Gifts are seen as the most in-group type of activity, followed by barter, then sale, then theft – the farther one goes along in the list, the less closely connected the different parties are seen to be. While this simple scalar notion elides many of the ambiguities of exchange, it does seem to be true that reciprocity establishes membership in some type of in-group, while non-reciprocity establishes an out-group.

In this light, examples in medieval literature and history of the refusal to engage in gift reciprocity – to accept gifts, to offer gifts – is a clear marker of sociocultural distance. Likewise, to refuse even to buy and sell marks an even greater sociocultural distance. But as we have seen, even violence can be a form of reciprocity, when used as one tool on a continuum of options for the resolution of conflicts. For example, taking hostages and holding them for ransom should certainly be considered a form of (common) medieval violence, yet it remains at the same time a form of reciprocity, if nevertheless more overtly hostile than gift-giving. But killing the vanquished or the prisoners is the limit case in which reciprocity ends. In the context of the medieval preference for taking hostages and ransoming them, purposeful killing itself could be seen as a gratuitous act – it makes no sense within a logic of reciprocity.

Reciprocity and non-reciprocity are fundamental to the medieval establishment of the category of alterity. One finds, in epics for example, that traitors and "Saracens" typically constitute full-scale Others, who are killed mercilessly in many instances. Interestingly, given the broad gamut of possibilities for reciprocity, the most typical opposition is between accepting gifts and killing, with killing being the direct result of refusing gifts. In *The Coronation of Louis*, for example (which will be discussed more fully in Chapter 9), the Saracens refuse offers of gifts from the Pope as he tries to save Rome (laisse 18), since they plan to pursue pure conquest, and also not coincidentally stress the superiority of their religion; William refuses offers of gifts from a pagan rival who seeks to avoid single combat, (laisse 23); however William then accepts an offer of a gift from a defeated foe, giving him the counter-gift of clemency, and immediately after, the foe converts to Christianity – the gift eliminates alterity (laisse 30); William refuses the gift of a rebellious traitor (laisse 43) and kills him instead (laisse 46);

---

9   See Linda 1994:Introduction; Humphrey and Hugh-Jones 1992:Introduction.

William refuses the gift of a foreign knight (laisse 60) and kills him (laisse 61). On the other hand, he never refuses gifts offered to him by those he has helped, as rewards after his brave deeds, and he never refuses to offer gifts to others who have been helpful or admirable. The scenes thus establish a categorization of others, whose alterity is marked by two events – refusal of gift, exchange and reciprocity, and death.

Interestingly, the one non-reciprocal relationship which later is converted to a reciprocal one is with the Saracen who converts, not with Christian aggressors or traitors. The latter have violated the code of reciprocity itself as it exists among Christians. The Saracens, on the other hand, are presented at least in this text as merely "culturally" other (using the term 'other' very loosely, as opposed to the stricter definition of non-reciprocity), and this is presented as a less important and more superable difference. In other words, the Saracen is militarily honorable, even open to obeying the rules of reciprocity, and thus can be integrated more easily than those who have violated the rules of reciprocity internally. The epic thus suggests that the gift and reciprocity are fundamental to in/out status, and that cultural differences such as religion, language, or race are secondary to, or constructed by, this first mechanism and criterion. Thus the acts of gratuity and non-reciprocity were less symbolic of some pre-existing relationship than the performative institution of a new one, and the act could occur just as well inside a group – to split it – as outside the group – to affirm it.

We have of course already met with examples of social-internal gratuity in connection with the gift. The examination of gift-giving in Chapter 2 showed that one key feature often noted in charters was the "spontaneity" of the gift. Indeed, for the gift to have maximum (religious) effect, and for maximum honor to accrue to the donor, it was crucial that the gift at least appear to be the result of a purely internal motivation, rather than arising from any external cause such as pressure or necessity or desire for something in exchange for the gift. Many charters, especially during later periods when the discourse of the gift itself became more problematic, explicitly mentioned that the gift donor was "smiling" (Le Goff 1997 in Bremmer and Roodenburg 1997), indicating the free will and lack of coercion involved. In a curious, paradoxical sense, the best gift to a religious institution – the one which produced the maximum spiritual benefit – was one that at least appeared to be unmotivated by any sense of spiritual shame, guilt or crisis. In the representational logic of the gift, the most honorable gift was, ultimately, the most unmotivated gift, the gratuitous gift – a gift given due to none of the (external) impulsions of reciprocity, and which explicitly underlined its disinterest in (or need for) horizontal reciprocity on the part of the donor, who gave purely "pro anima sua" as the commonest phrase went.

Gratuity in giving found its equivalent in gratuity in taking – or in gratuitously commanding that others do or give. The ability to command the meaningless, gratuitous act from someone else was used as a mark of the power of a lord – and also as a mark of the lack of integrity of the one who was so commanded. In the "Conventum" between William V of Aquitaine and Hugh of Lusignan from the

1020s – a unique document which records a conflict between Count William and his vassal Hugh from a purely secular perspective, and in great detail – William is attributed several remarks which stress his ability to impose any act whatsoever on Hugh, no matter how unmotivated, unnecessary or gratuitous: in asking for certain vassals to be handed over to him, the count tells Hugh "Non eos tibi interrogo propter tuum malum, sed etiam per hoc quod meus tu es ad facere meam voluntatem" ("I am not asking them from you because of your wrongdoing, but because you are mine to do my will") (l. 543). He refuses a logic of reciprocal morality in favor of one of pure power. Then later, questioning his vassal's resistance to his wishes, he says "Quare non agis conventum cum Bernardo? Tantum ex me tu es ut si dicerem tibi rusticum facere in seniori, facere debueras." ("Why won't you make an agreement with Bernard? You are so dependent on me that if I told you to make a peasant your lord, you ought to have done it") (l. 544).[10]

In response to this pressure, Hugh engaged in numerous unilateral, aggressive maneuvers to force the count to accept Hugh's own desires for power, including seizing several of the count's castles and essentially holding them for ransom until his rights to one of them were recognized. Hugh struggled to maintain a relationship of balanced reciprocity with his lord, and turned to the reciprocal violence of the "guerra" to maintain it.[11] The count, meanwhile, seems to have been using a rhetoric of gratuity as a means of underlining the non-reciprocal nature of the relationship, or at least the sense that his reciprocations were freely offered, not impelled by any actions, gifts, services or even attacks offered by the vassal.

A final historical example of gratuity, and the one which most closely resembles that of Roland, is another promise to do something above and beyond the call of duty: to do it better than, more than, faster than would seem to be reasonable or necessary. William of Poitiers reports that William the Conqueror told a captured spy from the English King Harold to return and tell Harold: "nec ullam aduersitatem ex nobis ei suscipiendam esse, qominus reliquam aetatem securus agat, nisi intra annuum spacium, ubi tutiorem locum suis pedibus sperat, me conspexerit" ("he will have nothing to fear from me and can live the rest of his life secure if, within the space of one year, he has not seen me in the place he thinks safest for his feet") (*Gesta Guillelmi*, 106–7).

This promise to invade within the year was clearly gratuitous in that it diminished much of the element of surprise that William might have hoped to benefit from, and it also placed extra pressure on him to ready the attack, for no apparent reason. The reason for the promise is essentially to increase his standing and honor among his followers, both immediately and even more so upon the accomplishment of the deed. Thus gratuity does not make sense within a logic of utility,

---

[10] The text is in Martindale 1969. Important studies are White 1992, 1996 and Beech 1966.

[11] See Beech 1966 on the socio-political situation of Poitou and Aquitaine at this time, and the increasing independence of castellan lords, as was typical of western Europe as a whole.

but it makes perfect sense within a logic of competitive honor. The two systems depend on each other, just as the notion of the symbol depends on the contrary notion of the sign.

Whether William said this or not is ultimately less important than the choice to report such a remark by the chronicler – himself a former knight. It clearly evokes the context of honor, giving and taking of the time. William of Poitiers goes on to stress explicitly the gratuity of the promise, noting that this was an "audacious promise" ("grande promissum") which left the Norman barons "marvelling" ("stupentes," pp. 106–7). They are reported to have doubted William greatly, and urged him not to follow through with the invasion, as well as to delay it beyond a year. But William replies that Harold, "non eo animi uiget robore quo uel minimum quid meorum polliceri audeat. At arbitrio meo pariter quae mea sunt, quaeque dicuntur illius, promittentur atque dabuntur" ("had not the bold-ness of spirit to dare to promise even the least of what belongs to me. On the other hand both the things that are mine and those said to be his will be promised and given at my will") (*Gesta guillelmi*, 108–9).

William's audacity as presented here compares favorably to that of Roland. And it is crucial to note the elements of taking and giving which are the vital context for William's words. The gratuity serves to underline the pure integrity which is at stake here, as William sets out to make himself king of all England. In addition, he is obviously promising to take the most fundamental kept or inal-ienable possession of a rival – the crown itself. Such an attempt is an extreme of non-reciprocity, and also offers the highest of symbolic values for taking, as well as opportunities for enormous amounts of subsequent giving. William (of Poitiers, of Normandy, or both) recognized that the pursuit of integrity required a gratuitous gesture centered on taking and giving.

In fact, a logic of gratuitous taking and of the challenge occurred broadly in medieval European society. Over and over one finds instances where characters choose to take the hard way to get what they want, to go to seemingly unnecessary lengths to get things, including things which they often have no need of anyway. William Ian Miller's study of hostile taking or "rán" in Norse literature underlines that this was a common practice in the culture of medieval Iceland (Miller 1986). He notes that in the Icelandic *Landnamabok*, which recounts the early settlement of the island, there are many instances where individuals refuse opportunities to receive land through gifts, or even to purchase it, preferring instead to take the land through duels or outright violence.[12] Similar ideas are described by Tacitus in the *Germania*. This is not to claim that *The Song of Roland* or other Old French epics are specifically "Germanic" in their literary or cultural heritage, or even that they were literarily influenced by Germanic elements, though this may very well be true to some extent. Rather, the characteristic of gratuity is integral to

---

[12] Miller 1986:49–50. See also Gurevich 1968:130: he notes that it was better to seize by force than to accept as gift.

gift cultures of the warrior aristocracy form, whether one is talking about medieval Germany, Iceland, England, France, Spain, or Italy.

In our historical examples, gratuity advertises integrity, both in the psychological sense of inner-directedness, and in the sociopolitical sense of independence from the compulsions of reciprocity – the immunity from being taken from, or from having to give to. Yet none of the examples involves either the death of the hero or the social destruction which accompanies it in, for example, *The Song of Roland*, *Raoul of Cambrai*, *Beowulf* or *The Nibelungenlied*. This is because the examples discussed above involved the use of the concept of gratuity as a symbolic tool by figures who were not truly in a situation of complete integrity – Hugh for example was successful at taking some of William of Aquitaine's castles, William the Conqueror was still William the would-be conqueror, and gifts to the Church also typically involved reciprocal relations with monasteries and abbeys. One could even propose that the trope of gratuity and integrity was borrowed or adapted from a more literary discourse where it could achieve its perfect form. This would be impossible to prove, though the historian Stephen White explicitly posits this idea in relation to the "Conventum."[13] The characteristic feature of the pure gratuity and integrity of the epic hero is that it is a fully realized form of non-reciprocity, which sunders the bonds even among those closest to him.[14]

In conclusion, the medieval hero can be defined as a specifically "literary" or narrative trope, in which the individual hero is represented as attaining – at the moment of death – complete integrity through his own internally-willed choice. He is shown to value that integrity above relationships with those around him, even his closest companions; above his ties to his kinsmen, his countrymen, and his culture; and above life itself. Note that all of these elements must be present – death alone, or simple scorn for those around one or one's own life or culture, or simply seeking death, do not make one a hero. The hero must perform his way to the top, and then place himself in impossible circumstances of his own making, gratuitously and knowingly engineered. Only then does he earn the right to die "heroically," with integrity, and thus to engage in a sacred, vertical exchange consecrated in the social memory of the epic.

The real-life medieval warrior-aristocrat, on the other hand, can draw on this trope as a model for identity formation and social action – in particular, on the

---

[13] See White 1992 and 1996. He suggests that legal disputes drew upon or at least resonated against models of potential procedure and resolution proposed in poetic sources.

[14] A recent study of the epic hero which resembles mine closely in a number of ways is Miller 2000. He focuses on the paradoxically social and individual nature of the hero (3–5), his inner-directedness and integrity (9, 121, 332), the way in which he raises issues and problems with boundaries (138ff), his use of symbolic modes of self-identity (188, 225), the gratuitous acts of the hero (214,330), and the need for him to be socially contained (3–4, 38–9). His analysis differs from mine principally in its lesser attention to socio-economic and historical context, and in its treatment of the hero as a direct social reflection rather than as a literary trope, and – ironically – that he makes much less use of economic or anthropological sources.

performative rise of the hero through giving and taking. But the listener to the epic must also use the trope as a point of reflection, and recognize that he must himself stop short of the apotheosis of the hero, and work hard to stop others short as well. The incredible social holocausts that mark the end of so many epics, with their impossible tens of thousands of deaths, as well as the extreme fates of the hero – whether assumption to Heaven in the arms of angels or the most brutal condemnations and deaths – serve to remind the listener that the world depicted is a world pushed to its speculative limits, and not a world to which the listener can – or would wish to – attain. Even the actual medieval king, who attains and enjoys sacral status and enters into vertical exchanges, attains integrity (at least theoretically) only in relationship to his own society. The hero attains this integrity in relationship to his own mind, body, will and life as well. While the king always remains under a generalized obligation to the society he represents, as its symbol, the hero has the luxury of escaping even this in his moment of engineered death. In the following chapter, we will explore further the tenuous relationship between the literary hero and warrior-aristocrat individuals and society.

7

The Supplemental Hero: *Raoul of Cambrai*

Roland is hardly unique as an example of the supplemental hero. In fact, supplementarity is a key feature of medieval heroes in several traditions. In the Middle High German *Nibelungenlied*, an epic from around the year 1200 which will be discussed in more detail in the following chapter, the hero Siegfried shows the same types of behavior. Arriving at the renowned castle of Worms, he is warmly greeted by the brothers of Kriemhild, whom he hopes to marry, but goes out of his way to increase the odds against his success:

> Mir wart gesaget mære   in mînes vater lant,
> daz hie bî iu wæren   (Daz het ich gerne erkant)
> die küenesten recken   (Des hân ich vil vernomen)
> kie ie künic gewunne;   dar umbe bin ich her bekomen. (St. 107)

> Ich bin ouch ein recke   und solde krône tragen.
> Ich wil daz gerne füegen   daz si von mir sagen
> daz ich habe von rehte   liute unde lant.
> Dar umbe sol mîn êre   und ouch mîn houbet wesen pfant.

> Nu ir sît sô küene,   Als mir ist geseit,
> sone ruoche ich, ist daz iemen   liep oder leit;
> ich wil an iu ertwingen   swaz ir muget hân:
> land unde bürge,   daz sol mir werden undertân. (St. 109–10)

> I was told repeatedly in my father's country that the bravest warriors that King ever had were to be found with you, and I have come to see for myself ... I, too, am a warrior and am entitled to wear a crown, but I wish to achieve the reputation of possessing a land and people *in my own right*, for which my head and honour shall be pledge! Now, since (as they tell me) you are so brave – and I do not care who minds – I will wrest from you *by force* all that you possess! Your lands and your castle shall all be subject to me!
> (p. 29 – my italics).

Siegfried, in this speech, displays a logic of possession which appears identical to that described by Tacitus in the *Germania*: "You cannot so easily persuade them to plough the soil or to wait for the harvest as to challenge an enemy and earn wounds as a reward. Indeed, they think it tame and spiritless to accumulate slowly by sweat what they can get quickly by losing some blood" (Sect. 14). It is better to take things by force than to acquire them through labor, gift or tribute, and Siegfried is even willing to go out of his way to prevent himself from being in a position to do the latter. He seeks to be able to wear a crown that was taken, not given to him. And he targets the most sacred, kept possessions for his taking – crowns and royal brides.

While this scene is typical of Siegfried, a more important moment in the text – indeed, the fulcrum around which the entire epic turns – also depends fundamentally on gratuity. After Siegfried has helped Gunther win the hand of Brunhild in Iceland, she resists Gunther's effort to consummate their relationship on their wedding night. Gunther, hung on the wall by a hook, calls desperately for Siegfried's help. Siegfried successfully wrestles Brunhild into submission, and then allows Gunther to finish the proceedings in the dark. But before leaving, Siegfried takes Brunhild's ring and girdle (St. 680; p. 93). There is no apparent reason for this, and the narrator in fact says, "ine weiz ob er daz tæte   durch sînen hôhen muote" ("I do not know whether it was his pride which made him do it").

After explicitly underlining the gratuity of this taking, the narrator concludes, "er gap ez sînem wîbe;   daz wart im sider leit" ("Later he gave them to his wife, and well did he rue it!") (St. 680; p. 93). Indeed, Siegfried's subsequent death, the war between the Burgundians and the Huns, and the apocalyptic destruction of all the warriors of both kingdoms at the end of the epic can all be traced back to Siegfried's gift of the ring and girdle to his wife and the dispute that erupts in the court between her and Brunhild due to this. The dispute exposes the fissures of the world of Worms in such a way that they must be addressed, and Siegfried's life is the price. There is no reason for Siegfried to take the items, or to give them to his wife, and he must know that the act can only lead to the potential for the greatest danger. Yet he engineers precisely this situation, and indirectly produces the events that will lead to his death. His death is however far less heroic in many senses than that of Roland, and the larger meaning of the epic differs considerably – a point to which we shall return in Chapter 8.

There is, however, a kind of reason here. The ring and the girdle are examples of the most personal symbols of integrity. They indeed literally mark the integrity of Brunhild's body, as a virgin, and indirectly, the integrity of the king. Siegfried has given a form of service to Gunther in helping him subdue his wife. He is entitled to expect a counter-gift of some form. Yet rather than await such a reciprocal counter-gift, he takes that which constitutes the personal sacred of Gunther and Brunhild. As Annette Weiner and Maurice Godelier both suggest, reciprocity is centered around giving which allows one to keep the ungivable. Unilaterally to take this ungivable is to short-circuit the entire system of reciprocity, by removing its transcendental anchor, (or supplement). Siegfried places himself in a position in relation to Gunther where Gunther cannot possibly reciprocate, since anything he might seek to give will be trumped by the ring and girdle which

Siegfried now possesses.[1] Thus Siegfried's taking is not truly unmotivated. But it remains gratuitous in that it abrogates the possibility of reciprocity, and serves to place the actor in a position of complete integrity in relation to those around him. Siegfried's action essentially places him in the same position vis-a-vis his new countrymen, as Roland was in with regards to the Franks. He becomes the consummate outsider, and the source of bitterness, jealousy and resentment on the part of all at the court.

Aron Gurevich has noted a similar moment in the *Eddas*, which parallels a similar scene in *The Nibelungenlied*. In the *Atlakviða*, Gunnar has been invited to Hungary in full knowledge of the danger that lies there, since his sister Kriemhild has sworn to avenge the death of her husband Siegfried. He is warned not to go by his companions. But he decides to depart, and even goes out of his way to render the situation more desperate, turning down offers of help. Gurevich writes that Gunnar's decision to depart is a "rationally unmotivated, impulsive decision, a desire to assert his own will, ecstatic, reckless willfulness, throwing a challenge at fate" (130). Thus the hero does not accept his fate, but creates it, he argues (134). He continues that the fate is death, but the death is not a tragedy in the Greek sense of the term, but a victory. He stresses that death is "the moment when the hero crosses into the world of glory" (123) and thus the moment of the hero's completion. He also points out that this is typically a solitary moment, that the heroic Germanic lays often lack a sense of group or national spirit (124–5), despite the supposed cultural solidarity of the time and the ideas of shame culture and the "comitatus." The individual hero goes where the group dares not – or should not – follow. He may come from the culture, but he ignores or surpasses it (140).

Gurevich is clearly describing the integrity which we have been discussing, and he here locates another moment where gratuity is the essential mark of this integrity. He also touches on the way in which this integrity is both the essence of the culture from which Gunnar arises, but also, in its heroic perfection, a surpassing of that culture, in which the hero becomes solitary, and potentially even Other to his culture or at least to its less-perfect members. And, one could add, in a world of wagers of honor, the highest wager is that which can only be met through the death of the hero. This particular scene does not center on giving and taking per se, but it is structured around the broader notions of reciprocity and its abrogation.

Similar scenes occur in other medieval texts, including *Beowulf*.[2] Gratuity and integrity lead quickly to death for Roland, Siegfried, Gunther, and Beowulf as well. But in their death – and its memorialization in epic texts – they also represent the only fully developed individuals of their cultures. Of course, such terms

---

[1]   The two items also stand metonymically in relation to the treasure of the Nibelungs – an endless source of giving which also marks Siegfried's integral, sacred status.

[2]   See Beowulf's refusal to use standard weapons and armor to fight Grendel, since Grendel cannot make use of them, in vv. 435–40 and 677–84 in *Beowulf*.

as "individual" have been widely regarded as problematic for early medieval society, especially that of the epic, which is so often seen as a world of social solidarity. Several scholars have argued that medieval "individualism" must be understood primarily in terms of quantitative differences between persons, rather than qualitative ones, so that there are no true, qualitatively distinct "individuals" of the modern form in early medieval culture (Vitz 1989). To a certain extent this analysis fits well with the concept of the hero being developed in this book – the hero is after all seen as the perfect embodiment of the central values of his culture. The seeker of heroism takes more, gives more, has a greater degree of integrity. He is quantitatively superior during his rise to greatness.

But the point of pure integrity, marked by the gratuitous gesture, can be seen as the point at which the hero dies to his culture – ceases to have a quantitative (or reciprocal) relationship to it – in order to live as an individual. The hero stands as the emblem of the way in which the logic of his culture becomes Other to the culture itself, as the pursuit of integrity through mechanisms of reciprocity leads to the end of reciprocity. But at the same time, to become socially Other is to become fully oneself.

The logic of the hero and of integrity, as examined in this book to this point, are essentially logics of the individual, and of the relationship of the individual to his own society in an aggressive gift culture. Personhood, in this context, must be understood in the context of the symbolic, personalized objects of taking, giving and keeping. And in such a culture, personhood is always incipient, always in the process of being developed from a grounds of non- or partial personhood. Thus one begins to see the fundamental disjunctions as well as connections between medieval and modern models of psychology and the sign. Lacan's theory, for example, dramatizes the loss and lacking that comes with entry into the Symbolic Order, in relation to a nostalgic notion of an original, integral person. Medieval epic culture, on the other hand, saw integrity not as an initial stage, but a final one, towards which one had to strive by the construction of symbols of identity, through symbolic acts of giving, taking and keeping. The hero can thus be seen as the no-longer-incipient, but completed individual, who has superseded the lacking which, for the medieval warrior, lay always ahead, never behind, since the future offered a brief, liminal end to that lacking. The medieval warrior aristocracy, however, seems to have found essentially intolerable the notion of such pure individualization, since the hero always dies as soon as he obtains it. This suggests the deeper sense in which the hero – the lone individual – must be seen as an Other to his culture.

But as we have seen, the mechanisms of individuation were also paradoxically the mechanisms of social solidarity: giving, taking and keeping acted to constitute homogeneous social unities as well as heterogeneous individual ones. This fact is a central sociocultural key to understanding the epic. It suggests the paradox that the mechanisms which excluded sociocultural others – the Saracens, most paradigmatically, or the traitor – also functioned to fragment the warrior culture internally, as heroes excluded – and were excluded from – their warrior peers.

Social solidarity came at the price of potential social self-destruction. Outward mechanisms of alterity generated inward forms of alterity. Or conversely, one could say that the sense of the Self as a fully realized individual was ontologically inseparable from the sense of the Other. In either case, the hero – the fully integral individual – and the Saracen or traitor, from this perspective, begin to converge. In the epic of revolt, this convergence becomes even clearer.

The Epic of Revolt and the Hero's Alterity

Perhaps the clearest example of the hero's alterity in all medieval literature is the Old French epic *Raoul of Cambrai*, the preserved version of which dates from around 1180. Raoul is virtually the perfect epic anti-hero. Yet the remainder of this chapter will examine the ways in which Raoul is finally not so different at all from Roland.[3] Both, it will suggest, operate with the same logic, and both are perfect incarnations of the ethos of their cultures. Together, they allow an appreciation of the dynamics of what we will call "tri-partite" alterity, in which the hero, the hero's group, and the outsider group exist in delicate balance.

In *Raoul of Cambrai*, the title hero is wrongly disinherited by the perennially weak King Louis, who gives away his father's lands when he dies, rather than allowing his widow to hold the lands, remarry, and pass them on to Raoul. Raoul complains, and is promised the lands of the next vassal to die. But when this turns out to be a man of the Vermandois family, with fours sons eager to inherit, Louis retracts the gift, leading to increasing bitterness on the part of Raoul, and ultimately catastrophe. Urged on by his uncle Guerri, Raoul eventually gives up on waiting for Louis and attacks the Vermandois lands. He burns a nunnery there, killing all inside, including the mother of his closest companion, Bernier. Bernier breaks with Raoul, and swears vengeance, and their feud, mixed with the general ambitions of Raoul, plays out through much of the remainder of the epic.

Initially, Raoul continues to take part in structures of reciprocity. Although he is passed over by King Louis when fiefs and other gifts are distributed, he remains hopeful of eventually receiving his due, and he engages in verbal interchange with Louis on many occasions, though the reciprocal exchanges are clearly fraught with violent tensions. As long as Raoul maintains a desire for negotiation and reciprocation, whether in words, deeds or possessions, he remains within the controlling, ordering structures of the warrior aristocracy. However, he finally reaches a symbolic liminal moment, which metaphorically signals his coming, more literal break with these traditions. Significantly, it occurs as he is playing chess. The game of chess was a *mise-en-abyme* of aristocratic society, complete

---

[3]   See Matarasso 1962:164–6, 171, 181ff, 211–14 for a study of some key similarities in the description of Roland and Raoul, and between Raoul and "typical" heroes more generally.

with careful rules, relationships and hierarchies of pieces – a complete social structure in miniature, one could say, with its kings, queens, knights, bishops and pawns. And to play chess is to accede to rules, as well as to engage in a form of carefully managed reciprocity,[4] where one gives (pawns) in order to keep ("sacred" kings). But the chess game goes awry in *Raoul*:

> As eschés joue R[aous] de Cambrizis
> si con li hom qi mal n'i entendi:
> G[ueris] le voit, par le bras le saisi,
> son peliçon li desront et parti.
> 'Fil a putain,' le clama – si menti –
> 'Malvais lechieres, por qoi joes tu ci?
> N'as tant de terre, par verté le te dï,
> ou tu peüses conreer un ro[n]ci.'
> R[aous] l'oï, desor ces piés sailli –
> si haut parole qe li palais fremi. (ll. 482–91)

> Raoul is playing chess like a man who meant no harm: Guerri sees him and seizes him by the arm, tearing his fur mantle. 'Son of a whore', he called him – quite without foundation – 'cowardly brute, why are you here playing games? I tell you truly, you haven't enough land to rub down an old nag on!' Raoul heard him; leaping to his feet, he speaks so loudly that the great hall shakes.

Urged on by his uncle Guerri, Raoul abandons his chess game and goes immediately before King Louis to demand his due, the text noting that "Devant le roi vienent cil aati./ Cele parole pas a pié ne chaï" ("They all hastened into the king's presence. [Raoul speaks to him as follows?] [*sic*] – he did not fall at his feet") (ll. 502–3). Rule-based behavior within social structures begins to dissolve, as will reciprocity. Faced with Raoul's rage and disrespect, Louis makes the fatal mistake of offering a non-personalized gift; that is, one which does not come with a specific history and conditions that would allow for a sense of balanced reciprocity between him and Raoul. He offers Raoul the lands of the next baron who should die, whomever that may be.

Here, Raoul could be seen as a virtual floating signifier seeking a place in the system. More specifically, however, he constitutes a surplus for whom no place in the social structure can now be found. The lands are all occupied, and they all have heirs, it turns out. Raoul is the quintessential form of dangerous excess – an individual who cannot be placed in relation to any specific lands, and thus in relation to any specific place in the structure of social relations; he is like an extra chess piece, a third black knight one might say, a form of Other who has no

---

[4] For another example of a chess game gone bad, which leads to non-reciprocity and revolt, see *Renaud de Montauban*, laisse 62 (ed. Thomas). For more discussion and references to chess in the epic, see Baumgartner and Harf-Lancner 1999:109. On chess and the aristocracy more generally, see Eales 1986.

place in the exchanges of the game. The dynamic of the rest of the epic is already established.

Louis soon regrets his promised gift, and tries to renege on it. Raoul, however, decides to take what should be his, irrespective of the words of Louis, his mother, his vassal Bernier, or anyone else. At this point, the chess metaphor is fully converted into reality, as he makes a fundamental break with the structures of linguistic and socioeconomic reciprocity that otherwise constitute the basis of his society. The pleadings of his mother (laisses 48–58) are useless, as will be those of everyone else. He procedes to burn down the abbey of Origny, incinerating all the nuns within, including the mother of his own closest follower Bernier, because the abbey belongs to his enemies. What follows is a downward spiral of blood and death, in which Raoul continually breaks with those closer and closer to himself, ending with the break with his loyal vassal Bernier, and then finally with his abandoning of his uncle Guerri and his followers on the field of battle, to die alone.[5]

Raoul thus passes through several moments of gratuity, non-reciprocity, excess and alterity, each of which strikes closer and closer to home – metaphorically in the context of the chess game, verbally in relation to his own family, and finally physically in his decision to burn down the abbey, in an act whose gratuitous defiance seems calculated in the text to produce a shock value. It is this final instance which perhaps marks the gratuity most clearly.

Yet the act is perhaps not unmotivated. In particular, it may not be so dissimilar from Siegfried's taking of the ring and girdle in *The Nibelungenlied*. Annette Weiner, in discussing the kept, addresses the issue of medieval aristocratic gifts to monasteries. This seems to offer a problem for the idea of the kept, especially in that, as Stephen White has noted, the preferred lands for gifts to monasteries were not those which had been purchased, but so-called inalienable, inherited lands – the lands most tied to the symbolic integrity of aristocratic families. Faced with this seeming contradiction, Weiner essentially suggests that such gifts actually constituted a form of banking of one's inalienable lands in a closely-associated monastery, where they would remain eternally, offering spiritual benefits. In a sense, such gifts thus allowed one to keep one's lands "forever," though the possession in the afterlife came in the form of conversion to spiritual benefits, even as the family on earth enjoyed continuing religious benefits as well. If such transfers are to be considered gifts at all, they should be considered vertical, rather than horizontal exchanges, offering privileged access to the sacred. They also served to constitute the receiving Church establishment in question as the sacred kept of a given family.

This analysis offers an intriguing way of theorizing Raoul's decision to burn the abbey at Origny. This abbey was the favorite abbey of the Vermandois brothers – his sworn enemies, as the holders to the fief to which he felt entitled. The resi-

---

[5]   Michelene de Combarieu du Grès cites this last moment as the true moment when Raoul surpasses the bounds of reciprocity and becomes "diabolical" (1999:17–9).

dence of Bernier's mother (Bernier is related to the Vermandois family) at the abbey strongly suggests this fact. One might imagine that, as was typical at the time, the Vermandois family would have given lands and other gifts to that abbey. Thus the abbey could be seen as the symbolic repository of the most sacred and kept parts of the Vermandois' integral patrimony. Line 1212 states that: "li fil H[erbert] orent le liu molt chier" ("Herbert's sons cared deeply for the place"), despite the fact that it was "worthless for purposes of defence" (l. 1214). In other words, it was not a locus of performative, military power, but of vertical access to the sacred. To destroy it was to strike at the heart of their integrity – and also to underline the refusal of reciprocity in the most powerful way possible.[6]

Should one then take Raoul as the monster that even the narrative suggests at numerous points that he is? One could argue, on the contrary, that an audience of medieval aristocrats might rather have had a (horrified) admiration for Raoul, and in particular for the relentless, unstoppable, unwavering, internally-directed force of will which drives him through the remainder of the narrative. He is, within the corpus of the chanson de geste, the epitome of Gurevich's hero of the will, purely internally driven, moving evermore outside the circle of society as defined by reciprocity. Note in particular that the narrative (or at least Guerri) depicts him quite harshly as he is playing chess, due to his lack of action – the last time in the narrative that this will be a problem. Subsequently he is not only "all action," but his very first deed is marked by a kind of "over the top" gratuity that could only have been designed to underline his ruthless will: the burning of the nuns despite the pleading of all around him.

While there is clearly a certain melodramatic quality to Raoul's "evil" here, yet at the same time, there is a transcendent quality to his integrity that, in the context of medieval admiration for hostile taking and aggressive action, might well have been perversely appealing to the epic's audience, as several critics have suggested.[7] Indeed, when he returns from the burning, the text says of him: "En toute France n'ot plus bel chevalier,/ ne si hardi por ce[s] armes baillier[r]" ("There was not such a fine knight in the whole of France, nor one so fearless at arms") (ll. 1371–2). Despite the narrative's numerous "proper" condemnations of Raoul's actions, he remains the central, fascinating focus of the text, following his goal to the death. The only final difference between Raoul and Roland, it seems, is the goal of their actions,[8] and even the goal can be seen as

---

[6]   See Calin 1974, where he argues that Origny is a feminine space, the specifically feminine qualities of which Raoul seeks to destroy – evoking the ideas in Ch. 5. See also Labbé 1999 for an analysis similar to mine of the integral function of the abbey.

[7]   See Calin 1974:3; Baumgartner and Harf-Lancner 1999:51; Kay 1994. These same qualities have appealed to the critical audience. See Boutet and Strubel 1979:61 ("l'énormité de son personnage") and Bezzola 1960:507–17. Matarasso 1962:195, 203–4 underlines the way in which Raoul is admirably "faithful to [him]self," thus recalling a key aspect of integrity – purely inner-directed motivations. Labbé 1999:154 speaks of his "démarche d'autoexaltation."

[8]   See Boutet and Strubels' suggestion that the "démesure" of Roland and Raoul are "metaphysically" the same, and differ only in their political orientation (1979:65–66).

secondary to the integrity which they both demonstrate as part of their pursuit of that goal. In stripping away the pretense of proper (religious) ends for those actions, Raoul raises the question of what is finally admirable – the end, or the pure will embodied in the actions themselves, in both Roland and Raoul's case.[9]

W.G. van Emden has argued, based on analyses of early chronicle accounts of the events on which many epics of revolt are based, that the time of the composition of *Raoul of Cambrai* – approximately 1180 – saw a fundamental shift in the representation of the rebellious baron. Using earlier epic material to bolster his argument as well, he suggests that the earliest rebels were depicted as being purely rebellious, without any clear motive, while King Louis was not shown as the weak and ineffective king that he appears to be in the later epics of revolt. The text we possess of *Gormont and Isembart* depicts the rebellious baron in this fashion still (Van Emden 1964). Dominique Boutet has made essentially the same points about Louis in particular, and Raoul as well indirectly, for the chronicles related to Raoul (Boutet 2000).[10] Thus, the text of *Raoul of Cambrai* that we now possess could actually be seen as vitiating the purity of his anti-reciprocity revolt and his absolute pursuit of integrity as an end in itself, as part of a more general tendency in the later twelfth century to "apologize" for the rebellious barons, render their revolt more explicable, and show them as finally repentant in the end. Yet our text maintains the essence of the prior situation. However much one may point to Louis' injustices as the cause of Raoul's rebellion, the fact is that Raoul's aggressive actions are actually targeted at those around him, in an ever-tightening circle that moves closer and closer to home, until the violence kills Raoul himself. Raoul thus falls in the line of narrative anti-heroes which include Milton's Satan, and Don Juan, in one sense.[11] But the central point of the argument here is in fact that Raoul is more fundamentally the exact opposite of these characters, in that his gratuity can actually be understood symbolically as the most perfect expression of the symbolic logic of his culture. He pursues the integrity which is the foundation of identity and power among the warrior aristocracy. As Sarah Kay has noted, everything that is said about Raoul in the text is said about someone else as well (Kay 1999b:85–6).

[9] Boutet and Strubel observe that "ce qui désigne le héros à l'admiration des foules, c'est bien ce déchaînement de force barbare et primitive; mais un tel héros, pour être supportable, doit revêtir au moins une apparence chrétienne" (1979:61). Of course on a social level, the point is that Raoul's behavior is "insupportable"; but the essence of the remark points first to the fact that Raoul is (on an ethnic and class level) able to be identified with by the audience and even admirable to it, and also that the gratuitous excess of his behavior can be seen within the context of the world-view of that very class and ethnicity. It is not an "other," a "diable" (Boutet), but the comportment of the warrior aristocracy itself which must be recognized in Raoul's "Christianity," which is less a religious label than a socio-cultural one.

[10] See also Matarasso 1962:84–7 on potential earlier versions of the text with Raoul as a pure aggressor, as he appears in chronicle sources.

[11] For an analysis of the character of Don Juan specifically in terms of the logic of honor and integrity, see Baroja 1966:110–1. For connections of Don Juan and Raoul, see Baumgartner and Harf-Lancner 1999:110 and especially Legros 1999.

It should be noted, however, that the violent impulsions of the text are not quite without constraint. At several points, Raoul himself seems to hesitate for a moment in his drive to integrity, only to be urged on by figures such as Aalais or Guerri – the same figures whom he has previously ignored in his own drive. Numerous readers have noted this vacillation, and even exchange of roles (Labbé 1999:60–1; Kay 1999b:91–2; Leupin 1988:94; Baumgartner and Harf-Lancner 1999:125). There is even a return to another chess game (laisse 75) which is however characteristically interrupted and left unfinished. One might suggest that this weakens the vision of Raoul as driven purely by internalized integrity desires. In a sense it does, since it opens up alternative possibilities of personality. Yet once Raoul moves into action after these moments of hesitation or reflection, the results are typically violent and unrestrained. In the circumstances, it seems more revealing to consider these moments as indicative of the way that the integrity drive works to narrow the circle of reciprocity and community around the individual to the point that the individual becomes alienated even from himself (as Alexandre Leupin also proposes, from the Lacanian perspective of fundamental "lack"). After all, a person's society plays a crucial role in making him who he is. As discussed earlier, within the society of the warrior aristocracy, identity was plural and relational. The drive towards integrity and dis-integration from society, while fundamentally learned from that society, also seems to destroy the individual even as the social logic is pursued to perfection. One is left with the choice of partial identity, within systems of reciprocity, or whole identity, but in a supra-social or extra-social form which is simultaneously perfect and deadly.

We are left with one final question, however. If Roland and Raoul are so similar, why is Raoul fundamentally condemned "metaphysically," while Roland is apotheosized? It is a commonplace of studies on Raoul that he revolts against God himself.[12] This point, however, raises more general questions about Raoul and Roland's relation to the sacred. Arguing from a Lacanian perspective, Alexandre Leupin suggests that *Raoul of Cambrai* dramatizes the missing Name of the Father, especially since King Louis, who represents the one figure of potential sacredness and transcendence, is seen as fundamentally degraded (Leupin 1988). In the context of this dilemma, Raoul in particular seeks (as do other characters more generally) to establish himself as the "transcendent origin of sense" (Leupin 1988:94) – to claim the place of the Father.

This analysis can be recast in terms of our vocabulary of giving, taking and keeping. In discussing *The Poem of the Cid*, we underlined the importance of the notion of performance within the social world of medieval Spain, with giving and taking both constituting acts which performatively produced the symbolic

---

[12] Some readers argue that Raoul fundamentally recognizes his sins and is forgiven at his death (see Combarieu du Grès 1999), while others suggest that the entire metaphysical "set-up" of this death scene shows little support for this idea (Kay 1984). I would agree with Kay that the repentance at death appears weak and perfunctory within the larger representational logic of the text as it precedes and follows this scene.

capital which paid for and at least temporarily solidified individual identity and linguistic truth. We also saw that this performative system was predicated on a transcendent sacred embodied in kingship: the Cid's taking and giving were fundamentally governed by a desire to attain the integrity which would allow access to this sacred, and they would be meaningless outside this context. His judicial performances likewise depended on the king's presence and supervision, and the access this opened up to the possibility of sacred, essentializing validation of his verbal claims. In that text, the sacrality of kingship offered a way to convert performative status and identity, if pushed to their limit, into essentialized, kept nobility and heroic status, as well as to convert performed linguistic truth into sacred, essential truth. There is thus a Name of the Father which one can attain.

In the world of *Raoul of Cambrai*, however, the sacred anchor of the system is missing. (This is not to say that "God is absent," but rather that the sacred king – the mediator through whom vertical reciprocity is made possible – no longer functions in this way.) Thus one sees only the possibility of performance, not essence. Performance is not convertible to stable social status. The king's loose play with supposedly heritable fiefs underlines this dilemma. Likewise, the failed trial scenes in the text point to the unconvertibility of verbal claim and performance to sacred, essential truth. And as a corollary to these points, personal identity must remain always unstable, open to performative renegotiations.[13] Raoul's frustration with Louis in his attempts to obtain a fief bespeaks more generally an ironically "metaphysical" anguish in the face of this realization – an anguish perhaps generally representative of the fears of a society where performance was so essential to status and power. One critic has remarked that we should perhaps see Raoul's "blasphemy" as a "blasphème comme appel" [to God] (Labbé 1999:57).

Yet the text seems to prefer this performative society in the end. Sarah Kay argues that the text consistently reveals "la valeur de l'effort humain" as against "l'insuccès du duel judiciaire" (1984:482) and more generally that "law" is less valued and less efficacious than interpersonal moral and affective relationships. She interprets this as an indication of a shift towards a more humanist, individualist society, marked by Christianity, and thus as a critique of the world of the warrior aristocracy (1984). But it could equally well be seen as an awareness of the need for some form of anchoring sacred for the performative world which the

---

[13] Dominique Boutet discusses the question of subjective identity in terms very similar to those used in analyzing *The Cid*: "le principe de son action violente est la volonté absolue de faire coïncider sa position dans la société féodale avec le statut que lui confère sa naissance. C'est, en quelque sorte, le drame de la disjonction entre le statut et le genus que retrace la première partie de la chanson" (2000:320). Boutet then argues that Raoul needs the fief, and the king's approbation, to render his conjoined self "idéalement immuable." But one must note that Raoul never truly accepts Louis' words as such otherwise (see Leupin 1988:93 on this as well). His need for the fief thus seems more like a fantasy of – or an attempt to personally project – a transcendent, essentializing sacred.

text seems to embrace.[14] The chaos of *Raoul of Cambrai* is the chaos that results when there is a failure of the social sacred, and when the individual consequently seeks to become sacred himself, to become the absolute giver and receiver of lands, the essential determiner of title – to lay claim to the Nomos, in Jacques Godbout's words, or to claim the Name of the Father, in Lacanian terms.[15] It is this social sacred function which must act to restrain the drive of the hero towards integrity, and to maintain both the individual and the society in a state of reciprocal, pluralistic imperfection which is essential to its functioning.

Roland, on the other hand, operates within a realm in which integrity can effectively provide access to the sacred. Indeed, *The Song of Roland* is essentially the recapitulation of a myth: the myth of the founding of the sacred itself. Two moments in the text point to this fact – one quite famously, the other much less so. Most famously, when Roland dies, the archangel Gabriel descends from Heaven to escort him there. Roland is literally apotheosized: his integrity leads directly to access to the sacred. Note that this is a personal access as well – not a mediated, social one as in *The Cid*. Roland thus becomes like a god or sacred ancestor – the very thing which societies typically deny to the individual, as seen in Chapter 4. Roland's unique status as an individual above and beyond the systems of reciprocity which otherwise govern his culture is underlined in the reaction of Aude to his death. She is told that he is dead, and then is offered another husband. Her reaction is to die. Far from indicating any proto-courtly sensibility, this scene serves to underline that Roland is irreplaceable ontologically – there is no one equivalent to him, not even Charlemagne's son Louis, who is offered as the replacement. This is striking, in that Louis as heir to the throne clearly represents another kind of access to the sacred – he will be, indeed, the human mediator between worldly and sacred. But Roland is not just a mediator: he has become sacred himself. More particularly, he has given an unreciprocable, vertical gift – the life of the hero. This is the gift which, from the viewpoint of mythical time, actually founds the sacred.

The epic itself, as ritual re-enactment of this founding, also participates in the sacred. The epic's unfolding within the quasi-mythical time of Charlemagne serves to underline this fact. The hero's gratuitous gestures work in the same way: they invite a death which is inseparable from an affirmation of sacred wholeness and integrity, scorning as it does any need for or attachment to relations of horizontal reciprocity, as well as all the potential temptations of worldly commodities. The otherness of Roland in relation to the Franks must also be read as a metaphor

[14] Leupin (1988) argues that Bernier – a bastard, ironically, in a text all about legitimate inheritance – is the only character who truly accepts and calls on the sacred (see v. 1709). Bernier locates "legitimacy" in a transcendental sacred, he suggests, and thus, in yet another irony, converts Raoul – who consistently defies the sacred – into the true "bastard" (1988).

[15] See Kay 1994 for a general analysis of the epic hero in terms of an extra-Christian, anthropological sense of the sacred. She argues that the hero could function as a vertical mediator between the secular and sacred, particularly in the moment of personal death (but renewal of the world).

for the otherness of the sacred – and of the language of the text's performance – to its audience as well, even though Roland's sacred, heroic perfection must no doubt have been the source of an equally powerful desire for identification on the part of the audience. The text constantly places Roland in opposition to the Franks – to Ganelon, but also to the barons when the decision is made to leave Spain, to Charlemagne, when the rear-guard is offered, and to Oliver when the debates about blowing the horn occur. When he dies he looks not back towards France, but away, towards Spain (l. 2367, 2376), even as his memory recalls the Frankish past (ll. 2377–81). Upon facing death, he attempts to shatter the sword Durendal that connects him to Charlemagne so that "jamais n'ert tel en France l'asolue" ("Never again will such a one be seen in holy France") (l. 2311): he hopes never to be imitable. The epic continually offers Roland as a point of identity for the audience, then withdraws him and makes him a point of alterity. In so doing, it repeatedly plays on the boundary of the liminal space of the supplement – this is indeed the function of the hero in the epic. But even this dramatic complexity does not fully capture the ambiguities of identity and alterity as they are played out in Old French epic.

The Triangle of Alterity

As much as Raoul and Roland are like the external, Saracen other, they are of course equally like their own societies. This paradox can be at least partially resolved by expanding the concept of alterity from a binary to a trinary model, in which the three points of a triangle are inhabited by the in-group, the out-group and the hero respectively. Roland rejects relations of reciprocity with both the Saracens and his own Franks. Meanwhile for the Franks, the Saracens are clearly Other, but so is Roland finally. And for the Sarracens, both Roland and the Franks are Other, though as the remarks of Ganelon during his negotiation with them make clear, Roland is clearly detached from the rest of the Franks in their minds as well, since Ganelon praises Charlemagne and his followers while blaming Roland for everyone's troubles:

> Dist Blancandrins: "Francs sunt mult gentilz home!"
> Mult grant mal funt e cil duc e cil cunte
> A lur seignur, ki tel conseill li dunent:
> Lui e altrui travaillent e cunfundent."
> Guenes respunt" "Jo ne sai veirs nul hume,
> Ne mes Rollant, ki uncore en avrat hunte." (ll. 377–82)

> Blancandrin said: "The Franks are most noble men! Great harm is being done by those dukes and counts who give such advice to their lord. They destroy and torment him and others too." Ganelon replies: "In truth I know of no one except Roland who will yet be shamed by this."

Thus, while the Franks and Saracens seem quite comfortable with a classic "us/ them" situation of alterity, for both of them, Roland appears to be the principal threat who will potentially destroy the situation of violent, but potentially stable reciprocity in which they find themselves.[16]

From the standpoint of the key group here whose viewpoint the epic ultimately takes – the Franks – alterity thus appears in two guises. The first is that of an exterior Other, defined in terms of differences of ethnicity, race, religion, language, geographical space, dress, appearance – everything except martial attitudes, in which they are seen as quite similar. Indeed, the logic of taking and giving, of which these martial attitudes are a part, is the one thing that seems to unite the two sides of Frank and Saracen. But it is precisely giving and taking which is missing between Roland and his fellow Franks. Thus Roland is a threat when he breaks off reciprocity – he must be kept within the web of reciprocity. Meanwhile, the Saracens, as Roland himself suggests at the beginning of the epic, are a threat to the extent that there is too much reciprocity between them and the Franks (in the form of the peace gifts offered, and eventually in the relationship with Ganelon). One must not reciprocate with the exterior Other, lest it become too familiar, but one must always make sure to keep reciprocating with those of the interior, lest they become Other. The goal of the Franks (and the Saracens) might be stated as a desire to maintain a bi-partite (Christian/ Saracen, culture-based) alterity, lest there be a collapse into sameness (through reciprocity with Saracens), but with the fear that the very act of maintaining this form of alterity – in particular by the hero – may produce a disastrous tri-partite alterity, as the logic which initiates one non-reciprocity and one form of integrity (between groups) threatens to unleash a second non-reciprocity and integrity (between group and individual), since the individual hero uses the external other as the means to establish his own internal heterogeneity and alterity. Indeed, as seen in this chapter, the development of a triangular relationship is essentially an inherent feature of this culture of violent performativity. Here it is useful to return to the terms used by Marilyn Strathern to describe performative identity (Chapter 1): for effective social action, the Franks need to suppress internal differences and produce an at least temporary image of homogeneity and unitary group identity. They also need artificially to create heightened and simplistic binary oppositions between their own in-group and the out-group Saracens. Great investments are obviously required for both projects, but unfortunately, the investment in the second one works against the goals of the first one.[17] In a similar manner, while Roland seeks integrity, Ganelon resists Roland's impulse

[16] Kinoshita 2001 studies what she calls the "crisis of non-differentiation" that is enacted in the epic. Kinoshita however focuses on the female figures – especially Bramimonde – as the fulcrums around which issues of alterity are resolved, rather than Roland.

[17] Emily Alba argues that exactly this realization is a central feature of the Norman historiographic tradition, and of the Normans themselves – see Alba 2001:4, 24, 108, 137. More generally, see Akbari 2000 for another study of a tri-partite structure of medieval identities (Asia, Africa, Europe, versus the more recent West versus East).

and seeks to draw him back into a form of reciprocal relationship, but establishes another reciprocal relationship – with the Saracens – in order to do so. Thus the two great fears of the Franks – the creation of internal alterity, the loss of external alterity – are enacted, as the rest of the Frankish society passively watches events unfold. In trying to strengthen external alterity, Roland also produces internal alterity, while in trying to strengthen internal (personal) reciprocity, Ganelon also produces external (group) reciprocity.

From Roland's standpoint, however – that of the hero-individual, rather than the group – things appear differently, since his goal is to construct group-internal heterogeneity. Roland "needs" the Saracens. They are the medium by which he enacts his own heroic alterity. The Saracens are in a sense merely a tool for him to bring about his death: they are the necessary other by/against which his final, transcendent self-identity can be established. Thus the Franks are the victims as much of Roland as of the Saracens – the victims of a process of identity formation and transcendence where one Other (the Franks' own apotheosis) can only define himself against the Franks through the mechanism of a confrontation with the Franks' Other – the Saracens. Raoul, on the other hand, creates his own other group (the Vermandois brothers) by his attacks on their sacredly held monastery. In so doing, he also injects an element of religious alterity into his epic (appearing as anti-Christian to many critics), while constantly moving farther and farther away from his own relatives and followers as well.

Interestingly the early, fragmentary epic *Gormont and Isembart*, the preserved version of which dates from the early twelfth century at the latest, captures both types of alterity – internal rebel and external enemy – in the same person even more explicitly. The texts pits King Louis of France against the Saracen leader Gormont. Isembard is a rebellious French vassal who joins forces with Gormont. The epic is often classified as part of the "rebellious barons" cycle, but Isembard is also a religious apostate. He thus combines the figure of Raoul with the figure of the Saracen. When Gormont is killed by Louis, Isembard rallies the Saracen troops, only eventually to fall victim himself to the Franks. Yet, in a striking way, his death recalls that of no less a hero than Roland.[18] Though Isembard carries out his destructiveness as both rebel and Saracen, he converts back to Christianity in the end, dying surrounded by the iconography of redemption just as Roland does:

> La u chai li Margaris,
> au quarefor de treis chemins,
> lez un bruillet espés foilli,
> de Damne Deu li membra si. (ll. 628–31)

---

[18] This point has been widely recognized, and its significance for the relationship between the two epics widely debated. See Ashford 1984–5 for complete references on the discussion, and a useful summary of past and present research issues surrounding the poem.

> Guarda aval, en un larriz,
> e vit un olivier fuilli.
> Tant se travaille qu'il i vint;
> sor la fresche herbe s'est asis;
> contre orient turna sun vis. (ll. 655–9)

There where the daisy fell at the meeting of three paths, beside a thickly forested wood, he recalled the Lord God.

He looked downwards, towards a heath, and saw a leafy olive tree. With great effort he reached it; he sat down upon the fresh grass; and turned his face to the east.

Like Roland, Isembard dies in an idyllic natural setting, well-watered and green (the word "lariz" being used in both texts). The olive tree associates him with final redemption, as well as with the figure of Oliver in *The Song of Roland*. And like Roland, he makes sure to direct his final gaze in a symbolic direction, staging a death "tableau" for those who will find him. Yet as Bédier notes, virtually alone among the rebellious barons of Old French epic, he is a complete rebel, and receives no tomb in an abbey, unlike the other repentant rebellious rebels (Bédier 1914:86). He seems to be simultaneously hero and Other, inextricably intertwined.[19]

Other elements of this epic establish parallels between the epic of revolt and the "geste du roi" of which *Roland* is a part: as Oliver is driven to strike Roland (and Raoul strikes Bernier), Isembard strikes the one who is closest to him – his father in this case. This underlines the way his rebellion breaks the bonds of reciprocity, and also suggests that the Christian/Islam dynamic of external otherness can be replicated internally – in terms of allies, of lord and vassal, or of father and son (ll. 37–9). The Christians and Saracens are also militarily, as in *The Song of Roland*, hardly distinguishable at many moments – King Louis for example mourns for the dead Gormont (see also ll. 530–3, 540–2), so that the "enemy" is ambiguously similar to the Self. This ambiguity can be most fully appreciated once one realizes that Isembard is essentially insider and outsider simultaneously – rebellious baron turned Saracen, but also exemplary proponent of the logic of integrity.[20] He pursues the integrity of the hero like any good Christian, but reveals how the integrity which is the logical perfection of the heroic system also, at the limit, necessarily turns against the system's greater long-term interests if allowed to reach that limit.

---

[19] See also Nichols 1963 on this ambiguity.

[20] See van Emden 1964 on Isembart's status as a gratuitous rebel. In his lack of grounds for revolt (unlike later examples of the rebellious vassal cycle) he epitomizes the pure logic of supplementarity, one might say from our perspective.

The Dilemma of Identity and Alterity

Hidden in this dilemma seems to be a medieval realization that the mechanisms of alterity, which seem to be crucial to the identity of the group, could, or would ultimately destroy that group itself, since their logic in relation to the other group always applied internally to one's own group as well. Thus the medieval epic offers a vision of identity and difference which looks surprisingly like Homi Babha's depiction of the fractured identity of the colonizer in relation to the colonized (1994:121ff, 145ff), or, for a reference closer to the world of the gift, Marianna Torgovnick's psychological reading of Malinowski among the Trobrianders (Torgovnick 1990:230ff). Obviously, the warrior aristocrats were themselves potential colonizers of the Saracens, as well as of peoples internal to Europe.[21] The fractured "colonizing identity" seems to play itself out repeatedly in the epic. But it appears to be deeper than the issue of colonization, which implies power differentials. It seems to involve the issue of aggression itself, no matter what the victim may be – stronger or weaker, internal or external. In the *Coronation of Louis*, one sees alternating rebellions: first French nobles, then a foreign enemy, then more nobles, then more foreigners, then more nobles. One must wonder what the real ontological difference between these groups was. Does that epic recognize that the drive towards integrity among the warrior aristocracy was finally intimately similar to the threat of the external invader – that both constituted Others which could stand in for each other? Thus no matter how narrowly the in-group might be defined – all Christians, all aristocrats, all warriors, all warriors loyal to the king, a single lord and vassal or companion or relation (Raoul and Bernier, Roland and Oliver, Isembard and his father) – the medieval mechanisms for defining that in-group in relation to the outsider, as used by the warrior aristocracy – giving and taking, reciprocity and integrity – threatened to disrupt the group itself. The more the concept of the gift and integrity was used to maintain a strict difference between Self and Other, the more threatening it could become internally.[22] Clear distinctions between Self and Other often tend to collapse in this world where performative giving and taking constantly comingle solidarity and violence in the process of identity formation.

As anthropologist Marc Augé has suggested, the question of the subject

---

[21] Peter Haidu has suggested that the Saracens are at least in part stand-ins for the medieval Christian peasantry, who were kept in a position of (class-based) alterity similar to that of the Saracens, and by the same essential mechanisms – violence and forms of institutionalized taking in the form of the exploitation of seigneurial demesnes (1993:49–55). The threat of the peasant revolt was perhaps equal to the threat of the external invasion, and medieval sources make clear that the reaction to each was roughly equivalent. Indeed, during the later popular crusades, the ambivalence over who the real enemy is suggests as much. In any event, models of colonization could certainly be applied internally to Europe. See especially Bartlett 1993.

[22] See Michael Harney's analysis of *The Cid* and *Roland* in similar terms: he focuses on kinship/lineage models as the central point of conflict, but these models center on issues of heritable versus performative status, and he notes the fundamental link between "rivalry" and "camaraderie" in what he terms "feudal" society (1997:85).

within society, and the question of the social group in relation to "other" social groups are intimately connected, even homologous questions in all societies (Augé 1998).[23] In particular, using tropical West African examples, but arguing for general legitimacy, Augé says that these societies understand the "subject" as always being founded on elements of both "identity" and "relational alterity." Subjects always are defined on two axes – the self/in-group axis of "identity", and the self/out-group axis of "alterity." The medieval epic suggests that the typical warrior-aristocratic subject was conceived in terms of similar elements of identity and alterity.

Similar findings are reported by Charles Hinnant (2002:115–6) in his studies of reciprocity in Old Testament societies, where the "divided family becomes the basis for ethnic differentiation and conflict" (115) and where more generally "the classic loci of socialization ... become the loci of ethnic differentiation and strife" (116). Antonio Callari's critical analysis of gift theory (2002) points to an even broader problematic. He suggests that the gift, as a mode of social ordering based on performance, is fundamentally incongruent with western notions of "society" which would be based on social "order," social "systems," or notions of proper, stable attributes in things, persons or institutions. Marilyn Strathern has made similar arguments in her study of Melanesian societies (1988). Callari writes that "the deliverance of the gift must take place in a deconstructive relation to the very idea of the social" (2002:256), primarily due to "the gift's eroding effects on the very notion of borders" (256). The gift then becomes an "Other from which to keep perspective on the notion of the social" (256).

It is beyond the scope of this work to decide here whether such a model gets at an anthropological universal. It does certainly point provocatively in that direction, however. What is relevant here is the idea that the hero was a trope for thinking about the questions of identity and alterity on both a personal and social level, and that the notions of giving and taking were in a sense the functional operators which set this trope to work on both its axes – the hero/in-group axis, and the hero+in-group/out-group axis. More generally, this trope, which is so intimately bound up with the society of the medieval warrior aristocrats, does seem to offer the modern reader a form of alterity which can indeed provide a renewed perspective on the notion of the social, and on the fundamentally social (as opposed to simply cultural) alterity of medieval society in relationship to the modern, western world.

The trope is also particularly revealing because it shows how notions of alterity and identity, in the context of performativity, remain entangled with notions of the sacred and essential. While it is a commonplace that the early epics in general, and *Roland* in particular, were imbued with the crusading spirit, others have argued equally forcefully that the Saracens are primarily simply Other, and that the specific issues of competing religions, or the moral imperative of

[23] He states that "it is impossible to dissociate the problems of group identity from those of individual identity" (1998:43).

the Christian religion, are merely subsidiary or even absent sometimes (Daniel 1984). Yet the second viewpoint and the first are inseparable as thought through the trope of the hero. All others are most deeply Other in their non-sacred status in relation to the hero. Roland thus necessarily fights "for God," though it is unclear if he is really fighting for the Franks: he seems to work against both the Franks and the Saracens. It is equally unclear whether the Franks are fighting for God, at least until Roland ritually re-enacts the formation of the sacred through his vertical exchange with God, and provides the rest of the army with such a motivation. Only then do they abandon their hopes of reciprocity with the Saracens and re-embrace a collective sacred which provides a transcendent, collective unity for the formerly fragmented and at times even unenthusiastic main Frankish contingent. Roland's sacred integrity ultimately fuses the Christian and secular, Frankish elements into a single whole.[24]

---

[24] Laura Ashe (1999) makes a similar argument about the fusion of the Christian and the secular in the poem, pointing out that the notion of fidelity applies equally to God and feudal lords. She suggests that Roland eliminates the mediating role of the Church in favor of a direct correspondence between individual integrity (to use my word) and the sacred.

8

Female Integrity and Masculine Desires
in *The Nibelungenlied*

Introduction

In classic gift theory, the most central gift of all is the woman, given by men in marriage exchanges. In theory, women would play the same symbolic role as other gifts – being symbolic rewards for internally-driven accomplishments, as well as symbols of ties between men. In *The Song of Roland*, Oliver essentially treats his sister Aude this way in his dealings with Roland. As a corollary to this claim, the most central danger in a classical gift economy would be that men would begin to desire women themselves, and to be diverted from their masculine-oriented world of symbolic relationships and accomplishments. The woman would move from object to subject, and men's actions would become motivated by externally-oriented desires.

This description is really a simplistic caricature of classic gift theory. Recent studies have shown the many failures of this simplistic model to explain social process adequately (Barraud *et al.* 1994:102–3; Gregory 1982:33, 63; Strathern 1988), and medievalists have likewise pointed out the ways in which the exchange of women is much more problematic than such theories would suggest, especially in that the women are hardly passive objects, but rather socially active subjects themselves (Kay 1995:15ff). But the caricature has a long history, not just in recent anthropological theory, but in the broader theories of culture expounded in some Western literature. In particular, medieval epics of the later twelfth and early thirteenth centuries presented – or at least attempted to present to their audience – just such a reading of the world of courtliness and the world of the romance genre. These texts suggested that the courtly world was a place where symbolic economies were short-circuited, where people craved material commodities for their own sake, where individual men risked dis-integration due to a desire for women. The texts suggested that women had ceased to be dependent symbols, and had become independent commodities whose independence was epitomized in the (apparently) new development of female subjectivity. Though the texts thus recognized the truth that more recent anthropological theory has also discovered, they rewrote this truth as a particular product of a certain history and social organization, and thus left it in theory amenable to resistance or repression. In this cultural diagnosis of the time, society as a whole faced disintegration because women as subjects had come to intervene actively in relationships between men.[1]

The Middle High German *Nibelungenlied* participated in just such a representation, presenting the woman as dangerous because of her supposedly new-found subjective identity. In the text, the hero Siegfried, having already won for himself the virtually limitless treasure of the Nibelungs, sets out from his home in Xanten in order to marry Kriemhild, a Burgundian princess whose reputation has reached him from afar – though the text establishes from the beginning Kriemhild's reluctance to marry. He arrives in Worms, the capital of the Burgundians, and approaches King Gunther about his plans. Although initially hoping simply to take Kriemhild as a secondary symbol of his own honor, Siegfried ends up falling in love with her and pursuing her as an individual, in a fashion that recalls Courtly Love.

After helping the Burgundians defeat the Saxons, Siegfried travels with Gunther to Iceland, and while disguised as a servant, uses magical powers to help him defeat Queen Brunhild in battle, so that Gunther may take for a wife this woman who, like Kriemhild, is reluctant to marry and be subservient to a man. Upon returning to Worms, Siegfried again uses his powers to conquer Brunhild in the bridal chamber in order that Gunther may consummate the marriage, and, as we saw in Chapter 7, Siegfried takes the opportunity to steal Brunhild's girdle. Later however, Brunhild is dismayed to see that her husband's sister, Kriemhild, is married to a man whom she believes to be a mere servant. Feeling dishonored, Brunhild bitterly insults Kriemhild and her husband, and, indirectly, her new in-laws also. The disputes between the two women over the honor they have through marriage escalate until Kriemhild pulls out Brunhild's girdle, proving that Siegfried supposedly dishonored her on her wedding night. Enraged, Brunhild plots with Gunther's brother Hagen to have Siegfried killed. Once Siegfried is dead, Kriemhild marries Etzel of Hungary, and invites the Burgundians to visit her in Hungary in order to have her revenge. She calls on her followers to destroy the Burgundians as part of their duty to her, and a holocaust is precipitated in which virtually everyone on both sides is killed. The Old German hero Hildebrand finally kills Kriemhild out of shock at seeing her take a sword and kill the bound and defenseless Hagen.

The text is most interesting in that it allows female subjective identity to develop to its maximal extent, so that the woman – Kriemhild – becomes a hero in pursuit of integrity just like a masculine hero. In so doing, it takes the surprising step of gendering the pursuit of integrity as feminine. Thus in this text, the two great dangers of the gift system – the integrity drive and the temptation of commodification – come together in a single, specifically Other figure: written out of the world of male heroism, these dangers are written onto the person of the

---

[1] See McCracken 1998 (on romance) and Kay 1995 (on epic as well as romance) for recent studies of the way in which this threat of the female subject was treated more generally at this time.

female protagonist, who both pursues integrity and also becomes a commodified source of desire for the male hero. In this chapter, we will explore the implications of this classificatory gesture for the end of the traditional society of the warrior aristocracy, the rise of romance, and the creation of a Western, feminine Other whose double becomes the Saracen princess.

The Epic Reads the Romance

The epic genre in the Middle Ages has always been conceptualized as prior to the romance genre, at least until quite recently. For this reason, literary historians often talk of the "contamination" of the epic by the (later) romance, whereas discussions of contamination of romance by the epic are in comparison much rarer.[2] Yet Sarah Kay has argued persuasively that later French epics (later twelfth- and thirteenth-century, for example) must always be read in dialogic relationship to the romances of the same period, since the two genres were fundamentally contemporaneous. The central dialogue which she locates in these texts is that of the poetics of the gift (epic) opposed to the poetics of the commodity (romance) (Kay 1995).

The argument in the present study would seem partially to contradict Kay's claims, in that it suggests that the axis of the gift shifted over time from opposition to non-reciprocal violence to opposition to the commodity. This shift certainly seems to have occurred, and it was due to changing socioeconomic patterns in the lives of the warrior aristocracy. But it represented only a relative shift in the importance of the two oppositional axes. The issue of commodification was always present in the discourse of the gift, and its importance in the Norman chronicles of the eleventh and very early twelfth centuries was clear. And, at least in the Germanic tradition, early forms of the romance genre itself had a long traditional history, in the guise of the bride-quest narrative (Andersson 1987). Thus Kay's argument can certainly be accepted, however with the key proviso of a relative shift in emphasis of the discourse of the gift over time.

Once one accepts the necessity of a dialogic reading, the key task is to determine what the two dialogues were, and how each genre talked to the other. Kay suggests that the romance tended to receive and respond to the epic through mechanisms of exclusion – the violence of the gift, for example, is suppressed (Kay 1995). Following up on this suggestion, one finds that the epic, in contrast, often read the romance through strategies of inclusion: it explicitly presented a romance-type world within its confines, and then critiqued and "contained" it ideologically. This is the real reason why modern readers have often talked of the contamination of the epic by the romance, while discussions of the contamination of the romance by the epic have been rarer.

---

[2] See Hoffmann 1987 for a historical perspective on the question of the epic and/or romance character of *The Nibelungenlied*.

The Nibelungenlied (specifically the text of the B manuscript), is a perfect exemplar of supposedly old, heroic, epic-like material supposedly contaminated by newer, romance-like sensibilities.[3] But one should not fall into the trap of seeing the "essence" of the B-manuscript as "old" and the romance contamination as "new." Rather, one must recognize that the B-manuscript of *The Nibelungenlied*, dating from 1190–1210, is itself already an explicit response to a romance influence which flourished in Germany beginning with the court epics and romances of the 1170s, produced by such figures as Henrike von Veldeke. The epic heroism of the text is thus already conditioned by that romance influence, and the romance courtliness in the text is already a rereading and re-presentation of that influence by the text as well.

Even more importantly, one must not fall into the trap of reifying practices of epic-like heroism or romance-like courtliness in the German world of the twelfth and early thirteenth centuries. Jerold Frakes has argued (1994) that *The Nibelungenlied* is perhaps the most politicized and propagandistic of all Middle High German texts. From this epic perspective, courtliness is simply a new type of discourse of commodification which replaced earlier ones. This is not to diminish the true novelties of the evolution of courtliness (see Jaeger 1995). But as read by the epic, the courtly becomes essentially a site where commodification can be (re)located.

In this vein, the argument here is that the text presents the world of courtly romance – and particularly the role of women within that world – as its Other. This other – itself a product of the ideological energies of the text – then serves as the "Other in the Present" which allows for the writing of History: in particular for the classic gesture of writing – that is, inventing – a History "Before the Other." The text first represents its social milieu in terms of a binary conflict of Self and Other, and then effectively reproduces the synchronic conflict in diachronic terms, in order to give historical priority to one partner in the conflict, and more fundamentally, in order to invent an epic past defined specifically in relation to an (invented) romance present.

While the dynamic of alterity just presented seems to differ radically from that found in previous epics examined, its underlying structure is quite similar, though with a crucial difference. The woman is presented as a threat parallel to that posed by the hero, in that she seeks integrity in relation to the men around her. She is thus another example of a form of socially internal alterity and non-reciprocity whose rise must be short-circuited and suppressed, like that of the hero – in this case, by making her an object of exchange and not allowing her to become a subject. Conversely, once the woman does become an independent

---

[3]   There are three thirteenth-century manuscripts of the text. Of these, A is shorter, and seems to have some stanzas deleted, but seems otherwise related to the B manuscript. C is longer, but has missing folio leaves, and also shows evidence of revisions. Virtually all of the manuscripts of the text have the later *Diu Klage* attached at the end, which was clearly a response to the original text. The B manuscript has come to be accepted by most as the standard version of the text.

subject – a commodity which is no longer in a secondary, symbolic relationship to men, but rather functions as a source of desire – then she is treated as a form of socially external alterity. Therefore – like the Saracen – she becomes someone with whom one should avoid exchanging. The figure of the woman in *The Nibelungenlied* thus collapses the roles of external and internal alterity into a single figure.

The Hero Distracted: Ambiguities of Epic and Romance

The Nibelungenlied opens with Siegfried's quest for Kriemhild, with whom he has fallen in love from afar. His decision to seek her out seems initially to be a classic instance of the romance bride-quest, carried out by the infatuated lover, and indeed, the first half of the text has consistently been judged to be more romance-like than the second half. Theodor Andersson in particular has showed its very close analogues with the Germanic bride-quest genre (1987).

But Siegfried's motives for the quest seem actually to resemble those of a typical epic-type hero when examined more closely. In particular, it is unclear whether he is more in love with Kriemhild herself – or at least the social representation of her, since he has never seen her, and will not for his first year in Worms – or with the honor and prestige which would accrue to him for winning such a prize. In the latter instance, one would say that Siegfried is more in love with himself and his own reputation than with Kriemhild. If such is the case, then Kriemhild must remain purely symbolic in order not to be a threat to Siegfried's integrity.

Siegfried's initial behavior indeed points towards this latter interpretation. His arrival at Worms is marked by a military challenge to Kriemhild's brothers, and Siegfried's primary interest seems to be in provoking an antagonistic response in order to gain honor in overcoming it. As seen in Chapter 5, he goes out of his way to create escalation in a manner quite similar to Beowulf or Roland, thus augmenting the difficulty of his task, as well as the amount of honor to be gained (p. 29).[4] Those at Worms point out explicitly to Gunther that "iu hât der starke Sîvrit unverdienet widerseit" (st. 116) ("mighty Siegfried has challenged you without provocation," p. 30). Were Siegfried understood as being motivated principally by love for Kriemhild, it is unclear why he would go out of his way to make his task more difficult. But if Kriemhild is conceived at least initially as a symbolic object, meant as a secondary testimony to Siegfried's primary achievement of heroic conquest, then his actions make more sense. And in fact, Siegfried announces not that he has come for Kriemhild, but rather to take "lant

---

    4   Pages numbers refer to the translation by Hatto (1969) listed in the bibliography, which is in prose format.

unde bürge" (st. 110) ("your lands and your castles," p. 29) – no mention is made of Kriemhild at all.

This moment is only the culmination of a series of developments. Siegfried in his youth is described as of "ellenthaften muot" (st. 21) ("put[ting] his strength to the test") in an apparently aggressive manner, since no mention is made of defensive necessity. He "versuochte vil der rîche" (st. 21) ("tried the mettle of many kingdoms," p. 20), the text adds. Regarding his first interest in Kriemhild, he says,

> ... sô wil ich Kriemhilden nemen,
> Die schoenen juncfrouwen von Burgonden lant
> durch ir unmâzen schoene. daz ist mir wol bekant,
> nie keiser wart sô rîche, der wolde haben wîp,
> im zaeme wol ze minner der rîchen küneginne lip. (st. 48–9)

> I shall *take* Kriemhild ... on account of her very great beauty, since even if the mightiest of emperors wished to marry, I know he would not demean himself in loving the noble princess.
>
> (p. 23, my italics)

Kriemhild is thus valuable due to the symbolic capital that accrues to the possessor/taker of such a valuable prize – Siegfried is concerned above all with social status. He goes on to say "swaz ich friuntlîche niht ab in erbit,/ daz mac sus erwerben mit ellen dâ mîn hant./ ich trouwe an in ertwingen beide liut unde lant" (st. 55) ("Whatever I fail to get from them by friendly requests, I shall take by my own valour. I fancy I shall wrest their lands and people from them," p. 24). Siegfried moves quickly from request to force, and his use of the word "fancy" suggests that the latter possibility is more to his liking. Furthermore, the focus shifts here from Kriemhild herself to "lands and people," by which he seems to mean the entire kingdom – of whose taking Kriemhild will be the symbol. Siegfried then echoes Roland in refusing his father's offer of additional knights to accompany him, choosing only twelve companions (st. 59; p. 24).

The text thus presents strong evidence for a performative view of the nature of authority and kingship, and its symbolic expression.[5] Following Siegfried's

---

[5]   See Bekker 1971 for an analysis of the interconnected roles of symbols and performance in the text which is perhaps the closest to the one I present here. He focuses in particular on the importance of the treasure and the Tarnkappe, as a "natural symbol" (106, and 104–6 more generally). He connects these to the "strength and wealth" (103–4) – in other words, taking and giving – which are crucial to the performance of kingship, which he argues predominates over essential kingship (71–4). He argues that Brunhild and Siegfried incarnate these qualities, but that Siegfried's inordinate love for Kriemhild leads him to violate kingship, and more particularly to violate "the adherence to symbols" (113) which is the essence of the social order (112–7). Siegfried is thus seduced by Kriemhild – who tends to value "the outward mark" (56) over the inner quality, and is therefore in our terms anti-symbolic – and the fateful argument between the two women is really a confrontation of symbolic and anti-symbolic tendencies (55–7).

challenge in Worms, the stage is thus set for an epic confrontation of warriors. Yet this does not occur. Try as Siegfried might to provoke a response, Gunther and his vassals refuse to take the bait, and Siegfried "dô gedâhte ouch ... an die hêrlîchen meit" (st. 123) ("was mollified by thoughts of lovely Kriemhild," p. 30). After they also agree to share everything they have with him – as hosts – he "wart ... ein lützel sanfter gemuot" (st. 127) ("was somewhat appeased," p. 31).

This opening scene must be read as fraught with irony and even farce. Indeed, it sets up the remainder of the epic in this way. From a courtly perspective, Siegfried comes across as a young, socially-inept and over-eager gunfighter, anxious to test his mettle yet again, trying over and over to provoke anger in the face of generosity and prudence. He finally turns out to be content with good hospitality and thoughts of the pretty girl, as if the preceding confrontation had been all bluster and bluff, more an act learned and aped from too many westerns – or epics – than from an innate desire for battle. But Siegfried is in fact a tried and tested knight, and a very dangerous one at that. Hagen has already recounted the tale of his virtual invincibility. Thus in a sense he more closely resembles a young, dangerously sociopathic gunfighter, who truly needs to be mollified by those older and wiser. Temporarily assuaged, one nevertheless waits for him to explode at any moment. At least from the perspective of courtly society, which will try to deal with him "mit zühten" (st. 120) ("courteously," p. 30), he is a dangerous mixture of epic-like aggression and youthful simplicity and naiveté – a much darker version of a young Percival.

But from the perspective of a warrior aristocracy, the scene appears equally ironic or even farcical. Faced with a single knight and twelve companions, standing in their own court, surrounded by all their countrymen, Gunther, his brothers, and his vassals back down from the challenge, again and again. As the text goes on, one begins to appreciate more and more what is hinted at here – the cowardice, inadequacy, and prevarication that characterizes the entire family and the entire court, especially Gunther. Indeed, in the very next adventure, Siegfried fights off the invading Saxons while Gunther waits back at court for news of events. Such behavior, from an epic perspective, looks like high farce, on the model of King Louis in the Old French William of Orange cycle. Thus the adjective "courteous" almost immediately acquires a very ambiguous, even derogatory tone in the text. Romance seems to mock epic, and epic to mock romance.

Yet such a simple binary opposition obscures the true degree of ambiguity. The exemplar of heroism turns out to be more than willing to play along with all the romance luxury and verbosity in order to have a chance to get the girl. If Siegfried is meant to serve as a rebuke to courtly softness, he is not a straightforward success, to put it mildly. Theodor Andersson has shown that several of the details discussed above in relation to heroic gratuity – refusing help, taking only twelve peers, for example – are also motifs of the bride-quest genre. Siegfried's true status and generic identity remain in question. The inter-generic tension between heroic epic and bride-quest, which seems simultaneously to parody each genre, captures the tension that surrounds Siegfried.[6] The text largely works out the implications of this opening scene in its critique of what it represents as contemporary courtliness and contemporary, fallen heroism.

Another example of Siegfried's ambiguous – and increasingly less heroic – status occurs after the battle with the Saxons is over: Siegfried is ready to depart, but decides to linger, essentially "durch der schoenen willen gedâhte er noch bestân,/ ob er si gesehen möhte" (st. 260) ("for the sake of the lovely young woman whom he hoped to be able to meet," p. 45). By the following chapter, it is clear that Siegfried is truly in love with Kriemhild herself – not as symbolic prize, but as an object of desire. The standard vocabulary of courtly love (Middle High German "minne") is used to describe his reactions to her (Av. 5; pp. 48–49). Siegfried completely fails in his role as integral hero, giving in to the temptation of commodity, which in the discourse of the hero must lead to the loss of the self. The final lines of this fifth adventure state that "wan daz in twanc ir minne: diu gap im dicke nôt./ dar umbe sît der küene lac vil jaemerlîche tôt" (st. 324) ("he was tormented by the passion she aroused in him, thanks to which, in days to come, the hero met a pitiful end," p. 52). Edward Haymes (1986:57–8) has noted a pun in st. 556, 2–4 where Siegfried accepts a gift from Kriemhild (which already raises suspicions within the logic of giving and receiving), wherein the pun (holt/holde) plays on Siegfried's status as "holde" (servant) in relation to Kriemhild – a point which the gift itself already makes clear.[7] Siegfried receives – and compromises integrity.

Ultimately, "farce" is too strong a word to apply to these scenes. I have exaggerated towards both ends of the spectrum somewhat in order to bring out the full potential implications involved. In reality, the scenes are a delicate balance of tragic irony and a type of "court envy" which seems fully capable of understanding Siegfried's temptations, even as it laments them and their supposed results. In a similar manner, the text tracks the intricate exchanges of the gift economy as it continues to operate in the courtly milieu, yet also examines the ways in which that economy is gradually losing its legitimacy. In particular, it shows the ways that the gift is losing its symbolic status and becoming more and more a part of the economy of the Real, in parallel to the problem of the hero and heroic culture. For example, gifts are as often given out of a position of need on the part of the donor – "buying help" one might say from another perspective – as from integrity. And recipients get gifts as often to motivate their action – "getting paid to act" from another perspective – as to reward it. Moreover, in

---

[6] For a similar reading of Siegfried as fundamentally ambiguous in his position as both epic hero and courtly knight, see Müller 2002:72–3.

[7] Haymes 1986, Ch. 5 presents a good general analysis of Siegfried's compromised position. He picks up on the focus in Bekker 1971 on symbolic economy, and argues that the text must be understood in the context of questions of dynastic stability which require stable symbols.

many cases, those doing the giving have acquired the things given not through
conquest or taking, but rather through theft or some other impropriety, so that the
gift has no authority or symbolic value behind it. And finally, many things which
should conceivably remain symbolic become commodified – most importantly,
Kriemhild. Not only is Siegfried guilty in this regard, but so too are Gunther
(most notably in the acquisition of his wife), Hagen (in his theft of Kriemhild's
treasure) and the Hunnish court (whose loyalty is bought by Kriemhild).

The men in the text seem especially upset at the idea of a female becoming an
acting subject in the gift economy. Yet they themselves are undermining the gift
economy in every other sense apparently without realizing it. Kriemhild is just
the most obvious and salient symbol of this corrosion, from the text's conservative perspective. The first half of the text, while fascinated by the world of the
court, ultimately contains and critiques that world: in one of the most elegiac
scenes of medieval literature, Siegfried goes on a hunting expedition and engages
in a magnificent display of martial prowess and gratuitous taking (of which the
hunt is a general symbol), but the death of the hero, which is expected after
such a moment of apotheosis, turns out to be literally a treacherous stab in the
back. Instead of the transcendence and access to the sacred which is linked to
the death of the hero in earlier epics, there is a sardonic indictment of the courtly
world, dominated by "von zweier frouwen bâgen" (st. 876) ("the wrangling of
two women," p. 118). The indictment is clearly extended to Hagen, Gunther, and
the world of the court of Worms more generally, and it is less the quarreling of
the women than the way in which the men let this quarreling become central to
their own motivations which seems to be at issue here.

Women Seeking Integrity

Despite this general indictment of men and their interest in things in themselves,
the text gradually focuses more and more of its indictment on the women. It uses
the discourse of reciprocity and integrity in order to elaborate this indictment:
the central critique of both Brunhild and Kriemhild is that they themselves aspire
not just to personhood, but to integrity.

Whereas earlier epics depict the dangers of such aspirations for any character,
this text focuses specifically on the dangers when a woman is involved – thus
displacing the general danger of integrity desires onto the figure of the female.
This is a crucial maneuver, because it suggests that the problem of integrity is the
result of a supposed "rise" of the female subject in the context of court culture,
rather than being a problem endemic to the epic world. It also focuses attention
on the female as actor, thus helping to "forget" the role of masculine desires in
the dilemma; and it finally suggests that the men's succumbing to the temptation of the commodity (including the woman) is a function of newfound female
subjecthood as well. Numerous scholars have noted that if Kriemhild followed
the same strategy as a man, she would be beyond reproach within the logic of

heroic culture.[8] But this perception simply points indirectly to the strategy of the text: to re-represent the integrity drive as a specifically female perversion, to which men are subjected, rather than as a general dynamic of the culture. And a further mechanism of that subjection is then supposedly the "courtly" promotion of commidifying desires. For the text, courtliness produces dangerous, integrity-seeking women, and also produces the commodity-desires that make men fall victim to them. Meanwhile the fact that courtliness (that is to say, commodification) is itself the product of quintessentially masculine desires is conveniently obscured, just as masculine integrity drives were.

Jan-Dirk Müller has pointed out that Kriemhild is unique in the text in the degree to which her subjective personhood is elaborated. He argues that while all the other characters must be understood as performing themselves within ever-changing social contexts, in such a way that they are more products of the contextual milieu than stable individuals, Kriemhild successfully resists the social roles which are imposed upon her, so as to become a consistent, internally-directed individual (2002:90–1, 123–5). He speaks of her "radikalen Verinnerlichung und Individualisierung" (2002:101–2). This is exactly what has been found in this book to be the characteristic mark of the integral hero – or at least, of those desiring such an identity.

Less clearly recognized has been the way in which desire for escape from performative identity cannot be dissociated from an escape from the exchange system wherein such identity is negotiated. This desire for escape is clearly enacted through the women's relations to treasures as sources of a limitless giving which would provide them with independence and integrity. The threat of the two women, as potentially integral figures with endless treasures is clearly recognized by the masculine figures. The text presents over and over scenes where men seem intent on destroying women's ability to give: once Brunhild has lost her competition with the disguised Siegfried and must marry, her treasure is given away far too liberally by Hagen's brother as they prepare to return to Worms, and she protests that she will have nothing left (st. 515–8; pp. 73–4); upon his marriage with Kriemhild, Siegfried acts to prevent his wife from receiving a dowry which would give her an independent source of wealth (st. 694–5; p.95), and she likewise protests; Kriemhild's treasure from Siegfried is stolen by her brothers (Av. 19). Gunther objects that "ir ist lîp und guot" (st. 1129) ("she is mistress of her person and property," p. 148), and this is exactly what troubles Hagen. Women's potential to be actors in the gift society is strenuously resisted by the most astute men (especially Hagen), who typically appropriate the women's wealth for the purpose of their own giving.

Kriemhild meanwhile also recognizes the possibilities of the same dynamic of the gift: though initially very reluctant to remarry (she is ironically encouraged by her own brothers), when she does reach the point of making the final

---

[8]   See Frakes 1994 for a historical survey of scholarly opinion on Kriemhild which closely matches my perspective here.

decision she "bat ... got vil dicke füegen ir den rât,/ daz si ze gebene hête golt silber une wât, sam ê bî ir manne, dô er noch was gesunt" (st. 1247) ("prayed to God again and again to vouchsafe to her the means of bestowing gifts of gold, silver, and fine clothes as she had done when her husband was alive," p. 160). She hesitates yet again, but finally yields when Rudiger promises her service and loyalty (st. 1255–7; p. 161) – in other words, the very things which the gifts would have functioned to obtain. She justifies her decision on the basis of this service, and on the wealth of Etzel which will allow her to attract additional warriors (st. 1259–60; p. 162). She immediately turns to her remaining stores of treasure and begins to reward Rudiger, but again, Hagen makes every effort to ensure that this remaining source of power be confiscated and given away by her brothers (st. 1268–77; pp. 163–4). The metaphorical violation of integrity here – a metaphorical rape, in essence – occurs when "dô kom ir bruoder Gêrnot hin zir kmeren gegân./ Mit gewalt des küneges den slüzzel stiez er an die tür" (st. 1276–7) ("Kriemhild's brother Gernot came to the door of her Treasury and thrust the key 'mit gewalt' ('with violence') into the door in the King's name," p. 164). The scene echoes the actual rape of Brunhild which, though concluded by Gunther, was enabled entirely by Siegfried. It also reveals the true nature of the masculine, commodifying desires which lie at the basis of the true crisis of the German warrior aristocracy.

Note that all of these scenes occur in relation to questions of marriage. This is no accident, for the issue of marriage is intimately tied to that of integrity. In particular, the desire not to marry is explicit in the text for both characters (Kriemhild: st. 17/p. 18; the entire trip to Iceland is of course required by Brunhild's reluctance to submit to marriage, and we have already seen her resistance to the marriage bed). It is a specifically female version of the integrity drive seen in male heroes. Neither character is able to avoid marriage in the end. Both end up marrying Siegfried – one directly, the other indirectly. Both are conquered by the one potential emblem of masculine integrity in the epic.

The fact that Siegfried lies at the nexus of the problem of integrity for all three characters is crucial. Siegfried's wrestling with Brunhild in order to allow her husband Gunther to consummate their marriage is overtly to prevent her from "tragen gelpfen muot" (st. 673) ("becoming an 'uppish' woman," p. 92), but more fundamentally, it is to ensure her reintegration into the male-dominated exchange system, from which only male heroes – not women – can aspire to escape. Siegfried appears to be the enforcer of an imperative of exchange much like that which Lévi-Strauss identifies in the incest taboo: women must not be kept (or keep themselves); they must enter into relations of reciprocity (controlled by men).

But as Kriemhild's metaphorical rape by her brother suggests, it is ironically the men who are incestuous. Whereas Lévi-Strauss never explains why one would want to avoid exchange, this text implicitly offers such a theoretical explanation: incest looks less like a desire to avoid exchange than a form of commodity-desire which wants to treat – and keep – the female as a sexual object, rather than using her as a vehicle for establishing relationships between men. A corollary to this commodifying tendency is the desire to obtain wealth in a highly illegitimate, non-honorable form, so that the symbolic content of the wealth is nil. Incest means turning tools of symbolic exchange into objects of desire. From the text's conservative, misogynistic perspective, incest is a form of "distraction" where male desire for the thing itself intervenes to destroy the gift system which is the basis of the masculine order. And Siegfried's rape of Brunhild is, on closer consideration, an example of the same phenomenon.

Siegfried's act in defense of male control of the system of reciprocity and integrity is fundamentally compromised due to the fact that he too is motivated by desire for a commodity. He acts out of a desire to help Gunther – and to submit himself to Gunther – in order to obtain Kriemhild. He denies to a woman the right to maintain or pursue integrity, but he does this as part of a strategy to abandon his own integrity. The irony, and the incestuous relationship with his future brother-in-law's wife, suggest the fraudulence of the text's more overt desire to blame women's subjecthood and pursuit of integrity for the problems of the warrior aristocracy.

Kriemhild initially manages to ignore Siegfried's compromised position as a quite unheroic dependent of Gunther. She has every reason to do so because her marriage to him will allow her access to the inexhaustible treasure of the Nibelungs. With this treasure indirectly in hand, she can give endlessly (through her husband), and thus has access to what is essentially the mark of the sacred in the text. She and Siegfried now share in the possibility of the unreciprocable gift. Once the situation is understood in terms of issues of integrity, it becomes apparent that Kriemhild's argument with Brunhild over Siegfried's true standing at court (Av. 14) is really an argument about the status of his – and her – integrity. Is Siegfried an integral hero, or is he a trickster who compromises his integrity for the sake of commodity-desire? The argument is essentially the moment when she must confront the compromised nature of Siegfried's own integrity – and therefore sacrality. Kriemhild initially seems to win the argument, in the sense that her display of Brunhild's ring and girdle leave Brunhild unable to respond further. By this point in the text however, Siegfried's compromised, ambiguous status has become more and more obvious, and his gratuitous, heroic gestures (such as the stealing of Brunhild's ring and girdle) more and more problematic. That act, while quintessentially gratuitous, is of course also directed as much at a woman – and performed for another woman – as it is for any of the men in the court. The "evidence" that Kriemhild cites to support her claim for Siegfried's continued integrity is fundamentally compromised by the way in which it was obtained – secretly and deceptively, but most importantly, while in the service of another.

More generally, it begins to appear as if the tables have been turned, in such a way that integrity, theft of integrity and performance of integrity all center on the female characters. In fact, Stephanie Pafenberg (1995) argues that Siegfried is killed due to a fear of Kriemhild and her power. In other words, the man is the symbolic extension of the woman's integrity, and one attacks her through him. The situation is arguably actually less straightforward, though it seems clear that the assault on Siegfried is an assault motivated by a fear of the potential of integrity, in which Kriemhild will share. To a very important extent, the "quarreling of two women" thus really is at the center of this world. The statement remains misogynist, but not in the straightforward sense that it misrepresents the events of the text as being the fault of the women. The text really does present the women as the central actors: the misogyny lies in the text's suggestion that the world it presents to the listener/reader faithfully represents the dynamics and gender of the integrity drive in the world of the medieval warrior aristocracy.

The text ends up implicitly suggesting that men would, in the absence of "subjectified" women acting out their own, independent desires, engage in exchanges centering on homosocial solidarity and peacefulness, but that courtliness has disrupted this process and unleashed a flood of violence. It elides the role of masculine desire in this courtly world, and instead focuses on the issue of female subjecthood. It thus displaces all the problems of the integrity-drive and violence which caused so much tension in the world of the warrior aristocracy, onto women as Other. And it rewrites the synchronic dilemma of the warrior aristocracy diachronically, suggesting that what was endemic to that world – the instability and violence of agressive masculine performance – was actually the result of a historical evolution away from that world and towards courtly culture, which let women get "uppish." Perhaps the strongest case for this rewriting is made indirectly by Theodor Andersson. He notes that five substantial episodes were apparently added to *The Nibelungenlied* text which were not a part of the hypothetical original "Ältere Not" (1987:124ff). He describes all five of these episodes as centering on "companionship"(125), "friendship" (126), "loyalty" (129), and "solidarity" (129, 130). Indeed Andersson argues that the central theme of the second part of the text is Hagen's "social re-integration" (133). In his – and many other – interpretations, the text itself diachronically moves more and more from the strife of men to the re-integration of masculine homosocial values and the condemnation of women for the disruption of those values.

While this accurately reflects the ideological and rhetorical strategy of the text, it does not capture the true labor done by it, which is gradually to repress and "forget" a (predominantly) masculine desire and the inherent paradox of the performative culture of the warrior aristocracy. The two fundamental dangers for the stability of the warrior aristocracy's symbolic economy were the drive to integrity, and the contrary, anti-symbolic desire for the thing itself. The epic genre could generally be said to be the exploration of this first danger, while romance broadly conceived, including the bridal romance, was in part an exploration of the second concern. Andersson has shown that the bride-quest genre has very ancient Germanic roots, and thus that a form of desire for the woman herself and literary depiction of this desire is almost as old as the heroic lay (1987:56–60). *The Nibelungenlied* essentially represses both problems, or at least writes them out of the ideal history of the warrior aristocracy: the integrity drive is depicted as a recent outcome of (foreign) romance tendencies which excessively empower the woman, and the bride-quest is effectively parodied and destroyed as an effective counternarrative. To the extent that bride-quest narratives succeeded (as they typically did), they offered a counternarrative to that of the heroic lay. But as Andersson notes (1987:86–8), the first half of *The Nibelungenlied* consistently parodies the bride-quest, and this quest ultimately fails. The text thus inscribes, contains, and destroys the legitimacy of this counternarrative, metaphorically clearing the past of all but a purified ethos of heroism contaminated by neither the danger of commodification nor the threat of integrity drives.

The Nibelungenlied's forward narrative momentum thus ironically represents a metaphorical return to a purely heroic past (in some imagined future), while at the same time suggesting the impossibility or at least great difficulty of such a return in a heroic world catastrophically disrupted by female agency epitomized by romance courtliness. In the strategy of this text, powerful female subjects in the present only serve to erase the notion or memory of powerful female subjects in the past, and potentially in the future as well, and these subjects' agency serves as a form of alterity against which proper masculine and feminine relationships of exchange and integrity can be implicitly defined.

There are of course real historical reasons why more powerful female agents might appear in epics and romances of the thirteenth century[9] – and why they might be perceived as the potentially most persuasive figure of Otherness. These historical changes are reflected most clearly in the medieval German responses to the B-text of *The Nibelungenlied*. The C-text, the *Klage*, and the *Kudrun* are all essentially attempts to rewrite the figure of the woman (Kriemhild) in far more sympathetic terms, and to oppose the conservative ideological project of the B-text. The very fact that these later texts rewrite Kriemhild so clearly is perhaps the best medieval testament for understanding the B-text as a conservative and – to many – objectionable attempt at othering.

The Repression of Male Desire

The integrity drive, as we have seen in this book, is simply the other side of a deeper insecurity – the unstable nature of performative identity. While the instability of this type of identity produced great stresses on individuals, it also produced similar stresses for the society of the warrior aristocracy as a whole, and could be highly disruptive to that society at times. In *The Nibelungenlied*, the transference of the problem of integrity – as well as commodification – onto Woman and History is simply the other side of the text's suppression of the true nature of masculine identity formation. This gesture of suppression is far from being unique to *The Nibelungenlied*. It is largely replicated in the treatment of the Saracen princess in medieval French epic. Several scholars have noted that

---

9   See McCracken 1998, especially the Introduction.

the Saracen princesses who appear so commonly in these epics are highly disruptive figures, and that the thing they most commonly disrupt is conceits of individual and cultural identity as imagined by masculine protagonists (Kay 1995,
especially pp. 47, 131, 137; Kinoshita 1995, 1001; Ramey 2001).

In discussing the mid-twelfth-century *Conquest of Orange*, which like *The
Nibelungenlied* features an interesting and powerful female protagonist, and
which also looks very much like a "courtly romance" epic, Sharon Kinoshita
argues that the Saracen princess is "the site of the excess that effaces the absolute
opposition between Christianity and heathendom" (1995:271).[10] In other words,
the Saracen princesses – both as self-fulfilled, integral Muslim, female figures,
and as sources of desire among Christian men – tend to break down radical us/
them distinctions upon which individual and social identity – especially masculine – are supposedly founded. The project of such scenes could be seen from
two perspectives. On the one hand, they parallel *The Nibelungenlied* in that they
write responsibility for commodifying, socially-disruptive desires as well as the
dangerous pursuit of integrity onto the Other. Conversely, they can be read as
forcing the patriarchal society of the warrior aristocracy to confront the reality
of the violent desires which other texts try to suppress, and as pointing out that
these desires always have a valence which treats or renders fellow warrior-aris-
tocrats as potentially Other.

But as we saw in Chapters 5 through 7, the hero himself – Roland, prototypi-
cally – represents just that same excess or surplus, and his ultimate function is
likewise to efface differences between himself and the Saracens (for the Franks,
at least), while highlighting how integrity-drives can produce an internal alterity
which always threatens the coherence of Frankish society. In *The Nibelungenlied*
as well as in the *Conquest of Orange*, following Kinoshita's argument, the woman
has replaced the hero as the trope – and source – of disruptive desire. But while
The Nibelungenlied focuses on the woman as both desirer of integrity and source
of masculine desire for the commodity, the romance genre focuses much more on
the second feature, though the origin of masculine desire is still is closely linked
to the depiction of full female subjecthood. This shift towards the romance model
(with texts such as *The Nibelungenlied* and the *Conquest* as intermediate forms)
would appear to be a fundamental turning point in the history of medieval and
indeed western society; it marks the point at which the integrity drive is seen as
less socially threatening than the temptations of commodification incarnated in
the woman.

Thus Roland, Kriemhild, and the Saracen princess are all written or composed
"out of" or "away from" the identity of the audience and onto an Other. As seen
earlier, the epic as a ritual performance seeks to render the hero "other", as a
response to potentially destructive masculine desires. It recognizes the legitimacy of those desires, but seeks to isolate, express and contain them by brack-

---

[10] See also Kinoshita 2001 on the similar role of the Saracen queen in *The Song of
Roland*.

eting them within a public, ritual space. The strategy is to make other in the texts what risks being enacted in real life. Yet the texts are quite forthright about the fact that the Other is an internal product of the society itself. The Saracen princess, the figure of Kriemhild – and the female source of desire more generally – serve conversely to disguise a form of masculine desire for the commodity which is otherwise all too readily recognizable. Rather than bringing a danger to light, Kriemhild and the Saracen Princess both hide a very visible danger, and allow it to be sublimated through conversion to Christianity, or brutally excised through death. From a post-colonial perspective, however, that which fascinates in the female, Saracen Other as well as in Kriemhild can be seen as the missing component of the Self which has been written out of the Self's identity – the desire for the commodity, and the desire for integrity.[11]

The similar "writing out" of the desire for integrity explains the fascination and desire directed towards the medieval hero as the figure of wholeness, who contains a missing, anchoring component of the Self in the form of his absolute integrity. But the very completeness of the hero's identity implicitly points to the need for incomplete, contaminated forms of identity for real, social individuals: the society of the warrior aristocracy functions best, the epics seem to argue, when sacral integrity exists as a motivating, anchoring principle for symbolic action and exchange, but when it remains uncompleted in individuals other than the few, socially-designated sacred exceptions (kings, for example). For all the problems which performative identities entail, individuals must not obtain an integral wholeness which would transcend the multiple identities negotiated in the endless acts of exchange in which they participate.

The figure of Kriemhild, or of the Saracen princess, denies or effaces this useful societal realization. While these figures point implicitly to the existence of non-integral identities within the male-dominated societies which produce them, they also seem to represent a belief in the possibility of the elimination or sublimation of improper desires. The representations of masculine strife and anxiety which surround these female characters provide inverse models of societies of solidarity, wherein the inherent tensions of performance would be eliminated, and integrity – on both an individual and a social level – would become possible with the removal of the female characters and the problems of commodification which surround them.

The Nibelungenlied ultimately represents a new – and surprisingly modern – conception of the commodity which recalls Marx's notion of commodity fetishism.[12] Marx shares with *The Nibelungenlied* the same conservative, nostalgic

---

[11] I am thinking in particular here of Homi Bhabha's analysis of the ambivalence of both colonizer and colonized, and of the hybridity of the identity of both. See Bhabha 1994, especially Chs. 4 and 6.

[12] This text is a clear example of what Brian Stock calls "traditionalistic" activity, which he distinguishes from "traditional" action (1990:164–5). Traditionalistic activity for him is "the self-conscious affirmation of traditional norms" (164). But as he notes, modernity itself is often the product of such traditionalistic action (166).

notion of the (male) agent whose work would remain originally a product or object which would be unalienated from – and symbolically dependent on – him. The commodity fetish is then a form of desire which is partly symptom, partly cause of the alienated condition of the individual in relation to the object, which becomes no longer object, but independent, Other subject. Once this subjectification occurs, the solidarity of the community collapses. In a critique similar to the one just offered of Marx, Marilyn Strathern has attacked the concept of the inalienable from an anthropological perspective, noting that the theoretical notion of the inalienable object of gift exchange represents a fantasmatic nostalgia for pure, secondary objects (Strathern 1988:7–19, 92–5, 103–5, 134–5). Sarah Kay's reading of the poetics of gift and commodity in medieval epic makes a related though inverse point, arguing that the epic depicts the threat of the other as the threat of the thing itself become "real" (1995:146–52, 166; see Ramey 2001:48 as well). Her study of issues of gender and exchange in the Old French domain suggests that the ultimate fantasy of the epic is that the hierarchy of men over things can subsist (1995:183). *The Nibelungenlied* serves in part to propose the same fantasy, though in a more desperate maneuver, it writes the retrospective history of this illusory possibility into the heroic past. But the text, in its writing of a history of the heroic time before the fetish of the object-become-subject, fails to provide any real theoretical reason for the end of that heroic time. In deconstructing the text, one finds concealed in it a virtually Durkheimian conception of the origin of the fetish in human – and specifically masculine – commodifying desire. It is this real origin which the text first hints at and even critiques in its early portrayal of Siegfried, but then suppresses in its implicit suggestion of a supposed "origin" of commodification in courtliness and romance.

Conclusion

This discussion allows us to consider briefly the writings of René Girard, whose most notable book, *La Violence et le Sacré*, addresses issues apparently central to this book, and which were discussed only briefly in a preceding chapter. Girard's central claims – that the violence internal to communities is vitiated through a sacrificial victim on whom all blame for the violence is placed, and that myth and ritual are mechanisms which eternally replicate this founding sacrifice – seem clearly applicable to *The Nibelungenlied*. Kriemhild could be identified with the role of the sacrificial victim. But elsewhere in the literature and practice of the warrior aristocracy, internal violence is quite directly confronted and acknowledged. One might try to argue that the hero represents another kind of sacrificial victim, made Other in order to be sacrificed in the public ritual performance of the epic. But the hero is also so closely identified with the community itself that it seems rather that the community – in the person of the hero – takes full responsibility for its own violence. It is not violence itself which must be written out of the community in *The Cid*, *Roland*, and similar texts, but only a certain type of non-reciprocal violence which is directed at the sacred, and which must be contained by the texts.

For this reason, though we have mentioned the "ritual" character of these texts and practices, they do not correspond to the kind of ritual or myth which Girard evokes, which acts to mystify social relations rather than to reflect on them. Girard's notion of the sacred and of ritual can be traced ultimately to Durkheim's classically colonialist understanding of them, as processes which obscure and conceal rather than as processes which enable reflection.[13] Such a view of myth predominated throughout the modernist period, culminating in the work of Lévi-Strauss. More recently, ritual and performance have come to be seen as vehicles as often – or even more often – used for opening up issues to negotiation, confronting social dilemmas, and meditating on the bases of power, order and authority as for attempting a cover-up of the loose ends of social life.

The Nibelungenlied, in this light, looks at first curiously like a colonialist text, writing the violence of its own society onto an Other in order to claim a mythical solidarity for its own past. The Other becomes a vehicle for the suppression of central elements in the identity of the text's composers. It is not alone in this regard, however. Although we will not pursue the point here in depth, as it would take us too far afield, courtly romance arguably engages in an inverse colonization of the warrior aristocracy as well; it writes the violence and disorder of the gift onto that group and its texts, through receptive readings of the epic in romance, while engaging in an eroticization of the gift within courtly love which represents it as a form of pure solidarity. Thus like Chivalry, both late epic (as in *The Nibelungenlied*) and romance try to lay claim to an imagined gift of solidarity – the very gift which has since come to dominate western theories of the gift. Although this book has argued that such theories are the product of modernism, one could equally well locate the deep origins of such modernism in the High Middle Ages. This era was a period which saw the rise of at least two fundamentally competing discourses of social order; and just as competition in the modernist era on a global scale has spawned colonialist gestures and anti-colonial, indigenous responses which pose the gift as a true form of anti-capitalist solidarity (Thomas 1991:185ff), the medieval confrontation seems to have produced similar colonialist and anti-colonialist responses. Given its conservative tendencies, *The Nibelungenlied* is perhaps better seen as an anti-colonialist text responding to the colonizing gesture of courtly romance, much like the indigenous discourses of the gift which have been produced in Melanesia and Polynesia. Patricia Ingham and Michelle Warren argue that the fundamental link between colonialism and the writing of history is that the colonizers' history tells the story of their move from "primitive" to "modern," while the colonized peoples come to mirror in the present the inferior past of the colonizer (Ingham

---

[13] Durkheim argues that the sacred as a category is instituted and used by humans to obscure the true, human origins of their own institutions, in order to render the institutions more distant, formidable – and unanalyzable. See Durkheim 1965.

and Warren 2003:1–2). *The Nibelungenlied*, on the other hand – like many resisting colonized peoples – represents the superior time as that of the past. The deeper lesson to take from this situation, however, is that no matter whether the discourse of the gift is the product of colonialist or anti-colonialist gestures, the context of colonial confrontation inevitably leads to an artificial simplification of the notion of the gift itself, and more particularly, a splitting – and often, gendering – of giving/solidarity and taking/violence into two separate domains, when in fact they must be recognized as fundamentally co-involved, whether in the twentieth century or the Middle Ages. We will return in the Conclusion to the larger question of the relationship between anthropology, colonialism, and the study of the Middle Ages.

9

Fractured Identities, and the Solution of Chivalry: William of Orange

As seen in Chapters 6 and 7, *The Song of Roland*, *Raoul of Cambrai*, and *Gormont and Isembard* examine the spectacular and often catastrophic consequences of crossing the boundary between social reciprocity and heroic, asocial integrity, for both the individual hero and the warrior aristocracy as a whole. Those texts emphasize the dangerous potential of the integrity-drive which underlies the performative system of giving and taking. But they also signal – through the specifically literary persona of the hero – their speculative and reflective nature and the supra-real quality of the events they narrate. The hero's gratuitous breaking of social reciprocity is also a breaking away from immediate identity with the epic audience itself. Despite the catastrophic violence narrated in the texts, they all insist on the redemptive possibilities of the act of narration itself as a social ritual and a form of reciprocity.

The mid-twelfth-century *Coronation of Louis*, part of the Old French William of Orange cycle, offers both a more comic and ultimately a more pessimistic view of the efficacy of performance. It portrays its hero, William of Orange, in a Quixotic light at times, and points to a continuing aristocratic fantasy – or better, nostalgia – for a sacred kept beyond the limits of reciprocity, which performance-based social structures seem unable to deliver. Like *The Nibelungenlied*, this epic offers a solution to the dilemma, but in this case, the solution lies in a reorientation of the integrity drive within the context of monastically-envisioned Christianity and a strongly religious conception of Chivalry.

Boundaries and Exemplarity

Despite its title, *The Coronation of Louis* is actually about the tireless efforts of *Guillaume Fierebras* to maintain the kingdom of the ninth-century French king Louis – and ultimately that of Louis' father Charlemagne – at the level of its historic and legendary boundaries. William first puts down a challenge to Louis' receiving of the crown, then twice defends Rome (part of the Carolingian Empire) from attack, and twice saves Louis from his own rebellious barons in France. The epic's exemplary function is often at the forefront, typically in quite pedantic ways: Charlemagne provides Louis with a long list of the do's and don'ts of kingship; the narrator scrupulously points out William's own scrupulously fair, just, faithful and Christian behavior with friends and enemies alike; and William goes to the trouble of reciting the full outline of Biblical history during the course of one of the long prayers intended for the edification of the epic audience.

Among the behaviors featured prominently in the poem are acts of exchange. The acts of exchange, and especially their range of types, from gift to sale to killing, act to establish and classify relationships, as is often the case. But this chapter aims to suggest that the range of exchange practices can be read as a form of medieval ethnography, acting to classify, describe and evaluate those who surround the in-group not just operationally, but reflectively.

Of course, in using the term ethnography, one risks a conflation of modern and medieval modes of representation. Modern anthropology – the science at least in part of ordering and classifying peoples – focuses on social and cultural differences as a key criterion by which this ordering is accomplished. But as William McGrane has argued in *Beyond Anthropology*, this criterion dates only from the nineteenth century. McGrane's study of the history of the concept of Otherness proposes that the basis of otherness has shifted over time in the West: equivalent to ignorance during the Enlightenment; to being non-Christian and ignorant of Christianity during the Renaissance; and to being anti-Christian during the Middle Ages.[1] As a further step toward disentangling the gift from its specifically modern theoretical context within anthropology, it is necessary to look more closely at the connections between the gift, religion, and alterity in the medieval epic. In *The Coronation of Louis,* the gift becomes the key concept for the epic's examination of the very idea of boundaries, of identity, and of their origins, as the text presents an etiology of boundaries and differing identities.

Exchange in general, and varieties of gifts in particular, are so pervasive in *The Coronation* that a complete discussion of all of them, or even a complete listing, would fill several pages.[2] As an example of William's activity in this regard, I will list simply his exchanges in a few laisses in the central part of the epic. Instances of the actual word "give" or "grant" are cited by verse number, while the larger context of the exchanges is given in terms of the laisse in question.

laisse 35 W's gift of money to a pilgrim who has spoken well of W's lineage (as opposed to those who have betrayed the king) without realizing he is talking to W.
laisse 36 W's promise of gifts of horses to his household knights.
laisse 38 W's promise of gifts of wealth and booty to those who will help him in his military endeavors.
laisse 39 W's gift of knightly accouterments to a gatekeeper who harshly criticizes W's enemies.
laisse 40 W's gift of aid to King Louis in the coming battle.

[1] McGrane 1989. See also Boon 1982 on the historical evolution of alterity.
[2] Boutet 1999:176, 180, argues that the gift is the dominant theme of the entire cycle.

laisse 56   W's promise of monetary gifts to those who will help him in battle, as well as of war booty such as horses and mules.

laisse 57   W's agreement to barter with one of his defeated victims.

laisse 58   W's gift of aid to Louis in the form of single combat.

laisse 59   W's refusal to give (2447) the symbolic glove, representing the right to single combat, to his nephew.

laisse 59   W wears the sword that Charlemagne gave (2502) him in the past.

laisse 60   W refuses to barter with a Saracen foe.

laisse 61   W prays for the Virgin to give him aid in battle.

laisse 61   W prays for God to give (2571) a Saracen enemy trouble.

laisse 61   God refuses to grant (2600) success to W's enemy.

laisse 61   W offers a gift of a horse to his nephew in recognition of his eagerness to help in the battle.

This list could certainly be extended, but it will serve to suggest the all-pervasive nature of exchange in this epic.

As already seen in Chapter 5, modes of exchange are used to classify relationships. On one end of the continuum lies conquest and violent seizure, which are presented as appropriate only group-externally: Louis must not "retolir" ("seize," l. 83) fiefs wrongly from orphans, or "tolir" (l. 84) money from widows. While such exchanges are inappropriate within the group, they are entirely appropriate as modes of interaction with the most Other of peoples – the non-Christians. William's refusal to barter with his Saracen foe in laisse 60 is an indirect way of saying the same thing. The foe suggests, "Faisons la paiz et seions ami,/ Et je et tu avrons Rome a tenir" ("let us make peace and as good friends retire; you and I will hold Rome with equal right") (ll. 2531–2). The offer is to establish a much closer relationship with the foe, through a more amicable mode of exchange, and to use a much more hostile mode of exchange against William's Christian allies, thus canceling out religious differences as an impediment to exchange and alliance. William refuses the exchange in explicitly religious terms: " 'Gloz,' dist Guillelmes, 'Deus te puist maleïr'" ("Wretch," says William, "may just God curse your life!") (l. 2533).[3] Note also that the term "gloz" denotes gluttony – an improper material desire for things themselves – so that integrity issues are raised explicitly, with the most foreign individuals and groups being the most clearly non-integral.

On the other hand, certain confrontations with the enemy are matters more of personal vengeance, and in these cases, William is in fact at least willing to barter with Saracen captives. In laisse 57, one such defeated enemy demands "pitié" (l. 2348), a quality which in this epic is explicitly linked to William's Christian virtue. By appealing to – and thus implicitly recognizing the validity of – William's religious identity as a Christian, the enemy removes the key criterion

---

3   See v. 808 for a similar refusal of an inter-group gift by William.

of difference, and takes the first step across the boundary between them. "Ber, ne m'oci, se tu Guillelmes iés,/ Mais pren mei vif, molt i puez guaaignier;/ Je te donrai un grant mui de deniers," ("Don't kill me, if you are William, be wise,/ you will gain more if you take me alive./ I shall give you wealth and goods of great price") (ll. 2349–51), says the enemy. He appeals to William's inner system of values (which are inseparable from his name and identity), then follows with the mention of wealth, which thus becomes a symbolic reward and consequence of William's primary, internal, religious motivation. The proposal is accepted.

Sale, on the other hand, places one even farther outside the group than barter. In particular, the term "vendre" is reserved in the epic for Judas, who sold the Christians (l. 755). In fact, it seems that in this epic sale is even worse than theft (by violent conquest), just as one would expect based on the symbolic economy of reciprocity.

In other words, exchange is all about moral evaluation and boundaries in this epic. A quick look at the list given above will serve to illustrate that the exchanges which occur all center around clear questions of friendship and hostility. They all occur at moments of crisis and danger, and serve to clarify the relations in question. They all exclude (theft, seizure, sale) or include (gift, barter) to a greater or lesser degree. As much as the battles themselves, these exchanges constitute the vocabulary of the boundary. Interestingly, this epic seems to move away from the complexity of giving and taking seen in earlier texts – there seems to be far less ambiguity between the two acts. Rather, the epic works to set up a neat scale onto which various relationships can be placed, and the categories of "friend" and "enemy" – gift and violence – seem to be more clearly delineated.

The Land without Boundaries

A closer look at the text, however, reveals many boundaries within Christian society itself: between loyal and rebellious barons, between William's exemplary vassalage and Louis' pathetic example of kingship, between those Saracens willing to convert to Christianity and those who are defiant to the end, or between aristocratic knights and the other menial characters who appear in the text, such as peasants and gatekeepers. Even the text of the epic itself is riven by boundaries as we possess it in manuscript form. *The Coronation* is often cited as the least unified of the base members of the William of Orange cycle, and readings of it typically separate it out into five sections, corresponding to the coronation, the defense of Rome, the rebellion of the barons, the second defense of Rome, and a second rebellion of the barons. The sections do indeed have little in common in terms of plot, and appear to be simply added on one after the other. But this form is fundamentally reflective of the larger theme of the work as a whole – the theme of boundaries. In a world of boundaries and strife, the text, each section of which calls for William to either reaffirm or attempt to abolish a boundary, is true to the dilemma of the nobleman of the eleventh and twelfth centuries. Life was an endless performative struggle over boundaries, which were everywhere, and everywhere in need of attention as they threatened to dissolve away.[4]

Of course the issue of boundaries is endemic to medieval epic as well as medieval society. The very categories of self and other are problematic, even impossible to disentangle, like the categories of gift and violence. But as seen above, *The Coronation* seems to suggest that boundaries can in fact be quite clearly defined: the problem is rather that they simply collapse very easily, and are constantly in need of attention. They also seem to have the potential to proliferate endlessly, according to all kinds of criteria – class, language, religion, and so on. These boundaries between groups (which occur throughout the William cycle more generally in great number) and their dramatization in acts of exchange are replicated in the very identity of William himself. In the cycle more generally, he plays numerous diverse and even contradictory roles, several of them while in disguise. He is alternately warrior, huntsman, hermit, monk, Saracen, merchant, and lover.[5] In many cases, these roles are adopted in order to allow him to engage in various kinds of exchanges – often with others who also occupy those roles. Recalling the notions of identity discussed in Chapter 1, one could say that, for effective social action, William is forced to suppress certain components of his identity in order to present a specific image to the world on different (exchange) occasions. But if this is the case, then the notion of exchanges as classificatory mechanisms begins to become problematic. While the discussion of *The Coronation* began by talking about how fixed relational identities are maintained, reinforced or renegotiated in this text through exchange, it seems equally valid to suggest the contrary: different types of exchange determine identity, and one is forced to adopt an identity in order to exchange. Exchange precedes identity.

From such a perspective, the "individual" becomes simply the site of multiple, relational encounters. The internal plurality of the individual is suppressed in any given exchange, yet also ironically emphasized in the taking on of each succes-

---

4 Dobozy 1997 offers an interesting reading of the ways in which medieval performers almost by definition raised issues of boundaries and alterity through their performances. She looks especially at the nature of the performer as social outsider to courtly audiences, and the way in which asking for gifts during performances served as a textual locus where these issues were brought most acutely into focus. On *The Coronation* in particular, Carol Kent has remarked that key events and moments in the text seem to fall at or cross the boundaries of laisses as well (Kent 1994–5). See also Kay 1995:200–1 for another consideration of jongleurs, requests for gifts, and the way these requests open up spaces for social reflection and response.

5 See especially Maddox and Maddox 1979 on this phenomenon in the cycle. On disguises in particular, see also Suard 1980. Perfetti 1992–3 argues, on lines similar to those I use here, that the disguises, and comic irony more generally, serve to "bring attention to the 'relativity' or arbitrariness of social codes" (183), challenge notions of language's intrinsic meaning (187) and play with social identities (190) – in other words, to reveal the performative character of language and identity, and to highlight the epic's own performative (as opposed to simply socially mirroring) function. See Luongo 1990 for a similar study of the "negazione di un'identità assoluta e unilaterale" (1990:225) in the texts.

sive role for each successive exchange (or refusal) with each successive group.[6] Thus the fragmented world full of boundaries is replicated in William's own identity in the cycle at large, and the ultimate boundary – between self and outer world – even turns out to be enormously fluid and porous.[7]

In such a world, for some at least, the dream of a place without boundaries, a place of wholeness, must have exercised a great attraction – like the fantasy of no longer exchanging which we met with earlier. Indeed, the two fantasies are theoretically inseparable here. A medieval warrior might have been tempted to wonder why boundaries existed in the first place, and where they came from. *The Coronation* offers not simply a study of boundaries and their modes of maintenance, but also a theory of boundaries themselves, or more properly, of their etiology. And in so doing, it offers a theory of alterity which combines elements of aristocratic and religious thought in a uniquely medieval – and uniquely twelfth-century – fashion.

At the center of the complex web of interactions and exchanges in *The Coronation* lies a founding gift – the gift from God of the Garden of Eden. On the scale of exchange which we have elaborated, it establishes a new positive reference point. It is not a prior gift, intended to evoke certain actions, nor is it a posterior gift designed to reward action. This is not to say that God does not expect worship and obedience in return: this requirement is incarnated in the one condition placed on the gift – that humans not eat of the Tree of Knowledge. But the gift clearly exceeds any possibility of reciprocation, and carries with it, in the purest ontological sense, no element of reward or recompense. It is unearned, overwhelming, and unreciprocable – a vertical, sacred gift. It is a gift marked not by performance, but by transcendent essence.

William himself tells this story during a prayer which he recites before going into battle. He begins appropriately at the beginning:

> Glorios Deus, qui me fesistes né,
> Fesis la terre tot a ta volenté,
> Si la closis environ de la mer;
> Adam formas et puis Evain sa per;
> En paradis les en menas ester;
> Li fruiz des arbres lor fu abandonez,
> Fors d'un pomier, icil lor fu veez;
> Il en mangierent, ce fu grant foleté;
> Grant honte en orent quant nel porent celer.
> De paradis les en covint aler,
> Venir a terre, foïr et laborer,

---

[6]   Michael Harney (1997:81) notes that the "epic experiences society as a constellation of binary oppositions" and that social labels express "relationships" rather than "memberships."

[7]   See Philip Bennet's Bakhtinian analysis of the heteroglossia of the William cycle, on several different levels (1999). The heteroglossia is simply another index of the plurality and instability of the world of the text, which the text itself captures stylistically and linguistically.

Et mortel vie sofrir et endurer.
Caïns ocist Abel par crüelté;
Adonc covint terre braire et crïer;
Uns crüels dons lor fu cel jor donez:
Riens n'eissent d'els n'i covenist aler. (ll. 695–710)

Glorious God, who set me in this place, and the earth to your will did once create, enclosing it round with great rushing waves, Adam you formed and then Eve his mate, led them to live in the Eden you made, and the fruit of all trees you gave them to taste; from the apple alone they were to abstain, which in their folly, they desired and ate. They could not conceal it – it brought them shame. Paradise they were bound to forsake; to plow and labor the earth they came, to endure and suffer mortal pain. Cruelly was Abel murdered by Cain; then the earth began to weep a wail, a cruel gift they were given that day; nothing leaves earth but to return again.

William continues the prayer all the way through to the resurrection. The resurrection essentially brings one to the then-current end of divine history, or up to the "present" of the Middle Ages, in the sense that after the resurrection, all is essentially an eternal present awaiting the final judgement. In other words, William has just narrated a history whose endpoint is the moment of his speech. As such, this history also must account for the conditions of the present medieval moment as well.[8] In particular, the Fall can be seen here as the inauguration of boundaries. Paradise represents a boundary-free land of plenitude. There is a boundary – the waves – but it encloses everyone, and thus serves to include rather than to exclude. Where there are no boundaries, there should be no need for the exchanges which elaborate those boundaries, and several medieval texts do point to a belief that in the land of plenty, there were no exchanges.[9] All is simply "abandonez" for humanity: "le fruit des arbres lor mesis a bandon/ Fors d'un pomier lor veastes le don" ("offered them all the fruits of the trees, one apple alone You forbade them to eat") (ll. 982–3).

But the vertical gift from God, which would provide a transcendental, boundary-free existence for humanity, is not respected. The Fall occurs. The first boundary is that between the Garden and the Earth (ll. 704–5). And with the first boundary comes the strife that is characteristic of boundaries: Cain's killing of Abel, as well as the labor and scarcity which necessitate economic exchange. The boundary and strife are finally the reason that William is reciting this prayer, which calls for aid in battle.

The many borders of *The Coronation* can now be seen as ironic figurations of

---

[8]   See Singerman 1985 for another discussion of the reflexive regard of the prayer on William's present moment. He also notes that William "throws out" the prayer as only a potential truth, whose veracity must finally be "performed" by God, in a way similar to the performative notion of truth analyzed in this book for *The Cid*.

[9]   See Cowell 1996, esp. 156–8, for a fuller discussion of the issue of exchange in medieval economic thought.

the one great, originary border, which surrounds the Garden of Eden and excludes humanity for evermore. That border is symbolic of the Fall from transcendence to performance – of the failure of the one, sacred, vertical gift, and its replacement by an endless series of performative exchanges which can never reestablish transcendency. In the post-lapsarian world, borders are always either collapsing when they should remain standing, or being put up where they shouldn't be by rebellious barons. The gift can never stabilize things. William is condemned to his long-suffering task of always defending, reestablishing, or attempting to abolish borders.

The same analysis could also be applied to William's identity itself: the wall around the garden of paradise – the one truly stable and encompassing boundary – could be read as a sort of skin around the body as well. The Fall into performance produces not just a chaotic social world of boundaries and boundary-crossing, but a chaotic, pluralistic individual identity as well, the text would seem to suggest. William must constantly either hold together or keep apart the world in general, along with himself in that world, and even his own internal self – all simultaneously, since they are all part of the same general task. As Marilyn Strathern notes of identity in such contexts, the individual essentially "contain[s] a generalized sociality within" which is the "composite site of the relationships that produced them" (1988:13). As long as identity formation is based on interactive performance within a complex society, it is bound to produce fluid, fragmented identities for the individual, which can only temporarily be stabilized, as seen in the conclusion to Chapter 1. The hero, in escaping reciprocity and achieving integrity, attains a form of identity which is no longer based on interactive performance, and is thus stable and transcendent. But as noted in Chapters 5 and 8, epic texts, understood as social rituals of reciprocity between performer and audience, stress the *desirability* of fluid, plural identities among actual members of the warrior aristocracy, given the cost to the society of heroic identity. Plural identity is an indicator of reciprocity, and reciprocity acts as a constraint on the integrity drive. Thus William's troubled identity is exemplary of that of the real-life warrior aristocrat.

William's task of identity formation and maintenance is all the more difficult because he seems never to be fully compensated, and those around him seem always to be failing in their loyalty and motivations. Exchanges, even gifts, never seem to be quite successful. The epic closes with a summary of the results of William's latest rescue of Louis' kingdom: "En grant barnage fu Looïs entrez;/ Quant il fu riches Guillelme n'en sot gré" ("Into great honor Louis ascends –/ but when he was rich he forgot his friend") (ll. 2694–5). The attempt at ethnography proves futile, and the intricate gradations and categories of exchange serve only to underline the impossibility of the effort. Likewise, William is metaphorically not recognized by Louis – his own identity is apparently not coherent enough to receive the symbolic rewards which would both recognize and solidify it.

This imperfection of Old French aristocratic society finally makes perfect sense within the logic of this epic, because the Fall is really the Fall of the originary Gift – the failure of that gift to be respected. This initial failure prefigures the many petty failures of loyalty and reward in King Louis' weak and hapless kingdom. The Christian Fall is thus invoked, in *The Coronation*, to account for the aristocratic failures of gift culture in the High Middle Ages, and for the failures of identity formation which William seems to constantly encounter.[10] And conversely, the model of gift culture is used to understand and refigure the Christian Fall. Because of this Fall, even the gift – the best form of exchange – is always contaminated with elements of violence, compulsion and ruse, the epic suggests. It can never attain the status of the pure, originary gift, free of violence, which could put an end to exchange and borders. Imperfect gifts and borders then follow as the logical consequence of each other. And behind the epic's seeming concern with exemplary instances of exchange and boundaries lies a deeper nostalgia which, in its etiology of borders, imagines their disappearance in the ideal, successful gift – a transcendent gift of grace.

This nostalgia ultimately replicates that of Derrida in his writing on the gift which was examined earlier. His invocation of a perfect gift – in other words, a completely forgotten gift, free of any contamination of compulsion, duty, or obligation – is also a gift which would be free of the economy of exchange. This text does not go so far as that, in that the initial constraint put on the gift by God always remains present. But it takes a major step towards imagining a purified, modern gift, devoid of violence, representing total solidarity.[11] Both Derrida and *The Coronation* deconstruct such a possibility, but only after nostalgically constructing it in the first place.

William the Redeemer

Given the social, political and economic imperfections and failures which surround William, one is tempted to look at this long-suffering hero as a potential redeemer of the failed gift. He seems to be the one figure in the epic whose motives are purely internal, untainted by calculation: when Louis calls yet again for his aid, at the end of the epic, William's nephew Bertran tells him:

> ... Car le laissiez ester.
> Car laissons France, comandons l'a malfé,

---

[10] He is not even recognized by his own wife at one point (*The Coronation*, ll. 1471–2).

[11] See David Schenk's (1988) reading of the text as specifically a "myth" of social "integration" (1988:8) which nevertheless imagines this integration occurring in fundamentally performative ways; Schenk emphasizes the oscillation between maintenance and destruction (1988:12). On the other hand, Aubailly 1987 argues that William specifically, and the epic hero more generally, function as archetypal models of the "élaboration d'un Moi" and of a "personnalité unifiée" (1987:224). He thus concludes that the text focuses on the same issues that interest us here, but sees a successful resolution of the issues, as the hero gains a personalizing fief, and then learns to submit himself to royal authority.

> Et cestui rei, qui tant est assotez;
> Ja ne tendra plein pié de l'erité. (ll. 2669–72)

> ... Let him be then. Let us leave him and France to the devil to
> tend, this king is such a fool, with all your help not a foot of his
> lands can he defend.

William ignores him, and goes off to do his (yet again un-rewarded – ll. 2694–5)
duty.

Given the nature of his task, however, and the risibility of young King Louis,
William comes to resemble perhaps more closely Don Quixote than Jesus Christ.
Much of the humor of the epic centers around William's comic frustration
and anger at the degraded state of aristocratic society. One of the great comic
moments of medieval literature occurs when Charlemagne is preparing to crown
his son Louis. He gives a long speech about the duties of a king, and closes with
the rhetorical statement:

> S'ensi le fais, j'en lorai Damedé:
> Prens la corone, si seras coronez;
> O se ce non, filz, laissiez la ester:
> Je vos defent que vos n'I adesez (ll. 68–71)

> If you are ready to give me your word, receive the crown and praise
> be to the lord. But let it be, my son, if you are not. Remember then,
> it is forever lost.

Louis, young and intimidated by all of this, takes his father at his word, and won't
step forward to receive the crown (l. 87). Charlemagne is enraged, and it is easy
to imagine William likewise. When someone else comically steps forward to
offer to replace Louis, he angrily kills the pretender, grabs the crown off the altar,
and unceremoniously plops it on Louis' head himself (ll. 142–6).

Despite the high comedy of the scene, it is also the moment in the text where
perhaps the most important gift and performance of all – the gift of the crown
which constitutes and undergirds the noble order – nearly fails, and is certainly
not completely successful. Here again, the sacred, vertical exchange (sancti-
fied by God) is botched, as in the Garden of Eden. The majority of the comic
moments of the text seem to center around various problems in exchange, typically internal to Christian, French society itself. Within this context, William
is not truly closely parallel to Don Quixote, because one senses in the text's
nostalgia a belief in the continued validity of the social model of the gift. While
one may laugh at William's dilemma, the high seriousness with which many of
his combats and religious prayers are treated serves to indicate the text's fundamental sympathy for his efforts, and thus to turn the laughter ultimately into a
moral vehicle of reproach (for the audience), even as it also serves to admit the
final impossibility of the text's own nostalgic desires.

Faced with this post-lapsarian dilemma, the text posits an alternative form of integrity, which William exemplifies. The text makes clear use of the ideas of the positive, posterior gift and the negative, prior gift, and thus establishes William's integrity through the vocabulary of reciprocity.[12] But in contrast to the heroes examined earlier, William's gratuitous integrity consists not in a violent rupture with his society, but rather in his devotion to King Louis and his gift of service to that highly imperfect and irregularly reciprocating monarch. His integrity lies in a gratuitous, unreasonable submission to reciprocity itself, rather than in a break with it, despite all the rational reasons for such a break which the text offers.

The archetypal prior gift which changes or conditions conduct and fundamentally compromises one's integrity is of course that received by Judas in the form of the thirty pieces of silver (v. 756). The fact that Judas acts in exchange for having already received the gift converts it from a gift to a sale – a commodification: "La fist Judas de vos grant crüelté;/ Il vos vendi par sa grant foleté" ("Then by Judas you were cruelly betrayed;/in his folly he sold you, to his shame") (ll. 754–5), says William praying to Jesus. The importance of this concept is stressed by its repetition at a later point in the text: "La fist Judas de vos la traïson:/ Il vos vendi ..." ("Then Judas commited his treacherous deed;/ he sold You") (ll. 999–1000). The appearance of this treason in the text in conjunction with the repeated acts of treason against Louis, along with William's repeated prayers to Jesus and repeated loyalty to Louis, serves to reinforce the connections between feudal and religious loyalty, and between pre-lapsarian gifts and post-lapsarian rewards. The extraordinary nature of William's loyalty to the weak and hesitant Louis is perhaps best demonstrated by his act of placing the crown on Louis' head at his coronation, thus indicating that his loyalty to Louis precedes any position of wealth, power or influence on Louis' part, and thus implicitly precedes any possibility of reward: he is already loyal, before Louis is crowned. Others may be loyal

---

[12] William distributes a number of gifts in the text, and almost without exception these are not intended to create ritual bonds and debt, but rather to reward exemplary behavior and faithfulness to existing bonds on the part of lesser individuals. Thus gifts recognize or even repay debts rather than creating them. William rewards a pilgrim with *dis onces d'or* for his high opinion of William's lineage and for his condemnation of those traitors who have deserted Louis (ll. 1458–84). He rewards a gatekeeper who again praises his lineage, condemns traitors to Louis and helps William overcome these enemies (ll. 1528–1655). The gatekeeper is made a knight in William's service, given all necessary arms and thus "de son servise li dona bon loier" ("for his service the count had paid him well") (l. 1655). Other gifts from William are for either service or good will from others (Bertran – ll. 2627–9), and the same is true of gifts he receives from the king Gaifiers in Rome (ll. 1352–64) and from Charlemagne (ll. 228–40). Where he does offer prior gifts, there is an implicit critique of the Franks around him, who are unwilling to act first, no matter what the rewards: he offers gifts in exchange for service as he tries to recruit an army (2255–67), so that gifts come close to appearing simply as a promised salary offered in advance, but to be delivered only after service is accomplished. But even here, he maintains the vocabulary of the gift: "Ja nuls frans om ne m'en tendra aver/Que toz nes doinse et encor plus assez" ("That I am a miser no man will say,/ I shall give all I have and then again") (ll. 2266–7).Thus it is William who is unerringly loyal, while the French as a whole – and by extension all of Christiandom – are consistently either hesitant to take arms, in need of lavish prior promises of reward, or outrightly rebellious.

before they are rewarded, in expectation of reward, but William's act is a sign of loyalty before the possibility of reward. The text further emphasizes William's extraordinary faith by noting the "coveitise" and "fals loiers" (ll. 35–6) that now reign in the world, suggesting the corrupted nature of words and gifts, which are sought rather than simply received, or performed for money or other interests. And where others at the coronation ceremony are unsure of Louis' capacities, or wish to wait for thirteen years and see if he will be ready (ll. 105–6), William has no room for doubts, contingencies, tests or proofs. Here is the exact opposite of the situation we saw reported for the Normans when loyalty was at issue in the chronicle of Robert Guiscard in Chapter 1: they supported someone who had the potential to reward them, and abandoned someone who was currently wealthy but did not seem to have the long-term potential for continued rewards. The Franks in the William of Orange cyle essentially behave in the same way towards Louis as the Normans, but William does the reverse, supporting someone with no integrity. He does so in order to indicate the extreme integrity of his own faith and devotion – to sacred kingship, and to feudal loyalty. Integrity becomes faith. Or more precisely, integrity no longer seeks to obtain access to the sacred kept through the practice of giving and keeping, using sacred kingship as a mediating vehicle. Rather, kingship becomes a secondary site of that which is primary – the faith itself. Abandoning a need for vertical exchanges and sacred mediation, integrity validates itself through a direct connection with sacred belief, through a performance of belief in the sacred.[13]

William's gesture represents a fundamental break with the dynamics of the sacred in the warrior aristocracy. In the texts examined earlier, the sacred was a given, which anchored the drive towards integrity. Now, William must actively affirm the sacred. While this would seem to indicate a very fragile status for the sacred, it actually greatly enhances its status; performance is no longer seen as anchored by a sacred which is ultimately supplementary to that performance. Rather, performance becomes a performance of sacred belief itself. The sacred enters directly into performance, in the act of faith. Performance is sacred.

This is the fullest sense of the long prayers in the text: they enact a sacred performance within the artistic performance of the text, recounting a history whose essential truth exceeds the bounds of the artistic performance in a way that none of the other events do. Thus the prayers sacralize the artistic performance in a fashion that prayers cannot in texts such as *The Song of Roland, Raoul of Cambrai*, or *Gormont and Isembard*. The prayers in this text function the way they do because they are uttered by a hero whose integrity is tied up in the actual performance of the prayers and a submission to their implications. The prayers are no longer simply requests for help in doing something else (which is what Roland's prayers are, for example); they are the doing itself.

But the entry of the sacred into the artistic performance can probably only be fully successful if we imagine the text as orally performed. A prayer is only

---

[13] See Nichols 1980 and Blumenfeld-Kosinski 1986 for studies of William as savior.

truly a sacral act as an *act* – as a spoken performance. Thus the activation of the sacred within the text depends on the text's orality. In fact, the opening of the text comes as close as any Old French *chanson de geste* to explicitly invoking a theory of oral-formualic composition, even as it posits a sacred intervention in the performance:

> Oiez, seignor, que Deus vos seit aidanz!
> Plaist vos oïr d'une estoire vaillant
> Bone chançon, corteise et avenant?
> Vilains joglere ne sai por quei se vant
> Nul mot en die tresque on li comant.
> De Looïs ne lairai ne vos chant. (ll. 1–6)

> Hear me, my lords, may God grant you his aid. Will it please you to hear a noble tale, a tale that is sung with charm and grace? The base minstrel makes his boast in vain – he speaks no word that has not been prepared. Of Louis the king I shall sing the tale.

The fifth line is somewhat more ambiguous than the translation suggests, but it clearly seems to invoke an authority for the performer, in the performance, that refuses prior or external sources of authority, unlike the performance of the base minstrel which it mocks. The line thus serves to locate the performance in a context of orality and presence – the same performative context which of course characterized the social world evoked in the text.[14] The sacred prayer works to sacralize the social performance of William as it is depicted by the epic; but it also sacralizes the artistic performance of the epic itself by the jongleur. The text offers itself, as the first line makes explicit, as a prayer to its audience.

Clearly, a text which posits itself as a gift, which is what most epics do, makes quite different claims on its audience than one which posits itself as a prayer. In place of a reception conditioned by the expectation of reciprocity and collaborative evaluation on the part of the listener, a prayer-text demands stronger adherence and makes a claim to potential moral criticism which is more difficult for the listener to resist. This correlates with the quite strong didactic tone of much of *The Coronation* which was noted earlier, as well as the tendency of the comic moments implicitly to critique the Franks as a whole, and thus the audience as well – rather than primarily the Saracens, as occurs in *The Song of Roland*.

---

[14] In his study of formulaic density in Old French epic, Duggan found that *The Coronation* featured the second highest density of any text, and was thus, in his view, highly likely to have been orally composed in performance as we now possess it in manuscript (Duggan 1973:25–7).

The Rise of Chivalry, and the Submissive Individual

The representation of performance and the sacred as fundamentally inseparable anticipates the larger claims of the ideology of Chivalry. William's gesture of gratuitous submission can be seen as an early version of the Chivalric belief system, which sees performative success as founded fundamentally on the sacred faith and willing obedience of the knight. Faith is posited, in the later manuals of chivalry, as that which can resolve the dilemma of performative society and identity, for faith becomes the ultimate performative act itself, and military victory is simply the subsidiary symbol and affirmation of this faith.

Such an idea did not arise from nowhere, of course, and the same idea of faith as fundamental to performance undergirds the belief in the efficacy of judicial combat which can be seen in *The Song of Roland* as well as many other texts. But the ideology of chivalry, in its strongest religious forms, extended this connection to all (authorized) military and political performance, rather than just to privileged moments of vertical exchange in which God and the Sacred were seen as co-participants, such as trials. Ramon Llull's *Llibre de l'Orde de Cavalleria* of the late thirteenth century offers a classic example: "per l'esperança que han en Déu han socors e ajuda de Déu, qui venç la batalla per raó de l'esperança e confiança que los cavallers han major en lo poder de Déu que en llurs forces ne en llurs armes" ("Thanks to the hope that they have in God, [knights] have help and aid from him, who [i.e. God] wins the battle thanks to the hope and confidence of the knights, which lies more in the power of God than in their own strength and weapons") (p. 76). Closer to the time of this epic, Etienne de Fougère's *Le Livre des manières* (composed in the 1170s) already begins to codify the importance of the notion of a performative submission to the sacred.[15] Chrétien de Troyes's romance *Perceval* likewise emphasizes the importance of faith and inner purity for successful performance of worldly tasks, and Wolfram von Eschenbach's *Parzival* further elaborates this theme. Where giving and taking have failed to produce a satisfactory social order, the solution proposed is to give oneself to God or his representative. As Etienne de Fougères says, "Donent grant dons por feire amis;/ quant ont doné et plus premis,/ ja n'avrunt plus maus anemis/ que cil qu'il ont es ennors mis" ("They give great gifts to create bonds;/ but when they have given much and promised more,/ they will never have worse enemies/ than those whom they have thusly honored") (ll. 25–8). He goes on to critique the endless instability of performative identity creation: "Ça et la veit, sovent se torne,/ ne repose ne ne sejorne./ Chasteaus abat, chasteaus aorne,/ sovent haitié, plus sovent morne" ("One is always looking here and there, always turning to something new,/ without either rest or repose./ Castles are taken, castles are adorned,/ often in joy, more often bringing sadness") (ll. 101–4). His alternative is that such men "obliër deit tot le son bon/ por le comun" and "sor tote rien aint Sainte Iglise" ("he must forget his own interest/ in favor of that of the commu-

---

[15] See Martin 1996:306–11 on the context of chivalry and faith in this work.

nity" and "love the Holy Church above all other things") (ll. 164–5, 173). He then goes on to propose a model of two swords, one literally in the hand of the warriors, the other figuratively in the hands of the churchmen (ll. 637–72), with both equally aiding each other. This idea eventually fundamentally changed the place of faith in the life of the warrior aristocracy.

This shift in the mode of identity formation and individual integrity marks the beginning of the closure of the warrior-aristocrat model of these concepts. In its place, for the warrior aristocrat, concepts of the individual much more closely tied to official (that is to say, documentary) Christian religion and theology rose to dominance. This particular form of individualism, subjectivity, and identity formation has been much more fully investigated than the warrior-aristocrat model examined in this book, thanks especially to the huge amount of documentation available. Indeed, for many scholars, the modern conception of the individual is fundamentally tied to the Christian model of the proper human relationship with God elaborated during the twelfth and thirteenth centuries. Louis Dumont, in his *Essays on Individualism*, makes this fundamental point (see especially Chapter 1). He begins with an interest in the same concepts I have explored in this book, focusing on the concept of "self-sufficiency" (1986:28–9), and noting that for "traditional, holistic" societies, the individual is typically defined as a kind of "supplement" to the society (1986:26). He then argues that such "out-wordly" models of individualism were converted into "in-wordly" models through the influence of the medieval church: an individual could establish a sense of integrity and identity in relation to God, while also remaining within Christian society (1986:32ff). The specific mechanisms of this conversion in the Middle Ages have been examined and debated in great detail, from many perspectives, including the philosophical (Garcia 1984), the theological (Chénu 1969, focusing on confession) and the political (Haidu 2004, focusing on the Peace of God movement as a key early component), to list just three exemplary treatments. The elaboration of the doctrine of religious Chivalry seems to have been one key mechanism in the creation of an in-wordly model for individualism.

It is important to recognize that apparently all societies, including traditional and holistic ones, have concepts of the individual. The key distinction lies in where that individual is conceptually located in relation to the society. Christian religious Chivalry, as exemplified by William's gratuitous gesture in *The Coronation of Louis*, offers the possibility for an in-wordly individualism which would be accessible to all through simple submission and faith, allowing them to integrate their secular vocation with sacred dictates, and to act as the agent of the sacred on Earth. Note the contrast between this position and the intermediary possibility which Sarah Kay points out in the epic *Girart of Roussillon*. There too, the clergy insist that "identity results not from exception [singularity] but from subjection" (Kay 1998–2003:21). And there too, Girart's key act in renouncing the pursuit of integrity is "voluntarily" done (34). She finds that "the uniqueness of one's own death can be reread as the uniqueness of one's own salvation" (34–5). But Girart "removes himself from human existence" (34) and retreats from the world in order to obtain this salvation. This epic is thus emblematic of an older, either/or potential for the warrior. In this clerical model, identity and salvation lie outside human society, and specifically outside the warrior society.

In contrast, William's gesture of performative faith in *The Coronation of Louis* marks the full integration of out-worldly-oriented salvation with in-worldy military performance, whereas the earlier warrior-aristocratic society offered a much more out-worldly model of military, performance-based identity, available to few if any, and at great cost to the society. Of course, as post-modern critics of the notion of the individual subject have revealed, the modern, Christian-derived, Western form of individuality may be equally or even more unavailable to the members of this society than the medieval heroic state was to the average warrior, and equally supplementary. But that is a question beyond the scope of this book, and nevertheless, the shift in the locale of the idealized individual remains crucial. Whereas a hero must work his way up the hierarchical levels of society through an ever-mounting series of performances in order finally to reach a point where sacred exchange is possible (beyond social reciprocity), each and every chivalric knight has at his disposal the potential of faithful submission from within society. Again using Dumont's words, in place of the individual incarnated in the overwhelming, inner-directed will of the hero, one eventually arrives at the concept of the individual as one of the many expressions of the will of God *in* the world (1986:56).[16] The offers of remission of sins made to participants in the First Crusade essentially served to convert all knights into potential Rolands who could gain direct access to salvation through the gift of their life and service.[17] Guibert de Nogent wrote that "the order of knights ... now ... may seek God's grace in their wonted habit, and in the discharge of their own office, and no longer need to be drawn to seek salvation by utterly renouncing the world in the profession of the monk" (*Patrologia Latina* CLVI, 685, cited in Keen 1984:48–9). The out-wordly model becomes in-worldly, and available to all.

It would require another book entirely to pursue fully the model of the individual elaborated by Chivalry. This book is really a pre-history of Chivalry, and it seems fitting to terminate with the transition to that new phase in the history of the warrior aristocracy. But it is important to underline again the conceptual breakthrough presented in *The Coronation of Louis*. This text from the middle of the twelfth century presents a model for maintaining the integrity drive, the gratuitous gesture, and the overwhelming gift, though in a new ideological

---

[16] Dumont argues that this development only culminates with Calvinism, but certainly the germ of the idea is found in Chivalry's conception of the knight as soldier of God.

[17] This was not actually the offer technically made to the knights, but there appears to have been quite a difference between the actual offer and its popular understanding. See Mayer 1972:25–40 for a discussion of the issues surrounding the crusading indulgence and the motivations for participation in the First Crusade.

framework. All of these elements became a part of the chivalric ethos in one way or another, and the fact that the elements of the previous model of identity were carried over so successfully into the chivalric one is suggestive of one reason for the latter's sociopolitical and literary success in the later Middle Ages.

Conclusion:
A New, Different Warrior Aristocracy

Modes of Reflection and Alterity, Medieval and Modern

For the most part in this book, we have not engaged directly with the complex medieval debate about the relative importance of oral and written traditions in the documented epic texts which we possess, though one important exception was the discussion of *The Poem of the Cid*. There seem to be strong arguments to believe that there were well developed traditions of both oral composition and performance in early medieval France, Spain, Germany, and elsewhere. It may not be possible to assert that the documented epic texts we possess are direct records of those traditions, nor would one want to argue that those traditions themselves were purely oral and uninfluenced by written texts or monastic culture. But there is good reason to believe that the texts in this book, in their themes and structure, reflect an origin and development in a culture where oral composition and/or performance was a predominant feature. This performance was public and given in settings that were, to a greater or lesser extent, ritualized. Much of the argument in Chapters 4 through 9 assumes that the reception of the texts occurred as "ritualized performances" in public, oral settings as defined in Chapter 4 (see references and definition, page 72). Similarly, much of the argument in Chapters 1 through 5 assumes that the performance of giving and taking occurred in such settings as well, part of the production of symbolic value.

As noted in Chapter 4, one of the central arguments of theorists of performance is that these events open up the lives of both the individuals present and the society as a whole to reflection and reconsideration. Central to this book are the demonstrations that the gift was a social trope for "thinking about" individual and social identity formation and power, and that the hero was similarly a narrative trope for thinking about the relationship between individual and society, and the limits of identity formation. In this light, medieval performances turn out to look very much like modern or even post-modern texts in their capacity for generating relationships of alterity. Writing of otherness and literary language, Gabriele Schwab argues that the "aesthetic mediation" of otherness through such language produces three relations of alterity: of the self to the culture, of one culture to another, and of the self to language itself (1996:xi). She claims that the experience of reading always involves some negotiation of otherness (9), and that it even constitutes a form of madness in the way that it produces a loss of boundaries (14). Medieval performances were of course marked by partial boundaries of time, place, and language in relation to the more normal flow of events – they were, by design, "other" to the world which surrounded them. And the alterity of performance opened up the possibility of experiencing the alterities of self to culture and of one culture to another. The boundaries established by performance allowed a better understanding of the problematic nature of social and personal boundaries. Just as Schwab seeks to show how "psychological and cultural aspects of reading are inextricably interwoven" (26), we can appreciate how these aspects of identity were inextricably connected in the culture of the warrior aristocracy, and how ritualized performances highlighted these connections.

From this perspective, the warrior aristocracy looks much more like "us" in its modes of social and aesthetic experience than has often been recognized. The claims which Schwab makes for "reading" could be made for "marked socio-aesthetic experiences" generally. While many of the classic stereotypes which medievalists have held of warrior aristocrats and of the epic rely on seeing that group as "other" in the quality of its experience of – and reflection on – the individual, that otherness seems far less evident now, though certainly the particular modes and tropes through which it occurred are quite different from those of the present; it is this latter difference which has often hindered our ability to see the relative *lack* of difference in the former.

The Missing Sacred

Rather than being surprised to find such qualities among medieval warriors or other anthropologically distant groups, we should consider our relationship to them. Vincent Pecora has argued that modernist and post-modernist literary theory and artistic production draw crucially on the anthropological energy of the sorcerer. What he calls the "alien, estranging force of modern poetry" (1994:348) is predicated specifically on a resistance to "the mass market" (348), and the elite work of art becomes quintessentially non-capitalist, and non-western. Both the writer and the "romantic anthropologist" become "shamans" who bring sacred secrets to their own culture (347–8).

Yet for Pecora, what the "shamans" arrive with turns out to look quite similar to what medieval scholars have often arrived with upon their return from visiting the warrior aristocracy: "the communitarian centrality of the gift" (351) and a view of ritual as "purely mimetic behavior" (355). Somehow, in the return, the alterity of performance which occurs in the other cultures is lost: their social, cultural and aesthetic energy brings forms of alterity to *us*, but their capacity to do the same thing for themselves is forgotten. That Other world can only endlessly enact their practices in a blind trap. As Michael Taussig has pointed out, the Other is closely linked in many western descriptions to mimetic "aping" (1993:xiv). The primitive is allied to the mimetic.

Taussig goes on to recuperate the notion of the mimetic, however, suggesting that in its most positive form, it always involves a mimicry of the other, and thus opens up the self to alterity. He then shows how the dynamic of the gift, between colonizer and colonized, replicates the dynamic of mimesis, and enacts many of the dilemmas of boundaries and alterity which we have been examining in this book (Taussig 1993, Ch. 7). The "spirit of the gift" parallels the "spirit of the mime" in distributing plural identities onto all involved in the processes of exchange or encounter (93). In such contexts, the gift becomes a site of immense tension, and either "violence or the threat of violence" are displaced onto this exchange (94). Thus whereas classic theories of the gift leave boundaries intact – especially the boundary between reflecting western subject and acting non-western object of study – an anthropologically-informed, post-colonial notion of gift practice works to trouble such boundaries. Like medieval moments of the gift, the exchanges become not just practices, but also tropes for thinking about and negotiating boundaries.

Yet Taussig insists that the mimetic faculty also allows us to "actively forget" that identities are constructed (1993:xvi), so that we can live as if "we live facts" (xv). In a similar sense, we have shown here that the gift in the Middle Ages acted simultaneously as a trope for reflection on boundaries, but also as a practice for establishing them within performative contexts. Taussig argues that the "sensuous" quality of the best kinds of mimesis both distributes plurality and alterity, but also allows for a sensuous embrace of the social as if it were the natural. Taussig removes reflexivity from the equation: identities are troubled and dissolved in a performative world where no participant can stand back and evaluate the on-going processes. True mimesis does not imitate something else – Nature, or the Other – it *is* that thing.

Such a view can be thought of as erasing the sacred, leaving only performance. But as we have seen, it is the sacred – often in the person of the fully integral hero – which established a baseline in relation to which the warrior aristocracy could "think" about itself in performance. This is essentially the argument of Maurice Godelier and Annette Weiner as well: social performance cannot exist without an anchoring concept of the sacred, even though the performance is by definition not "sacred." Likewise, neither medieval warrior-aristocrat culture nor the medieval ritual of the epic could have existed without the hero – the integral, sacred anchor of the performative world. But the hero is (by definition, this book argues) not part of that world, or more properly, is not allowed to become a part of that world, any more than individuals engaged in social performance are allowed to seize hold of the sacred "nomos" for themselves. Once we grasp this fact, we can respond to the failure that Pecora's account of the modernist "shaman" exposes: modernist anthropology has tended to "come back from abroad" without the sacred kept which remains out of circulation. It has failed to see or find this component of performance in the cultures it studies. Lévi-Strauss argued that culture was founded on the necessity of exchange. The sacred kept played no important role in his thought. And likewise, medieval studies has too often come back with a medieval hero who is intimately tied to – even a "simple" mimetic representation of – the prosaic medieval world of the warrior aristocracy; the sacral or integral nature of the hero is missing. Because of this, the hero's alterity to his own culture disappears, and with it the ambiguity of the gift and of violence, leaving a view of the warrior aristocracy that looks like a repeat of what Adam Kuper calls the "invention of primitive society" (Kuper 1988), with its focus on (progressively) evolving systems of lineage and social order marked by a gradual "birth" or "rise" of the individual, authorial distance, reflective consciousness, and all the rest.[1]

Medieval Studies, Anthropology, and Colonialism

To rob the hero of his alterity is a classic colonizing gesture, since it robs the warrior aristocracy of its point of self-perception, self-analysis and self-critique, and reduces it to a solid group, which mimics its own practices in an endless cycle which can only end in the violent social "tragedy" to which the epic supposedly bears witness. As a corollary to this point, we must recognize that the notion of "gift" (that is to say, "solidarity") versus "violence" (that is to say, "fragmenta-tion"), with the two terms of the opposition seen as unambiguous binary oppo-sites, is also a fundamentally colonialist notion. The opposition captures two different, key elements of "colonial structuralism." Not only does it feature a clear binary opposition (which a better understanding of performance, the hero and the sacred would reveal to be illusory), but the opposition in question – of whole and fragment – is intimately linked to structuralist anthropology more generally. James Clifford has critiqued the notion of "whole cultures" and the a-diachronic ethnographic monograph from a post-colonial perspective (Clifford 1988:21ff), arguing that the wholeness is largely a construction needed by the anthropologists against which to frame modernist social "fragmentation" and historical "evolution," but also modernism's supposed privileged perspective on the Other.[2]

In addition, the opposition of whole and fragment evokes the larger failure fully to appreciate artistic, aesthetic performance in traditional settings. Marc

---

[1] Robert Young (1990:124) offers an interesting analysis of the structuralist project in relation to its suspicion of violence as inherently western. In retrospect, the desire to locate violence in the West can be seen as key to the tendency of structuralist studies of the gift to find non-violence precisely in the gift-giving, non-western, solidarian Other.

[2] See Lévinas 1999 on the relationship between structures of wholeness and totality, western concepts of knowledge, and the question of alterity. He argues that knowledge is not only conceived as a wholeness, but as an intentionality or act of will (1999:14). Such a concep-tion recalls the medieval integral hero. He also speaks of "a surplus of signification ... that could be designated as glory" (1999:27; see also 33), which again evokes a key component of the medieval hero. The medieval hero is the emblem of a kind of social knowledge and self-consciousness which takes on other forms and identities in the modern West. For more on Lévinas's Other and the Derridean supplement, see Young 1990:15–16.

Manganaro has noted that modernist anthropology's notion of a "culture" (incarnated in the ethnographic monograph) replicates modernist literary theory's notion of "form" as an integral whole (Manganaro 1990b:10). These notions of wholeness are both responses to senses of contemporary social "fragmentation" (1990b:29). Oral-formulaic theory (Lord 1960) and "strong" orality theories (Ong 1982), with their strong formalist tendencies, are good examples of approaches which, though literary, generate notions of "culture" which strongly resemble those critiqued by Manganaro. They rely ultimately on structuralist theories which see ("whole") language systems as constitutive of society. The uncritical application of oral formulaics to medieval epic as a theory of reception and audience (as opposed to a theory of production) is one reason why the true nature of the hero and ritualized performance has not been appreciated. It is this "wholeness" – which elides internal differentiation, contestation, ambiguity, and incompleteness – which is the essence of the colonizing gesture.[3] One need not get to know various individual natives, because one can simply understand "the natives." A proper medieval view of the hero – as mark of the "gratuity" of artistic performance, and as theoretical marker of the simultaneous completeness and excess of the otherwise incomplete performative world of the gift – is essential to resisting such tendencies.

Medieval studies of the warrior aristocracy, in other words, have participated in a mode of analysis which is parallel to – and indeed, borrowed from, to a degree – structuralist anthropology, which is itself related to larger modes of colonialist thought. The Middle Ages, and particularly the warrior aristocracy, become simple, whole, primitive, and unreflective, like colonized, "primitive" peoples. Brian Stock has examined how the eighteenth century elaborated a notion of "tradition" which involved ideas of unchanging norms and a lack of reflexivity, and how this notion was applied to the Middle Ages (Stock 1990). While he argues that the nineteenth and twentieth centuries produced a vision of the Middle Ages as evolving progressively, the various books which Stock cites reveal (as he himself points out) that this evolutionist project is predicated on "the myth of medieval tradition as a reference point for immobile values" (1990:161).[4] That reference point has often been the early warrior aristocracy: it is against this group that the "discovery of the individual" (Colin Morris, 1972) or the "rise of romance" (Eugène Vinaver, 1971) are framed (both texts cited by Stock). Barbara Rosenwein, writing in 1998 on the issue of anger in the Middle Ages, critiques Norbert Elias's view of the "civilizing process" that supposedly allowed "primitive, childlike" medieval emotionalism to evolve towards rational, civilized self-control, but notes that even today, medievalists' own viewpoints about emotion are split between those who see medieval people as existing at an

---

[3] See Boon 1982, Ch. 7 on the relationships between structuralism and romantic notions of the primitivism echoed in the literary theories of formalism and structuralism (1982:208–11).

[4] See Biddick 2000 for a reading of the "medieval" in Said as similarly "immobile."

earlier stage in a process of "development" (if not "evolution") and those who see medieval emotion as simply different in its social forms and functions (Rosen-wein 1998b:238–41). The warrior aristocracy in particular, even for medievalists, remains too often the last historical "other" before the birth of "modernity," just as medievalists have complained (ironically) that the entire Middle Ages often occupies the same position for various modernists.[5]

Decolonizing the Gift and Reciprocity

In contrast, under the influence of post-modernism, one can begin to return to the early modern anthropologists and sociologists and better appreciate the ambigui-ties they found in the notions of the gift and the sacred. As Michèle Richman stresses, Mauss recognized the German irony in the word gift, which contained also the sense of "poison" (Richman 1990:203), and Durkheim's notion of the sacred likewise included both a sanctioned and transgressive sacred (204) which looks quite like the sacred of the warrior aristocracy, divided between a "social" sacred and the transgressive sacred represented by heroes such as Raoul of Cambrai. Thus post-modernism does not so much reveal complexities of the gift, performance and alterity as begin to uncover what was covered up by the discourses of structuralism and colonialism. Of course, all theories cover and un-cover different things: post-modernism simply seems to be a fairly effective tool for decolonizing. It is even more effective for thinking about the gift for the very particular reason that "the gift" (as generalized reciprocity) is virtually the founding concept of anthropological structuralism, while the founding post-structuralist critiques of structuralism focused on notions such as the "floating signifier" which were fundamental to the analysis of gift-giving in Lévi-Strauss (see Lévi-Strauss 1987:62–4). As Jacques Derrida's recent response to Marcel Mauss suggests (1992), the gift lies at the very center of twentieth-century critical theory as well as at the center of the response to structuralism and colonialism.

But such an intricately entangled concept is all the more difficult to use effec-tively within those enveloping tangles.[6] As we have seen, the post-structuralist response to the theory of the gift is necessarily entangled dialogically with the theory it critiques. Post-colonial attempts to erase the blockage between the present and the past and thereby erase a certain kind of alterity produced by the writing of colonialist history (Ingham and Warren 2003:1–6) always carry the risk of eliding other forms of alterity without which the past always ends up looking *too much* like the present, thereby entangling it in models of analysis

[5] An overview of this last phenomenon, with more detailed references, can be found in Dagenais and Greer 2000, Cohen 2000 (the Introduction and several of the chapters), Holsinger 2002, and Ingham and Warren 2003 (Introduction).

[6] See Nicholas Thomas's exemplary study, *Entangled Objects* (1991), and especially pp. 185ff on "The Discovery of the Gift" for an investigation of the relationships between anthro-pology, colonialism, and theories of the gift in the context of the Pacific.

which are anachronistic. In closing, let us consider that the concepts of the hero and the "sacred supplement" can indeed allow us to see the warrior aristocracy – as a group and as individuals – in a way which bridges forms of illusory alterity between that culture and our own, thus overcoming some of the limitations of classical gift theory. Yet the openly acclaimed violent performativity which characterized the early medieval practice of giving and taking, which organized the warrior aristocracy internally, and which enabled access to the sacred, represents a true, profound form of alteric practice that always threatens to intrude between that culture and its academic students and readers of the present.

WORKS CITED

PRIMARY SOURCES
(alphabetical by author or title; original texts first, translations second)

Beowulf. A Dual-Language Edition. Howell D. Chickering, Jr., ed. and transl. New York: Anchor Books, 1977.

Le Charroi de Nîmes, Chanson de geste du XIIe siècle. Duncan McMillan, ed. Paris: Klincksieck, 1978.
  Le Charroi de Nimes. An English Translation with Notes. Henri J. Godin, transl. Oxford: Basil Blackwell, 1936.

"Conventum inter Guillelmum Aquitanorum comes et Hugonem Chiliarchum." Jane Martindale, ed. *English Historical Review* 84 (1969):528–48.

"Agreement between Count William V of Aquitaine and Hugh IV of Lusignan". Paul Hyams, transl. Internet Medieval Sourcebook, www.fordham.edu/halsall/source/agreement.html, accessed 11/5/02.

Le Couronnement de Louis. Ernst Langlois, ed. Paris: Champion, 1966.
  Guillaume d'Orange. Four Twelfth Century Epics. Joan Ferrante, transl. New York: Columbia University Press, 1991.

Les Deux Redactions en vers du Moniage Guillaume. Wilhelm Cloetta, ed. Paris: Fermin-Didot, 1906.
  Guillaume d'Orange. Four Twelfth Century Epics. Joan Ferrante, transl. New York: Columbia University Press, 1991.

Doon de Maience. M.A. Pey, ed. Paris: Franck, 1859.

The Ecclesiastical History of Orderic Vitalis. Marjorie Chibnall, ed. and transl. 6 vols. Oxford: Clarendon, 1969.

Les Enfances Vivien. Magali Rouquier, ed. Geneva: Droz, 1997.

Etienne de Fougères. *Le Livre des Manières.* R. Anthony Lodge, ed. Geneva: Droz, 1979 (translations my own).

Gaufredo Malaterra. *De rebus gestis Rogerii Calabriae et Siciliae Comitis et Roberti Guiscardi Ducis fratris eius.* Ernesto Pontieri, ed. Bologna: Nicola Zanichelli, 1927 (translations my own).

The Gesta Guillelmi of William of Poitiers. R.H.C. Davis and Marjorie Chibnall, ed. and transl. Oxford: Clarendon Press, 1998.

The Gesta Normannorum Ducum of William of Jumieges, Orderic Vitalis, and Robert of Torigni. 2 vols. Elisabeth M.C. Van Houts, ed. Oxford: Clarendon Press, 1992 (translations my own).

Girart de Roussillon. Mary Hackett, ed. Paris: A & J. Pickard, 1953.

Girart de Vienne. Wolfgang van Emden, ed. Paris: Société des Anciens Textes Français, 1977.

The Song of Girart of Vienne by Bertrand de Bar-Sur-Aube. Michael A. Newth, transl. Tempe, AZ: Arizona Center for Medieval and Renaissance Studies, 1999.

Gormont et Isembart: Fragment de Chanson de Geste du XIIe siècle. 3rd edn, rev. Alphonse Bayot, ed. Paris: Champion, 1931 (translations my own).

Guillaume de Lorris and Jean de Meun. *The Romance of the Rose*. Ernst Langlois, ed. Paris: Firmin-Didot, 1914–24.

Hervis de Mes: chanson de geste anonyme (début du XIIIème siècle). Jean-Charles Herbin, ed. Geneva: Droz, 1992.

Histoire de Guillaume le Maréchal. P. Meyer, ed. 3 vols. Paris: Société de l'Histoire, 1891–1901 (translations my own).

Llull, Ramon. *Llibre de l'Ordre de Cavalleria*. Marina Gustá, ed. Barcelona: Edicions 62, 1980 (translations my own).

Das Nibelungenlied. Nach der Ausgabe von Karl Bartsch. 15th edn. Wiesbaden: Helmut de Boor, 1959.

The Nibelungenlied. A.T. Hatto, transl. London: Penguin Books, 1969.

Poema de mio Cid. Colin Smith, ed. Oxford: Oxford University Press, 1972.

The Poem of the Cid. Rita Hamilton, transl. Manchester: Manchester University Press, 1975.

Raoul of Cambrai. Sarah Kay, ed. and transl. Oxford: Clarendon Press, 1992.

Renaud de Montauban. Jacques Thomas, ed. Geneva: Droz, 1989.

Le Roman de Rou de Wace. 3 vols. A. J. Holden, ed. Paris: A. & J. Picard, 1970.

The History of the Norman People: Wace's Roman de Rou. Glyn S. Burgess, ed. Woodbridge, UK: Boydell Press, 2004.

The Song of Roland: An Analytical Edition. Gerard Brault, ed. 2 vols.

The Song of Roland. Glyn Burgess, trans. London, Penguin Books, 1990.

Storia de' Normanni di Amato di Montecassino. Vincenzo de Bartholomaeis, ed. Rome: Istituto Storico Italiano, 1935 (translations my own).

Tacitus. *Agricola; Germania*. Anthony R. Birley, transl. Oxford: Oxford University Press, 1999.

William of Apulia. *La Geste de Robert Guiscard*. Marguerite Mathieu, ed. Palermo: Istituto Siciliano di Studi Bizantini e Neoellenici, 1961 (translations my own).

SECONDARY SOURCES
(alphabetical by author, date)

Abou-Zeid, Ahmed. 1966. "Honour and Shame among the Bedouins." In Peristiany 1966:243–60.

Adams, William Y. 1998. *The Philosophical Roots of Anthropology*. Stanford: Center for the Study of Language and Information.

Adler, Alfred. 1975. *Epische Spekulanten: Versuch einer synchronen Geschichte des altfranzösischen Epos*. Munich: Wilhem Fink.

Aebischer, Paul. 1972. *Préhistoire et protohistoire du Roland d'Oxford*. Bern: Francke.

Aitchison, N.B. 1994. "Kingship, Society, and Sacrality: Rank, Power, and Ideology in Early Medieval Ireland." *Traditio* 49:45–75.

Akbari, Suzanne Conklin. 2000. "From Due East to True North: Orientalism and Orientation." In Cohen 2000:19–34.

Akehurst, F.R.P. and Stephanis Cain Van d'Elden, ed. c.1997. *The Stranger in Medieval Society*. Minnapolis: University of Minnesota Press.

Alba, Emily. 2001. *The Normans in their Histories: Propaganda, Myth and Subversion*. Woodbridge, UK: Boydell.

Andersson, Theodore M. 1987. *A Preface to the Nibelungenlied*. Stanford: Stanford University Press.

Appadurai, Arjun, ed. 1986a. *The Social Life of Things*. London: Cambridge University Press.

———. 1986b. "Introduction: commodities and the politics of value." In Appadurai 1986a:3–63.

Ashe, Laura. 1999. "'A Prayer and a Warcry.' The Creation of a Secular Religion in the *Song of Roland*." *Cambridge Quarterly* 28:349–67.

Ashford, Josette Britte. 1984–85. "Etat présent des recherches sur *Gormont et Isembart*." *Olifant* 10:188–209.

Aubailly, Jean-Claude. 1987. "Mythe et épopée dans la geste de Guillaume." *Olifant* 12:221–45.

Augé, Marc. 1998 [1994]. *A Sense for the Other: The Timeliness and Relevance of Anthropology*. Amy Jacobs, transl. Stanford: Stanford University Press.

Baldwin, John W 2000. *Aristocratic Life in Medieval France: The Romances of Jean Renaut and Gerbertde Montreuil, 1190–1230*. Baltimore: Johns Hopkins University Press.

Barbero, Alessandro. 1991. "Noblesse et chevalerie en France au Moyen Âges. Une réflexion." *Le Moyen Age* 97:431–49.

Baroja, Julio Caro. 1966. "Honour and Shame: A Historical Account of Several Conflicts." In Peristiany 1966:79–138.

Barraud, Cécile, Daniel de Coppet, André Iteanu and Raymond Jamous. 1994 [1984]. *Of Relations and the Dead: Four Societies Viewed from the Angle of Their Exchanges*. Stephen J. Suffern, transl. Oxford: Berg.

Barthélemy, Dominique. 1996. "Noblesse, chevalerie et lignage dans le Vendômois." In Duhamel-Amado *et al.*1996:121–39.

Bartlett, Robert. 1993. *The Making of Europe: Conquest, Colonization and Cultural Change 950–1350*. Princeton: Princeton University Press.

Barton, Richard E. 1998. "'Zealous Anger' and the Renegotiation of Aristocratic Relationships in Eleventh- and Twelfth-Century France." In Rosenwein 1998a:153–70.

Bataille, Georges. 1985. *Visions of Excess: Selected Writings, 1927–39*. Allan Stoekel ed. and transl. Minneapolis: University of Minnesota Press.

———. 1988 [1967]. *The Accursed Share: An Essay on General Economy*. Robert Hurley, transl. New York: Zone Books.

Baudrillard, Jean. 1968. *Le système des objets*. Paris: Gallimard.

———. 1972. *Pour une critique de l'économie politique du signe*. Paris: Gallimard.

———. 1973. *Le miroir de la production, ou l'illusion critique du materialisme historique*. 2nd edn. Paris: Casterman.

Bauman, Richard. 1977. *Verbal Art as Performance*. Rowley, MA: J. Newbury House.

———. 1986. *Story, Performance, and Event: Contextual Studies of Oral Narrative*. Cambridge: Cambridge University Press.

————— . 1989. "American Folklore Studies and Social Transformation: A Performance-Centered Perspective." *Text and Performance Quarterly* 9,3:175–84.

Baumgartner, Emmanuèle and Laurence Harf-Lancner. 1999. *Raoul de Cambrai: L'impossible révolte*. Paris: Champion.

Bédier, Joseph. 1914. *Les Legendes épiques: Recherches sur la formation des chansons de geste*. 4 vols. Paris: Champion.

Bedos-Rezak, Brigitte Miriam, and Dominique Iogna-Prat, eds. 2005. *L'individu au Moyen Age*. Paris: Aubier.

Beech, George. 1966. "A Feudal Document of Early Eleventh-Century Poitou." In Gallais and Riou 1966:Vol. I:203–13.

Bekker, Hugo. 1971. *The Nibelungenlied: A Literary Analysis*. Toronto: University of Toronto Press.

Bennet, Philip E. 1999. "Hétéroglossie et carnaval dans le cycle de Guillaume." *Littérature Epique au Moyen Age. Hommage à Jean Fouquet pour son 100eme Anniversaire*. Greifswald: Reineke-Verlag, 135–50.

Bennett, Matthew. 1998. "Violence in Eleventh-Century Normandy: Feud, Warfare and Politics." In Halsall 1998:126–40.

Bezzola, Reto. 1960. *Les Origines et la formation de la littérature courtoise en occident (500–1200)*. 2e partie, t. 2. Bibliothèque de l'école des hautes études. Sciences historiques et philologiques. Fascicule 313. Paris: Champion.

Bhabha, Homi. 1994. *The Location of Culture*. London: Routledge.

Biddick, Kathleen. 1998. *The Shock of Medievalism*. Durham, NC: Duke University Press.

————— . 2000. "Coming out of Exile: Dante on the Orient Express." In Cohen 2000:35–52.

Bisson, Thomas N. ed. 1995. *Cultures of Power: Lordship, Status, and Process in Twelfth-Century Europe*. Philadelphia: University of Pennsylvania Press.

Bloch, R. Howard. 1983. *Etymologies and Genealogies: A Literary Anthropology of the French Middle Ages*. Chicago: University of Chicago Press.

————— and Stephen Nichols, eds. 1996. *Medievalism and the Modernist Temper*. Baltimore: Johns Hopkins University Press.

Blumenfeld-Kosinski, R. 1986. "Praying and Reading in the *Couronnement de Louis*." French Studies 40:385–92.

Boon, James A. 1982. *Other Tribes, Other Scribes: Symbolic Anthropology in the Comparative Study of Cultures, Histories, Religions, and Texts*. Cambridge: Cambridge University Press.

————— . 1999. *Verging on Extravagance: Anthropology, History, Religion, Literature, Art ... Showbiz*. Princeton: Princeton University Press.

Bouchard, Constance. 1987. *Sword, Mitre and Cloister: Nobility and the Church in Burgundy, 980–1198*. Ithaca: Cornell University Press.

————— . 1991. *Holy Entrepreneurs: Cistercians, Knights and Economic Exchange in Twelfth-Century Burgundy*. Ithaca: Cornell University Press.

————— . 1998. *'Strong of Body, Brave and Noble': Chivalry and Society in Medieval France*. Ithaca: Cornell Univesity Press.

Bourdieu, Pierre. 1966. "The Sentiment of Honour in Kabyle Society." In Peristiany 1966:191–242.

————. 1977 [1972]. *Outline of a Theory of Practice*. Richard Nice, transl. Cambridge: Cambridge University Press.

————. 1992. "Rites as Acts of Institution." In Peristiany and Pitt-Rivers 1992:79–90.

Boutet, Dominique. 1993. *La Chanson de geste: Forme et signification d'une écriture épique du Moyen Age*. Paris: Presses Universitaires de France.

————. 1999. *Formes littéraires et conscience historique: Aux origines de la littérature française 1100–1250*. Paris: Presses Universitaires de France.

————. 2000. "Le roi Louis et la signification politico-historique de Raoul de Cambrai." *Romania* 118:315–35.

———— and Armand Strubel. 1979. *Littérature, politique et société dans la France du Moyen Âge*. Paris: Presses Universitaires de France.

Brault, Gérard. 1978. *The Song of Roland: An Analytical Edition*. 2 vols. University Park, PA: Penn State University Press.

Bremmer, Jan and Herman Roodenburg, eds. 1997. *A Cultural History of Humour: From Antiquity to the Present Day*. Cambridge: Polity Press.

Brown, Warren. 2001. *Unjust Seizure: Conflict, Interest, and Authority in an Early Medieval Society*. Ithaca: Cornell University Press.

Calin, William.1974. "Un univers en Décomposition: Raoul de Cambrai." *Olifant* 1,4:3–9.

Callari, Antonio. 2002. "The Ghost of the Gift: The Unlikelihood of Economics." In Osteen 2002a: 248–65.

Campbell, J.K. 1966. "Honour and the Devil." In Peristiany 1966:139–70.

————. 1992. "The Greek Hero." In Peristiany and Pitt Rivers 1992:129–50.

Carpentier, Elisabeth and Michel Le Mené. 1996. *La France du XIe au XVe siècle: population, société, économie*. Paris: Presses Universitaires de France.

Chénu, Marie-Dominique. 1969. *L'Éveil de la conscience dans la civilisation médiévale*. Montreal: Vrin.

Cixous, Hélène. 1981. "Castration or decapitation." *Signs* 7:41–55.

————. 1989. "The Laugh of the Medusa." In David H. Richter, ed. *The Critical Tradition: Classical Texts and Contemporary Trends*. New York: St. Martins, 1090–1102.

Clanchy, M.T. 1993. *From Memory to Written Record*. 2nd edn. Oxford: Basil Blackwell.

Clifford, James. 1988. *The Predicament of Culture: Twentieth-Century Ethnography, Literature, and Art*. Cambridge: Harvard University Press.

Cohen, Jeffrey Jerome, ed. 2000. *The Postcolonial Middle Ages*. New York: St Martin's.

Combarieu du Grès, Micheline, de. 1999. "'et in hora mortis nostrae.' Sur 'l'aristeîa' de Raoul." *Littératures* 41:5–31.

Contamine, Philippe. 1984 [1980] *War in the Middle Ages*. Michael Jones, transl. New York: Basil Blackwell.

Cook, Robert Francis. 1987. *The Sense of the Song of Roland*. Ithaca: Cornell University Press.

Cordoba, Jose Maria Garatre. 1967. *Espiritu y milicia en la España medieval*. Madrid: Publicaciones españolas.

Cowell, Andrew. 1996. "The Fall of the Oral Economy: Writing Economics on the Dead Body." *Exemplaria* 8:145–67.

————. 2002. "The Pleasures and Pains of the Gift." In Osteen 2002a:280–97.

Crouch, David. 1988. "Strategies of Lordship in Angevin England and the Career of William Marshal." *The Ideals and Practice of Knighthood II*, Christopher Harper-Bill and Ruth Harvey, eds. Woodbridge, UK: Boydell.

————. 1990. *William Marshal: Court, Career and Chivalry in the Angevin Empire 1147–1219*. London: Longman.

Dagenais, John and Margaret R. Greer. 2000. "Decolonizing the Middle Ages: Introduction." *Journal of Medieval and Early Modern Studies* 30:431–48.

Daniel, Norman. 1975. *The Arabs and Mediaeval Europe*. London: Longman.

————. 1984. *Heroes and Saracens: An Interpretation of the Chansons de Geste*. Edinburgh: Edinburgh University Press.

Davis, John. 1987. "Family and State in the Mediterranean." In Gilmore 1987a:22–34.

Demartini, Dominique. 2005. "Le Discours amoureux dans le Tristan en prose: Miroir et mirage du 'je'." In Bedos-Rezak and Iogna-Prat 2005:145–65.

Den Bok, Nico. 2005. "Richard de Saint-Victor et la quête de l'individualité essentielle: La sagesse de daniélité." In Bedos-Rezak and Iogna-Prat 2005:123–43.

Derrida, Jacques. 1974 [1967]. *Of Grammatology*. Gayatri Chakravorty Spivak, transl. Baltimore: Johns Hopkins University Press.

————. 1992 [1991]. *Given Time: I. Counterfeit Money*. Peggy Kamuf, transl. Chicago: University of Chicago Press.

Deyermond, A.D. ed. 1977. *"Mio Cid" Studies*. London: Támesis.

————. 1982. "The Close of the Cantar de mío Cid: Epic Tradition and Individual Variation." In Peter Noble, Lucie Polak and Claire Isoz, eds. *The Medieval Alexander Legend and Romance Epic: Essays in Honour of David J.A. Ross*. Millwood, NY: Kraus, 11–18.

di Bella, Maria Pia. 1992. "Name, Blood, and Miracles: The Claims to Renown in Traditional Sicily." In Peristiany and Pitt-Rivers 1992:151–65.

Dobozy, Maria. 1997. "Creating Credibility and Truth through Performance: Kelin's Encomium." In Akehurst 1997:92–103.

Douglas, David C. 1969. *William the Conqueror: The Norman Impact on England*. London: Methuen.

Douglas, Mary and Baron Isherwood. 1979. *The World of Goods*. New York: Basic Books.

Dresch, Paul. 1998. "Mutual Deception: Totality, Exchange, and Islam in the Middle East." In James and Allen 1998:111–33.

Dreyfus, Hubert. L. and Paul Rabinow. 1988. *Michel Foucault: Beyond Structuralism and Hermeneutics*. Chicago: University of Chicago Press.

Duby, Georges. 1953. *La Société aux XIe et XIIe siècles dans la région mâconnaise*. Paris: Armand Colin.

————. 1968 [1962]. *Rural Economy and Country Life in the Medieval West*. Cynthia Postan, transl. Colombia: University of South Carolina Press.

————. 1973. *Guerriers et paysans VIIe-XIIe siècle: Premier essor de l'économie européenne*. Paris, Gallimard.

————. 1988a [1979]. *La Société chevaleresque. Hommes et structures du moyen age (I)*. Paris: Flammarion..

————. 1988b [1979]. *Seigneurs et paysans. Hommes et structures du moyen age (II)*. Paris: Flammarion.

———. 1990 [1973]. *The Legend of Bouvines: War, Religion and Culture in the Middle Ages.* Catherine Tihanyi, transl. Berkeley, University of California Press.

Duggan, Anne J. ed. 2000. *Nobles and Nobility in Medieval Europe: Concepts, Origins, Transformations.* Woodbridge, UK: Boydell Press.

Duggan, Joseph J. 1973. *The Song of Roland: Formulaic Style and Poetic Craft.* Berkeley: University of California Press.

———. 1989. *The Cantar de mio Cid: Poetic Creation in its Economic and Social Contexts.* Cambridge: Cambridge University Press.

Duhamel-Amado, Claudie and Guy Lobrichon, eds. 1996. *Georges Duby: L'écriture de l'histoire.* Brussels: De Boeck-Wesmael.

Dumont, Louis. 1986. *Essays on Individualism: Modern Ideology in Anthropological Perspective.* Chicago: University of Chicago Press.

Dunbabin, Jean. 2000. *France in the Making 843–1180.* 2nd edn. Oxford: Oxford University Press.

Durkheim, Emile. 1965 [1915]. *The Elementary Forms of Religious Life.* Joseph Swain, trans. New York: Free Press.

Eales, Richard. 1986. "The Game of Chess: An Aspect of Medieval Knightly Culture." In Harper-Bill and Harvey 1986:12–34.

Escobedo, Antonio. 1993. *Estructuras Léxicas Verbales del "Cantar de Mio Cid".* Granada: University of Granada Publications.

Evans, Stephen S. 1997. *The Lords of Battle: Image and Reality of the Comitatus in Dark-Age Britain.* Woodbridge, UK: Boydell.

Evergates, Theodore. 1995. "Nobles and Knights in Twelfth-Century France." In Bisson 1995: 11–35.

Flori, Jean. 1986. *L'Essor de la chevalerie. Xie–XIIe siècles.* Travaux d'histoire éthico-politique, 46. Geneva: Droz.

Foley, John Miles. 1991. *Immanent Art: From Structure to Meaning in Traditional Oral Epic.* Bloomington: Indiana University Press.

———. 1995. *The Singer of Tales in Performance.* Bloomington: Indiana University Press..

Fossier, Robert. 1982. *Enfance de l'Europe: Xe–XIIe siècles*: *Aspects économiques et sociaux.* 2 vols. Paris: Presses Universitaires de France.

Foucault, Michel. 1975 [1977]. *Discipline and Punish: The Birth of the Prison.* Alan Sheridan, transl. New York: Random House.

———. 1979. *Discipline and Punish.* Alan Sheridan, transl. New York: Vintage (re-edn of preceding entry)

———. 1988. *Politics Philosophy Culture. Interviews and Other Writings 1977– 1984.* Alan Sheridan et al transl. Lawrence Kritzman, ed. New York: Routledge.

Fox, Robin. 1994. *The Challenge of Anthropology: Old Encounters and New Excursions.* New Brunswick, NJ: Transaction Publishers.

Fradenburg, Louise. 1997. "'So That We May Speak of Them': Enjoying the Middle Ages." *New Literary History* 28:205–30.

Frakes, Jerold C. 1994. *Brides and Doom: Gender, Property, and Power in Medieval German Women's Epic.* Philadelphia: University of Pennsylvania Press.

France, John. 1999. *Western Warfare in the Age of the Crusades. 1000–1300.* Ithaca: Cornell University Press.

Gal, Susan. 2001. "Language, Gender, and Power: An Anthropological Review." In
    Alessandro Duranti, ed., *Linguistic Anthropology: A Reader*. Malden, MA: Black-
    well, 420–30.
Gallais, Pierre and Yves-Jean Riou, eds.1966. *Mélanges offerts à René Crozet*. 2
    vols. Poitiers: Société d'Etudes Médiévales.
Ganshof, F.L. 1947. *Qu'est-ce que la féodalité?* Bruxelles: Office de Publicité.
Garcia, Jorge J.E. 1984. *Introduction to the Problem of Individuation in the Early
    Middle Ages*. Munich: Philsophia Verlag.
Geary, Patrick. 1986. "Sacred Commodities: The Circulation of Medieval Relics." In
    Appadurai 1986a:169–91.
———. 1996. "Moral Obligations and Peer Pressure: Conflict Resolution in the
    Medieval Aristocracy." In Duhamel-Amado 1996:217–21.
Gillingham, John. 1999. "The Age of Expansion, c. 1020–1204." In Keen 1999:59–
    88.
Gilmore, David D., ed. 1987a. *Honor and Shame and the Unity of the Mediterranean*.
    American Anthropological Association Special Publication no. 22. Washington,
    D.C.
———. 1987b. "Honor, Honesty, Shame: Male Status in Contemporary Andalusia."
    In Gilmore 1987a:90–103.
Girard, René. 1972. *La Violence et le sacré*. Paris: Grasset.
Godbout, Jacques. 1998. *The World of the Gift*. Donald Winker, transl. Montreal:
    McGill-Queen's University Press.
Godelier, Maurice. 1999. *The Enigma of the Gift*. Nora Scott, transl. Chicago:
    University of Chicago Press.
——— and Marilyn Strathern, eds. 1991. *Big Men and Great Men: Personifications
    of Power in Melanesia*. Cambridge: Cambridge University Press.
Golding, Brian. 2001. *Conquest and Colonization: The Normans in Britain, 1066–
    1100*. Rev. edn. New York: Palgrave.
Greenblatt, Stephen. 1980. *Renaissance Self-Fashioning. From More to Shakespeare*.
    Chicago: University of Chicago Press.
Gregory, C.A. 1982. *Gifts and Commodities*. London: Academic Press.
Grisward, Joël. 1981. *Archéologie de l'épopée médiévale: structures trifonctionelles
    et mythes indo-européens dans le cycle des narbonnais*. Paris: Payot.
Gurevich, A.Y. 1968. "Wealth and Gift-Bestowal Among the Ancient Scandinavians."
    Scandinavica 7,2:126–38.
———. 1985. *Categories of Medieval Culture*. G.L. Campbell, transl. London:
    Routledge and Kegan Paul.
———. 1992. *Historical Anthropology of the Middle Ages*. Chicago: University of
    Chicago Press.
———. 1995. *The Origins of European Individualism*. Oxford: Blackwell.
Haidu, Peter. 1993. *The Subject of Violence: The Song of Roland and the Birth of the
    State*. Bloomington: Indiana University Press.
———. 2004. *The Subject Medieval/Modern: Text and Governance in the Middle
    Ages*. Stanford: Stanford University Press.
Halperin, Rhoda H. 1994. *Cultural Economies: Past and Present*. Austin: University
    of Texas Press.
Halsall, Guy, ed. 1998. *Violence and Society in the Early Medieval West*. Woodbridge,
    UK: Boydell.

Hanley, Catherine. 2003. *War and Combat, 1150–1270: The Evidence from Old French Literature*. Cambridge, UK: D.S. Brewer.

Harney, Michael. 1992. "Movilidad Social, Rebelión Primitiva y la Emergencia del Estado en al *Poema de mio Cid*." In Jean Ramón Resina, ed. *Mythopoesis: Literature, Totalidad, Ideología*. Barcelona: Editorial Anthropos, 65–101.

———. 1993. *Kinship and Polity in the Poema de mio Cid*. Purdue Studies in Romance Literatures, vol. 2. West Lafayette, IN: Purdue University Press.

———. 1997. "Social Stratification and Class Ideology in the Poema de Mio Cid and the Chanson de Roland." In *Medieval Iberia: Essays in the History and Literature of Medieval Spain*, Donald J. Kagay and Joseph T. Snow, ed. New York: Peter Lang, 77–102.

Harper-Bill, Christopher and Ruth Harvey, eds. 1986. *The Ideals and Practice of Medieval Knighthood*. Woodbridge, UK: Boydell.

Hart, Thomas R. 1977. "Characterization and Plot Structure in the 'Poema de mio Cid'." In Deyermond 1977:63–72.

Haymes, Edward R. 1986. *The Nibelungenlied: A History and Interpretation*. Chicago: University of Illinois Press.

Hinnant, Charles H. 2002. "The patriarchal narratives of *Genesis* and the ethos of gift exchange". In Osteen 2002a:105–17.

Histoire et société: Mélanges offerts à Georges Duby. Aix-en-Provence: Publications of the University of Provence, 1992.

Hodges, Richard. 1988. *Primitive and Peasant Markets*. Oxford: Basil Blackwell.

Hoffmann, Werner. 1987. "Das *Nibelungenlied* - Epos oder Roman? Positionen und Perspektiven der Forschung." In Knapp, 1978:124–51.

———. 1992. *Das Nibelungenlied*. 6th edn. Stuttgart: J.B. Metzler.

Holsinger, Bruce. 2002. "Medieval Studies, Postcolonial Studies, and the Genealogies of Critique." *Speculum* 77:1195–227.

Holton, R.J. 1985. *The Transition from Feudalism to Capitalism*. New York: St. Martin's Press.

Homans, George C. 1974[1942]. *English Villagers of the Thirteenth Century*. New York: Norton.

Housley, Norman. 1999. "European Warfare c. 1200–1320." In Keen 1999:113–35.

Hüe, Denis, Ed. 1999. *L'orgueil à démesure: Etudes sur Raoul de Cambrai*. Orléans: Paradigme.

Humphrey, Caroline and Stephen Hugh-Jones, eds. 1992. *Barter, Exchange and Value: An Anthropological Approach*. Cambridge: Cambridge University Press.

Hyde, Lewis. 1983. *The Gift: Imagination and the Erotic Life of Property*. New York: Random House.

Hymes, Dell. 1981. *"In vain I tried to tell you": Essays in Native American Ethnopoetics*. Philadelphia, University of Pennsylvania Press.

Ingham, Patricia and Michelle Warren, eds. 2003. *Postcolonial Moves: Medieval Through Modern*. New York: Palgrave MacMillan.

Jaeger, C. Stephen. 1995. "Courtliness and Social Change." In Bisson 1995:287–309.

James, Edward. 1988. *The Franks*. Oxford: Basil Blackwell.

James, Wendy and N.J. Allen, eds. 1998. *Marcel Mauss: A Centenary Tribute*. New York: Berghahn Books.

Jameson, Fredric. 1991. *Postmodernism or, The Cultural Logic of Late Capitalism.* Durham: Duke University Press.

Jamous, Raymond. 1992. "From the Death of Men to the Peace of God: Violence and Peace-making in the Rif." In Peristany and Pitt Rivers 1992:167–92.

———. 1994. "Iqar'iyen." In Barraud, Cécile, Daniel de Coppet, André Iteanu and Raymond Jamous. 1994:88–100.

Jones, George F. 1963. *The Ethos of the Song of Roland.* Baltimore: Johns Hopkins University Press.

Kaeuper, Richard W. 1999. *Chivalry and Violence in Medieval Europe.* Oxford: Oxford University Press.

Kagay, Donald J. and Joseph T. Snow, eds. 1997. *Medieval Iberia: Essays on the History and Literature of Medieval Spain.* New York: Peter Lang.

Kagay, Donald J. and L.J. Andrew Villalon, eds. 1998. *The Final Argument: The Imprint of Violence on Society in Medieval and Early Modern Europe.* Wood-bridge, UK: Boydell.

Kay, Sarah. 1984. "La composition de *Raoul de Cambrai.*" *Revue Belge de Philologie et d'Histoire* 62:474–92.

———. 1994. "The Life of the Dead Body: Death and the Sacred in the Chansons de geste." *Yale French Studies* 86:94–108.

———. 1995. *The Chansons de geste in the Age of Romance: Political Fictions.* Oxford: Clarendon.

———. 1998–2003. "Singularity and Spectrality: Desire and Death in Girart de Roussillon." *Olifant* 22:11–38.

———. 1999a. "L'éthique dans Raoul de Cambrai." *Littérature française et comparée* 13:5–10.

———. 1999b. "Le Caractère des personnages dans les Chansons de geste." In Hüe 1999:79–105.

Keen, Maurice. 1984. *Chivalry.* New Haven: Yale University Press.

———. 1999. *Medieval Warfare: A History.* Oxford: Oxford University Press.

Keller, Hans-Erich, ed. 1987. *Romance Epic: Essays on a Medieval Literary Genre.* Kalamazoo: Medieval Institute Publications and Western Michigan University.

Kellogg, Judith. 1989. *Medieval Artistry and Exchange: Economic Institutions, Society, and Literary Form in Old French Narrative.* New York: Peter Lang.

Kent, Carol A. 1994–95. "Fidelity and Treachery: Thematic and Dramatic Structuring of the Laisse in an Episode of the Couronnement de Louis (laisses 43–54)." *Olifant* 19:223–38.

Kinoshita, Sharon. 1995. "The Politics of Courtly Love: La Prise d'Orange and the Conversion of the Saracen Queen." *Romanic Review* 86:265–87.

———. 2001. "Pagans are Wrong, Christians are Right: Alterity, Gender and Nation in the Chanson de Roland." *Journal of Medieval and Early Modern Studies* 31:79–111.

Knapp, Fritz Peter, ed. 1987. *Nibelungenlied und Klage: Sage und Geschiche, Struktur und Gattung.* Proceedings of the Passauer Nibelungengespräche, 1985. Heidelberg: Carl Winter.

Kohler, Erich. 1970. *Ideal und Wirklichkeit in der höfischen Epik.* Tubingen: Max Niemeyer.

Komter, Aafke E., ed. 1996a. *The Gift: An Interdisciplinary Perspective.* Amsterdam: Amsterdam University Press.

————. 1996b. "Women, Gifts and Power." In Komter 1996a:119–33.

Kopytoff, Igor. 1986. "The Cultural Biography of Things: Commoditization as Process." In Appadurai 1986a:64–91.

Koziol, Geoffrey. 1992. *Begging Pardon and Favor: Ritual and Political Order in Early Medieval France*. Ithaca: Cornell University Press.

Kuper, Adam. 1988. *The Invention of Primitive Society: Transformations of an Illusion*. London: Routledge.

Labbé, Alain. 1999. "La Croix, l'épée et la flamme: autour de l'incendie d'Origny dans Raoul de Cambrai." In Hüe 1999:147–85.

Lacarra, Eugenia Maria. 1980. *El Poema de Mio Cid: Realidad, Historica e Ideologia*. Madrid: Juranzas.

Lafages, Catherine. 1992. "Royalty and Ritual in the Middle Ages: Coronation and Funerary Rites in France." In Peristiany and Pitt-Rivers 1992:19–50.

Laidlaw, James. 2002. "A free gift makes no friends." In Osteen 2002a:45–66.

Le Gentil, Pierre. 1969. *The Chanson de Roland*. Cambridge: Harvard University Press.

Le Goff, Jacques. 1988. *The Medieval Imagination*. Arthur Goldhammer, transl. Chicago: University of Chicago Press.

————. 1997. "Laughter in the Middle Ages." In *A Cultural History of Humour: From Antiquity to the Present Day*. Jan Bremmer and Herman Roodenburg, eds. Cambridge, UK: Polity Press, 40–53.

Legros, Huguette. 1999. "Raoul de Cambrai et Dom Juan." In Hüe 1999:187–200.

Lejeune, Rita. 1951. "Les Noms d'épée dans la Chanson de Roland." In *Mélanges Mario Roques,* (Paris, 1951), vol. I:149–66.

Leupin, Alexandre. 1988. "Raoul de Cambrai: la bâtardise de l'écriture." *Romanic Review* 79:89–104.

Lévinas, Emmanuel. 1999 [1995]. *Alterity and Transcendence*. Michael B. Smith, transl. New York: Columbia University Press.

Lévi-Strauss, Claude. 1969. *The Elementary Structures of Kinship*. Rev. edn. James Harle Bell, transl. John Richard von Sturmer and Rodney Needham, eds. Boston: Beacon Press.

————. 1973 [1955]. *Tristes tropiques*. John and Doreen Weightman, transl. New York: Penguin.

————. 1987 [1950]. *Introduction to the Work of Marcel Mauss*. Felicity Baker, transl. London: Routledge and Kegan Paul.

Linda, Janet Tai. 1994. *Trust, Ethnicity and Identity*. Ann Arbor: University of Michigan Press, 1994.

Little, Lester K. 1978. *Religous Poverty and the Profit Economy in Medieval Europe*. Ithaca: Cornell University Press.

Lord, Albert Bates. 1960. *The Singer of Tales*. Harvard Studies in Comparative Literature, 24. Cambridge: Harvard University Press.

Luongo, Salvatore. 1990. "Tra periferia e centro del discorso epico: Note sulla *Prise d'Orange.*" *Medioevo Romanzo* 15:211–34.

Lyon, Bryce D. 1957. *From Fief to Indenture: The Transition from Feudal to Non-Feudal Contract in Western Europe*. Cambridge: Harvard University Press.

Maddox, Donald and Sara Sturm-Maddox. 1979. "Intertextual Discourse in the William Cycle." *Olifant* 7:131–48.

Malinowski, Bronislaw. 1961 [1922]. *Argonauts of the Western Pacific*. New York: E.P. Dutton.

Manganaro, Marc, ed. 1990a. *Modernist Anthropology: From Fieldwork to Text*. Princeton: Princeton University Press.

――― . 1990b. "Textual Play, Power, and Cultural Critique: An Orientation to Modernist Anthropology." In Manganaro 1990a:3–50.

Marcus, Michael A. "'Horsement are the Fence of the Land': Honor and History among the Ghiyata of Eastern Morocco." In Gilmore 1987a:49–60.

Martin, Hervé. 1996. *Mentalités médiévales: Xie–XVe siècle*. Paris: Presses Universitaires de France.

Martindale, Jane. 1969. "Conventum inter Guillelmum Aquitanorum comes et Hugonem Chiliarchum." *English Historical Review* 84:528–48.

Matarasso, P. 1962. *Recherches historiques et littéraires sur Raoul de Cambrai*. Paris: Nizet.

Mauss, Marcel. 1967 [1925]. *The Gift: Forms and Functions of Exchange in Archaic Societies*. Ian Cunnison, transl. New York: W.W. Norton and Co.

Mayer, Hans Eberhard. 1972. *The Crusades*. John Gillingham, trans. Oxford: Oxford University Press.

McCracken, Peggy. 1998. *The Romance of Adultery: Queenship and Transgression in Old French Literature*. Philadelphia: University of Pennsylvania Press.

McGrane, Bernard. 1989. *Beyond Anthropology: Society and the Other*. New York: Columbia University Press.

Miller, D. 1995. "Consumption and Commodities." *Annual Review of Anthropology* 24:141–61.

Miller, Dean. 2000. *The Epic Hero*. Baltimore: Johns Hopkins University Press.

Miller, William Ian. 1986. "Gift, Sale, Payment, Raid: Case Studies in the Negotiation and Classification of Exchange in Medieval Iceland." *Speculum* 61:18–50.

――― . 1993. *Humiliation and Other Essays on Honor, Social Discomfort, and Violence*. Ithaca: Cornell University Press.

Montgomery, Thomas. 1983. "Mythopoeia and Myopia: Colin Smith's *The Making of the Poema de Mio Cid*." *Journal of Hispanic Philology* 8:7–16.

――― . 1987. "The Rhetoric of Solidarity in the *Poema del Cid*." *MLN* 102:191–205.

――― . 1990. "Marking Voice and Place in the *Poema del Cid*." *La Coronica* 19:49–66.

Moore, R.I. 1987. *The Formation of a Persecuting Society: Power and Deviance in Western Europe, 950–1250*. New York: Blackwell.

Morris, Colin. 1972. *The Discovery of the Individual, 1050–1200*. London: SPCK for the Church Historical Society.

Müller, Jan-Dirk. 1998. *Spielregeln für den Untergang: Die Welt des Nibelungenliedes*. Tubingen: Max Niemeyer.

――― . 2002. *Das Nibelungenlied*. Berlin: Erich Schmidt.

Nelson, Janet L. 1986. *Politics and Ritual in Early Medieval Europe*. London: Hambledon Press.

――― . 1998. "Violence in the Carolingian World and the Ritualization of Ninth-Century Warfare." In Halsall 1998:90–107.

Nichols, Stephen G. 1963. "Style and Structure in *Gormont et Isembart*." *Romania* 84:500–35.

———— . 1980. "Signs as (Hi)story in the *Couronnement de Louis.*" *Romanic Review* 71:1–9.

Noble, Peter S. 1986, "Knights and Burgesses in the Feudal Epic." In Harper-Bill and Harvey 1986:104–10.

Ong, Walter J. 1982. *Orality and Literacy: The Technologizing of the Word.* London: Routledge.

Osteen, Mark, ed. 2002a. *The Question of the Gift: Essays Across Disciplines.* London: Routledge.

———— . 2002b "Gift or Commodity." In Osteen 2002a:229–47.

Pafenberg, Stephanie B. 1995. "The Spindle and the Sword: Gender, Sex and Heroism in the Nibelungenlied and Kudrun Author." *Germanic Review* 70:106–15.

Painter, Sidney. 1933. *William Marshal: Knight-Errant, Baron and Regent of England.* Baltimore: Johns Hopkins University Press.

Parry, Jonathan. 1989. "On the Moral Perils of Exchange." In Parry and Bloch 1989:64–93.

———— . and M. Bloch, eds. 1989. *Money and the Morality of Exchange.* Cambridge: Cambridge University Press.

Patterson, Lee. 1987. *Negotiating the Past: The Historical Understanding of Medieval Literature.* Madison: University of Wisconsin Press.

Pecora, Vincent. 1994. "The Sorcerer's Apprentice." *Modern Language Quarterly* 55,4:345–82.

Perfetti, Lisa. 1992–93. "Dialogues of Laughter: Bahktin's Theory of Carnival and the Charroi de Nîmes." *Olifant* 17:177–95.

Peristiany, J.G., ed. 1966. *Honour and Shame: The Values of Mediterranean Society.* Chicago: University of Chicago Press.

———— . 1992. "The *Sophron* – a Secular Saint? Wisdom and the Wise in a Cypriot Community." In Peristiany and Pitt-Rivers 1992:103–28.

———— and Julian Pitt-Rivers, eds. 1992. *Honor and Grace in Anthropology.* Cambridge: Cambridge University Press.

Pitt-Rivers, Julian. 1966. "Honour and Social Status." In Peristiany 1966:19–78.

Pitt-Rivers, Julian. 1992. "Postscript: The Place of Grace in Anthropology." In Peristiany and Pitt-Rivers 1992:215–46.

Polanyi, Karl. 1968. *Primitive, Archaic and Modern Economies.* Garden City, NY: Anchor Books.

———— . 1977. *The Livelihood of Man.* New York: Academic Press.

Poly, Jean-Pierre and Eric Bournazel. 1991[1980]. *The Feudal Transformation: 900–1200.* Caroline Higgitt transl. New York: Homes & Meier.

Ramey, Lynn Tarte. 2001. *Christian, Saracen and Genre in Medieval French Literature.* Studies in Medieval History and Culture, Vol. 3. New York: Routledge.

Resina, Juan Ramón. 1984. "El Honor y las relaciones feudales en el *Poema de Mio Cid.*" *Revista de Estudios Hispánicos* 18:417–28.

Reuter, Timothy, ed. and transl. 1978. *The Medieval Nobility: Studies on the Ruling Classes of France and Germany from the Sixth to the Twelfth Century.* Amsterdam: North Holland Publishing.

———— . 1999. "Carolingian and Ottonian Warfare." In Keen 1999:13–35.

Reynolds, Susan. 1984. *Kingdoms and Communities in Western Europe, 900–1300.* Oxford: Clarendon.

―――. 1994. *Fiefs and Vassals: The Medieval Evidence Reinterpreted*. Oxford: Oxford University Press.

Riché, Pierre. 1993. *The Carolingians: A Family who Forged Europe*. Michael Idomir Allen, transl. Philadelphia: University of Pennsylvania Press.

Riches, David, ed. 1986. *The Anthropology of Violence*. Oxford: Basil Blackwell.

Richman, Michèle. 1990. "Anthropology and Modernism in France: From Durkheim to the Collège de sociologie." In Manganaro 1990a:183–214.

Rodríguez-Puértolas, Julio. 1977. "El 'Poema de Mio Cid': nueva épica y nueva propaganda." In Deyermond 1977:141–60.

Rosenwein, Barbara, ed. 1998a. *Anger's Past: The Social Uses of an Emotion in the Middle Ages*. Ithaca: Cornell University Press.

―――. 1998b. "Controlling Paradigms." In Rosenwein 1998a:233–47.

Sahlins, Marshall. 1963. "Poor Man, Rich Man, Big-man, Chief: Political Types in Melanesia and Polynesia." *Comparative Studies in Society and History* 5:285–303.

―――. 1972. *Stone Age Economics*. New York: Aldine Publishing.

Schenk, David P. 1988. *The Myth of Guillaume. Poetic Consciousness in the Guillaume d'Orange Cycle*. Birmingham: Summa Publications.

Schwab, Gabriele. 1996. *The Mirror and the Killer-Queen: Otherness in Literary Language*. Bloomington: Indiana University Press.

Schwarz, Barry. 1996. "The Social Psychology of the Gift." In Komter 1996a:69–80.

Shell, Marc. 1978. *The Economy of Literature*. Baltimore: Johns Hopkins University Press.

―――. 1982. *Money, Language and Thought*. Berkeley: University of California Press.

Simmel, Georg. 1950. *The Sociology of Georg Simmel*. Kurt Wolff, ed. and transl. Glencoe, IL: Free Press.

Singerman, Jerome E. 1985. " 'Si com c'est veir': The Polemical Approach to Prayer in Le couronnement de Louis." *Romania* 106:289–302.

Smith, Colin. 1983. *The Making of the Poema de mio Cid*. Cambridge: Cambridge University Press.

Spierenburg, Pieter. 1991. *The Broken Spell: A Cultural and Anthropological History of Preindustrial Europe*. New Brunswick, NJ: Rutgers University Press.

Stock, Brian. 1983. *The Implications of Literacy: Written Language and Models of Interpretation in the Eleventh and Twelfth Centuries*. Princeton: Princeton University Press.

―――. 1990. *Listening for the Text: On the Uses of the Past*. Baltimore: Johns Hopkins.

Strathern, Marilyn. 1988. *The Gender of the Gift: Problems with Women and Problems with Society in Melanesia*. Berkeley: University of California Press.

Suard, François. 1980. "Le Motif du déguisement dans quelques chansons du cycle de Guillaume d'Orange." *Olifant* 7:343–58.

Tabuteau, Emily Zack. 1988. *Transfers of Property in Eleventh-Century Norman Law*. Chapel Hill: University of North Carolina Press.

Taussig, Michael. 1993. *Mimesis and Alterity: A Particular History of the Senses*. New York: Routledge.

Testart, Alain. 1993. *Des dons et des dieux: Anthropologie, religion et sociologie comparative*. Paris: Armand Colin.

Thomas, Nicholas. 1991. *Entangled Objects*. Cambridge: Harvard University Press.

Torgovnick, Marianna. 1990. *Gone Primitive: Savage Intellects, Modern Minds*. Chicago: University of Chicago Press.

Turner, Victor. 1986. *The Anthropology of Performance*. New York: PAJ.

van Emden, W.G. 1964. "Isembart and the Old French Epic." *Nottingham Medieval Studies* 8:22–34.

Vance, Eugene. 1986. *Mervelous Signals: Poetics and Sign Theory in the Middle Ages*. Lincoln: University of Nebraska Press.

Verbruggen, J.F. 1997. *The Art of Warfare in Western Europe During the Middle Ages: From the Eighth Century to 1340*. Sumner Willard and Mrs. R.W. Southern, transls. 2nd edn. Woodbridge, UK: Boydell.

Vinaver, Eugène. 1971. *The Rise of Romance*. Oxford: Clarendon.

Vitz, Evelyn Birge. 1975. "Type et individu dans 'l'autobiographie' médiévale." *Poétique* 24:426–45.

——— . 1989. *Medieval Narrative and Modern Narratology: Subjects and Objects of Desire*. New York: New York University Press.

Walsh, John K. 1970–1. "Religious Motifs in Early Spanish Epics." *Revista Hispanica Moderna* 36:165–72.

Warren, Michelle. 1999. "Roger of Howden Strikes Back: Investing Arthur of Brittany with the Anglo-Norman Future. In *Proceedings of the Battle Conference, 1998*. Christopher Harper-Bill, ed. Woodbridge, UK: Boydell, 1999: 261–72.

——— . 2000. *History on the Edge: Excalibur and the Borders of Britain, 1100–1300*. Minneapolis: University of Minnesota Press.

Wathelet-Willem, Jeanne. 1966. "L'épée dans les plus anciennes chansons de geste. Etude de vocabulaire." In Gallais and Riou 1966:435–49.

Webber, Ruth. 1986. "The Cantar de Mio Cid: Problems of Interpretation." In *Oral Tradition in Literature*. J.M. Foley, ed. Columbia: University of Missouri Press, 65–88.

Weiner, Annette B. 1992. *Inalienable Possessions: The Paradox of Keeping-While-Giving*. Berkeley: University of California Press.

West, Geoffrey. 1977. "King and Vassal in History and Poetry: a conrast between the 'Historia Roderici' and the 'Poema de Mio Cid.'" In Deyermond 1977:195–208.

White, Stephen D. 1988. *Custom, Kinship, and Gifts to Saints: The Laudatio Parentum in Western France, 1050–1150*. Chapel Hill: University of North Carolina Press.

——— . 1992. "Stratégie rhétorique dans la Conventio d'Hugues de Lusignan." In *Histoire et Société*: Vol II: 147–58.

——— . 1995. "Proposing the Ordeal and Avoiding It: Strategy and Power in Western French Litigation, 1050–1110." In Bisson 1995:89–123.

——— . 1996. "Politics of Fidelity: Hugh of Lusignan and William of Aquitaine." In Duhamel-Amado 1996:223–30.

——— . 1998. "The Politics of Anger." In Rosenwein 1998a:127–52.

Young, Robert. 1990. *White Mythologies: Writing History and the West*. London: Routledge, 1990.

Zink, Michel. 1985. *La Subjectivité littéraire: Autour du siècle de Saint Louis*. Paris: Presses Universitaires de France.

INDEX

Adalbert of Laon, 32
Adorno, Theodor, 80
"Altere Not" (hypothetical earlier version of *The Nibelungenlied*), 146
alterity: and non-reciprocity, 103, 109–10; and relationship to the sacred, 132–3; and violence, 80–86, 175–6; medieval theories of, 158–61; tri-partite, 119, 127–33
Amatus of Montecassino, 58, 63 n.32
amor (Old Spanish word), meaning of, 69, 83–4; *see also* "love" and fear, relationship of
'Ane'ane, people of Melanesia, 93–4
Anglo-Saxons, 29 n.35, 79
Annales School, 6
Aristotle, 37 n.2
Atlakviða, 117
Aude, character in *Song of Roland*, 126, 134
autobiography, medieval, 49

Babha, Homi, 131, 149 n.11
banal lordship, 32–3, 50
barter, 75, 109
Bataille, Georges, 5, 13, 108 n.8
Baudrillard, Jean, 5
beard, unplucked, as symbol of integrity, 70
Bedouins, people of Egypt, 55, 97
Benedictine Rule, 25 n.28
Beowulf, 79, 117 n.2
Berbers, people of Morocco – *see* Iqar'iyen
Bertran of Born, 62
"big man," in Melanesia, 20, 35–6, 90, 93
blood, symbolic importance of in *The Cid*, 64, 72, 74–6
boundaries: ambiguity of (external vs. internal), 84–5, 100–1, 127–31, 156–8; exchange and establishment of, 154–6; gift and, 154–6, 172; lack of in Paradise, 159; medieval etiology of, 154, 158–61
Bourdieu, Pierre, 9, 37–8, 51, 55, 89
Bretons, described by William of Poitiers, 31 n.39

Brevis relatio, 46 n.20
bridal romance, Middle High German – *see* bride-quest narratives
bride-quest narratives, in medieval Germany, 136, 138, 140, 146–7
Burgundy, military expeditions from, 59–60

Calabria, relations with Normans, 52
Carolingian era, 12, 32, 57–8
castles, as bases for taking and exploitation, 59
Chanson d'Antioche, 68
Charles Martel, 57
Charroi de Nîmes, Le (Old French epic), 54
chess, as metapor for medieval society, 119–22, 124
Chivalry, 14, 62–3, 153, 166–9
Chrétien de Troyes, 166
Cid, The Poem of the, 13, 64–86, 95–9; ambiguity of boundaries in, 100–1; orality, 72–74, 170; performance in, 70–6, 107, 124–5, 131 n.22; the sacred, 95–9
Cixous, Helene, 5
colonialism, and anthropology, 173–5, and medieval studies, 174
commodity: and alterity, 150; and relationships to markets, 78–9; danger of for warrior aristocracy, 43, 49, 76, 78, 94, 96, 141–3; definition of, 42–3, 49, 78–9
Conquest of Orange, The (Old French epic), 148
"Conventum" (between William V of Aquitaine and Hugh of Lusignan), 110–11, 113
Coronation of Louis, The (Old French epic), 14, 68 n.8, 109–10, 131, 153–69
counter-gifts, 15, 20, 30, 105
courtly romance (literary genre) – *see* romance, courtly
Crusade, First, 168
Crusade, Fourth, 58
Crusades, texts concerning, 67–8

warfare, medieval, 57–63; as basis of
economy, 57–8; as producer of symbolic
value, 59–61; in relation to giving and
taking, 61
warrior aristocracy, definition of, 3
wealth, as secondary symbol of honor, 40–5
William I, Duke of Normandy (William the
Conqueror), 13, 53, 57–8, 78; and sacred,
87, 91; gratuitous gestures, 111–12;
strategies of giving, 25–33, 66; symbolic
action, 43–8, 60, 83
William V of Aquitaine, 110–11, 113
William Longsword, 30, 44
William of Apulia, 29, 32, 38, 44

William of Jumièges, 25 n.29, 27 n.32
William of Orange (epic character), 61,
153–69
William of Orange cycle (Old French epic
tradition), 140, 153, 156–7, 164
William of Poitiers, 25–6
William Marshall, 28 n.33, 76–8
Wolfram von Eschenbach, 166
women: as dangerously desirable
commodities, 134–8, 141–3, 147; as
giving "subjects," 137–8, 142–4, 146;
as secondary symbols, 138–9; as Other,
135–50; sacred, "kept" status, 97–9, 122
n.6